Ethnography of the costumes of the Monpa and Brokpa people
Western Arunachal Pradesh, eastern Bhutan and southern Tibet

MICHIKO WAKITA
with contributions by Timotheus A. Bodt

亡き夫重雄(1947-2022)に捧ぐ

Dedicated to my late husband, Shigeo (1947-2022)

© 2025 Michiko Wakita　Printed in Japan
No part of this book may be reproduced in any form
without prior permission in writing from the publisher.

Hozokan Co., Ltd.
20 Nijuninkocho Shimogyo-ku, Kyoto-shi, Kyoto-fu 600-8153, Japan
TEL：+81-75-343-0030

ISBN　978-4-8318-6294-5 C3039

モンパとブロクパの衣装民族誌

アルナーチャル・プラデーシュ西部、ブータン東部、チベット南部

脇田道子=著
寄稿 ティモテユス・アドゥリヤヌス・ボット

タワン僧院での 説法に集まったモンパの人びと
Local Monpa people gathered in formal dress for the public teaching at Tawang Monastery. (October 2013)

チョエコル祭では、参加者はメラとゲンゴーの村の周囲を重い経典を担いで一日かけて歩く。
During the *Choekor* festival, participants spend a day walking around the villages of Merak and Gengo, carrying heavy sacred texts. (Near Gengo, July 2019)

目次

まえがき …………………………………………………………………………… 10
地　図 ……………………………………………………………………………… 20

第1章　地域の概要 ……………………………………………………………… 24
第2章　モンパの民族衣装を読む ……………………………………………… 34
第3章　牧畜民ブロクパの谷、メラとサクテン ……………………………… 90
第4章　染める・織る・運ぶ ……………………………………………………130
　　　　コラム　モンパの多目的バッグ、ダンガー …………………………150
第5章　シンカに必須の腰当て布 ………………………………………………158
第6章　民俗芸能に残る衣装 ……………………………………………………164
第7章　仏教行事を通じた国境を越える交流 …………………………………182
第8章　第二の故郷を創る―ペマコのモンパ― ………………………………196
第9章　西カメン県のモンパの隣人たちの
　　　　民族衣装 …………………………………………………………………218
第10章　タワンの手漉き紙作り …………………………………………………238

参考文献 ……………………………………………………………………………259
あとがき ……………………………………………………………………………266

凡例

1. 第8章本文および第4章のコラムの著者はティモテユス・A・ボット（Timotheus A. Bodt）である。その他のすべての章の著者は脇田道子である。
2. 写真は、撮影者名の記載のないものは、すべて当該章の著者が撮影したものである。
3. 英語以外の現地用語についてはイタリック体で表記している。第8章の英文については、チベット語は、（Tib. sbas-yul）のようにワイリー方式で表記している。

TABLE OF CONTENTS

Preface ⋯⋯ 10
Maps ⋯⋯ 20

Chap.1. Regional Overview ⋯⋯ 24
Chap.2. Observing the Traditional Costumes of the Monpa ⋯⋯ 34
Chap.3. The Herder(Brokpa)'s Valleys, Merak and Sakteng ⋯⋯ 90
Chap.4. Dyeing, Weaving and Trading ⋯⋯ 130
   Column: The Monpa's Multi-Purpose Bag: the *Dangnga* ⋯⋯ 150
Chap.5. The Back Apron is Essential for *Shingka* ⋯⋯ 158
Chap.6. Costumes in Folk Performing Arts ⋯⋯ 164
Chap.7. Cross Border Exchanges Through Buddhist Events ⋯⋯ 182
Chap.8. Creating a Home Away From Home: Pemakö's Monpa ⋯⋯ 196
Chap.9. Traditional Attires of the Neighbours of the Monpa in West Kameng District ⋯⋯ 218
Chap.10. Handmade Papermaking in Tawang ⋯⋯ 238

References ⋯⋯ 259
Afterword ⋯⋯ 268

Explanatory Notes

1. The author of Chapter 8 and the column in Chapter 4 is Timotheus A. Bodt. The author of all other chapters is Michiko Wakita.
2. All photographs were taken by the author of the chapter unless the photographer is credited.
3. Local terms other than English are in italics. The Tibetan terms in Chapter 8 are written in the Wylie transliteration, for example (Tib. sbas-yul).

まえがき Preface

　2019年3月に『モンパ―インド・ブータン国境の民』(法藏館)を上梓した。同書は、2014年に慶應義塾大学社会学研究科に提出した博士論文「モンパの民族表象と伝統文化の動態に関する文化人類学的考察―インド、アルナーチャル・プラデーシュ州を中心として」を元に、加筆・修正したもので、すべて日本語で書かれている。インド、ブータン、中国(チベット)の国境地帯に住むモンパの人々の衣装については、その第2章「民族表象としての衣服」に詳しく書いた。

　本書は、その第2章を全面的に書き直し、カラー写真を多用した。その上、前書には十分は盛り込めなかったブータン側のサクテン地区、メラ地区の牧畜民ブロクパの人々やアルナーチャル・プラデーシュ州西カメン県のモンパ以外の集団の衣装についても取り上げた。本書が英語でも書かれているのは、現地の人々に読んでいただきたいからである。

　まず、なぜ衣装に着目したのかという理由を簡単に述べておこうと思う。1995年3月に初めて北東インドのアルナーチャル・プラデーシュ州を旅した。1987年にインドの24番目の州に昇格した同州は、かつて北東辺境管区(North East Frontier Agency：略称NEFA)と呼ばれていた。現在も中国が領有を主張しているなど地政学上多くの問題を抱える地でもあり、1992年に解禁されるまで外国人の訪問は許されなかった。

　初めての旅で、下スバンシリ県のズィロの博物館を訪ねた際に、ブータン東部のダクパやブロクパと呼ばれる牧畜民が着ている民族衣装とよく似た衣服に、「モンパの衣装」という説明書きがあった。それは、ブータンにおける国民服である一枚布で身体を包む女性の「キラ」や男性の「ゴ」とは、明らかに形状や素材、色が異なっている。モンパは、州西部のタワン県、西カメン県に居住する民族集団だが、当時この二つの県はまだ外国人には開放されておらず、実際にこの衣装を着用しているモンパの人々に出会ったのは、入域が許可された1998年から1年後のことであった【0-1】。

【0-1】民族衣装を着てタワン僧院を訪れた若いモンパ女性たち。
Young Monpa women in traditional dress visiting Tawang Monastery.
(Tawang, June 2023)

【0-2】メラのブロクパ女性たち。
The Brokpa women in Merak. (Merak, July 2012)

　一方、ブータンは1974年に外国人観光客に門戸を開き、私も1976年から訪問を続けている。ブータン西部から始まった観光客受け入れであるが、ブロクパと呼ばれる牧畜民が住むタシガン県のサクテン、メラの村々は、長い間外国人の入域が禁じられてきた。その二つの谷への観光客受け入れが始まったのは2010年9月のことである。幸い特別許可が得られ、2006年3月から2008年7月の間に3回、つまり観光が開始される前にこの地域を訪ねることができ、現在も訪問を続けている【0-2】。

　タシガン県には、インド側のモンパと同じ言語を話す、ダクパと呼ばれる人々がいるが、その存在を日本に紹介したのが西岡京治・里子夫妻である。コロンボプランによる農業専門家として1964年からブータンに滞在していた夫妻は、1965年に馬でタシガン県まで旅している。その日本語の著書『神秘の王国』（1978年、学習研究社）の中に、東ブータンで訪れたダクパの村で見聞した衣装についての貴重な記録がある。村の名前ははっきりしないが、彼らの衣装は写真で見る限り、現在のサクテンやメラの人々のものとほぼ同じである。だが、衣服の部位の名称は、サクテンやメラのブロクパ語ではなく、インド側の

タワン県のモンパが使う呼称と共通している。

　実は、モンパという名称は、チベット人がヒマラヤ山脈南麓のモンと呼ばれる広大な地域に住む人々を呼ぶときの総称で、かつてはシッキムやブータンの人々もモンパと呼ばれていた。実際の自称は居住地名、時にはその旧名の最後に「〜の人」を意味する「パ」を加えるのが一般的である。例えば、タワンの人であればタワンパ、ゼミタンの人であれば、土地の旧名に由来するパンチェンパ、ディランの人であればディランパである。ダクパも本来は、タワン県西部のダクパ地域に住む人々の名称である。

　インド独立後に、インド政府は宗教や文化の独自性、社会経済的後進性、そして隔絶度の高い山岳地域に居住しているなどの基準に該当する部族集団を、憲法上「指定トライブ」とした。アルナーチャル・プラデーシュ州の多くの民族集団同様、モンパも指定トライブとなったが、モンパは総称に過ぎず、異なる言語や出自を持つ人々を包摂している。これらの集団の中には、ブータンのシャルチョプやダクパ、ブロクパと共通した言語を話す人も含まれ、そのことが衣装やその部位の名称にも反映しているのである。

　衣服は身体を包み隠すだけでなく、それを着る者の民族・地域・職業・階層・既婚か未婚かなどの属性を表す記号として機能する場合もある。また、その地域の文化や伝統を象徴することもある。一方、衣服は、「交易」や「支配的な文化」、「他集団との接触」、「時の流行」などさまざまな要因により変化しやすいものでもある。モンパの場合には、「支配的な文化」とは過去にはチベットの文化、現在はインドの文化で、周辺には小さい民族集団が隣接して生活している。山岳地帯に住むブータンのブロクパにも隣接するモンパと共通するチベットの文化的影響が強く残されていて、彼らの文化は独自のものである。現在は、ブータンの主流の文化がブロクパにとっての「支配的な文化」となっている。

　私が初めてモンパやブロクパが住む地を訪れた時、最初に抱いた疑問は、女性が着ている衣服の染料と素材についてである。女性の貫頭衣シンカと上着のトトゥンの材料は、エリ蚕という蚕の糸から織られたもので、インドではエリ・シルク、あるいはエンディ・シルクなどと呼称されていて、ブータンやチベットではブラと呼ばれている。日本では野蚕絹の中に分類されている。その糸をさまざまな赤系の色に染める染料は、ラック・カイガラムシの雌の粘着性の排出物ラックから抽出されるものである。このエリ・シルク、ラック染料のいず

れもがインド平原部やブータンのモンガル、タシガン、ペマガツェル県の2,000 m以下の土地で産出されるもので、それを着る人々の住む村では生産されないものであったからだ。

　調べてゆくとシンカやトトゥンは、ブータン東部のタシガン県のラディなどの村や、ブータンとの国境付近のアッサム州のボドやラブハと呼ばれる人々の村で織られていることがわかり、それをタワンやディランに交易のために運んでいた人たちにも会った。最近になって、メラや西カメン県には自分たちで織る女性たちも出てきている。ディランにいくつかある織物センターでも、アッサムやマニプルからの女性たちによってシンカやトトゥンが織られているが、それは2002年頃にインド政府が主催した染織講習会が行われた後のことである。年配の人々に質問をしてゆくと、タワンやサクテン、メラの女性は、もともとウールのホームスパンの貫頭衣を着ていたという回答が得られ、極めて稀なケースだが、その実物を目にすることができた。ウールの布であれば、自分たちで糸を紡ぎ、各戸のベランダに立てかけられた後帯機で織る女性たちを現在でも多くの村で見ることができる。また、標高の低い地域では、かつてはイラクサで織った衣服が着られていたこともわかってきた。それらが次第に変化し、白や臙脂色の野蚕絹に変わり、現在では言語の違いを越えて、多くのモンパやブロクパの民族衣装へと定着してきたのである。

　また、貫頭衣という形状にも注目してみると、この形はかつてサクテンやメラ以外のブータンにもあり、カメン県のモンパ以外の民族集団にも見られるものである。それだけではなく、アルナーチャル・プラデーシュ州北東部のシー・ヨミ県（かつての西シアン県の一部）メンチュカ谷に住むメンバや、東ブータンから移住してきたとされるチベット自治区のペマコの門巴（メンバ）族、メンチュカ谷の北のチベットのコンポ地方の人々も、貫頭衣を民族衣装としている。そこには、人々の移動や交流、そしてそれぞれの集団のアイデンティティの表象が示されている【0-3】。

　私がこの国境地域を初めて訪ねてから四半世紀の間に、人々の生活環境も大きく変わり、その変化は衣服にも少しずつ見られるようになっている。かつて着ていたウールの貫頭衣がほぼ姿を消したように、男性の衣装の中にも、目にする機会が少なくなったものがいくつかある。数年後に、本書を携行して同じ場所を訪ねても、まったく見られなくなってしまうものがあるかもしれない。

2010年頃までは、ディラン近郊の家の軒先や道端でダンンガー、通称モンパ・バッグと呼ばれるカラフルなバッグ用の布を織る人々をよく見かけたが、その数も訪問する度に減っている。

　チベットでは、ジンチョウゲ科の植物の靱皮で漉かれる手漉き紙を「モンの紙」という意味でモン・ショクと呼んでいたことからわかるように、ブータン東部やモンパの村では盛んに手漉き紙が生産されていた。今でも残るそれらの紙漉きは、ヒマラヤ山麓に残る貴重な文化遺産でもある。モンパの村では、工場製の安価な衣服や靴、バッグ、そして紙などが入手できるようになり、手仕事による素朴だが味わい深い工芸品は次第に少なくなり、質の低下が見られるようにもなっている。本書を急いでまとめたいと思った理由もそこにある。

【0-3】コンポ地方のウールの貫頭衣と同じようなドレスを着たメンバ女性。
　A Memba woman in a woollen tunic dress similar to that of the Kongpo region. (Menchukha, September 2010)

　インド、ブータン、そして中国との国境地帯に住む人々から多くのことを学んできた。本書が読者の皆様、とりわけ私の研究に協力してくださった現地の友人たちにとって、この地域の人々の移住や交流についての理解のささやかな一助となれば幸いである。

　本書に関しては、オランダの言語学者ティモテユス・アドゥリヤヌス・ボットから多くの助言を受けた。彼とは2013年1月にタワン僧院のドンギュル祭で出会い、親交を結んできた。彼の助言と、第8章の本文と第4章のコラムの寄稿に対して謝意を表しておきたい。

2025年3月 東京にて
脇田道子

Preface

In March 2019, Hozokan, Kyoto published my book entitled "The Monpas: People of the Borderland between India and Bhutan". That book is the revised and expanded edition of my doctoral dissertation, "A Study of Cultural Anthropology on the Dynamics of Ethnic Representation and Traditional Culture of the Monpas: With a Focus on Arunachal Pradesh, India" which was submitted to the Graduate School of Sociology, Keio University in 2014, and is written in Japanese. The costume of the Monpa people, who live in the border areas of India, Bhutan and China (Tibet), is described in detail in Chapter two "Clothing as Ethnic Representation" of my 2019 publication. The present book is a complete revision of that Chapter, with many color photographs. Additionally, this book covers the costumes of the people of Sakteng and Merak on the Bhutanese side of the border and the non-Monpa groups of West Kameng district, Arunachal Pradesh, which were not fully included in the previous publication. I have written this book in English as well, because I want local people to read it.

First of all, let me briefly explain why I focused on costumes. In March 1995, I made my first trip to Arunachal Pradesh, a state in northeast India, which was promoted to the status of India's 24th state in 1987 and was once known as the North East Frontier Agency (abbreviated NEFA). The state faces a number of difficult geopolitical and national security issues, including China's territorial claims to the region. For this reason, foreigners were not allowed to visit the state until the ban was lifted in 1992.

On my first trip to Arunachal Pradesh in 1995, I visited the district museum at Ziro in Lower Subansiri district. In that museum, I found some clothes with as description "Costume of the Monpas". The clothes were similar as those worn by the Dakpa and Brokpa people of eastern Bhutan. These garments are distinctly different in shape, material, and color from the Bhutanese national dress *kira* for women and *go* for men. The Monpa people were living in Tawang and West Kameng districts in the western part of Arunachal Pradesh, but at that time, these two districts were not yet open to foreigners. Hence, I didn't actually meet the Monpa people wearing these costumes until a year after these two districts were opened to foreigners in 1998 【0-1】.

Bhutan, on the other hand, had opened its doors to foreign tourists in 1974, and I have been visiting the country since 1976. Tourism in Bhutan began from the western part of the country, but Sakteng and Merak villages of the Brokpa people, the highland yak-herding pastoralists located in the easternmost part of the country, were closed to foreigners until September 2010. Fortunately, I could get special permits and I was able to visit the area three times between March 2006 and July

2008, i.e., before the start of tourism, and I continue to visit the area even today 【0-2】.

It was Keiji Nishioka and his wife Satoko who introduced the Dakpas, a people who speak the same language as one of the Monpa groups on the Indian side, to Japan. The couple had lived in Bhutan since 1964, when Nishioka was posted as an agricultural specialist under the Colombo Plan, and they travelled to Trashigang district by horse in 1965. In their book in Japanese, "Shinpi no Oukoku" (*The Mysterious Kingdom*, 1978, Gakushu Kenkyusha), there is a valuable record of costumes seen and heard about in a Dakpa village they visited in eastern Bhutan. The name of the village is not clear, but their costumes, as far as the photographs show, are almost identical to those of the Sakteng and Merak people today, but the names of the parts of the garments are not in the Brokpa language but share the names used by the Monpa people of Tawang district in adjoining Arunachal Pradesh.

In fact, the name Monpa is a generic term used by the Tibetans to refer to the people living on the southern flanks of the Himalayas in a vast area called Mon, and in the past, the people of Sikkim and Bhutan were also called Monpa. As a matter of fact, their local alias or self-identification is mainly the name of the place of residence, which is the old name of the place occasionally, with the addition of "pa", meaning people, at the end. If you are a resident of Tawang, it is Tawangpa; if you are a resident of Zemithang, it is Pangchenpa, derived from the old name of the place; if you are from Dirang, it is Dirangpa. Dakpa was also originally a name for the people living in the Dakpa region of western Tawang district.

After India's independence, the Indian government constitutionally designated tribal groups as "Scheduled Tribes" if they met the criteria of religious and cultural uniqueness, socioeconomic backwardness, and residence in highly segregated mountainous areas. Like many ethnic groups in Arunachal Pradesh, the Monpa people became a Scheduled Tribe and they were recognized as Monpa. But in practice this name is an umbrella term that encompasses people of different languages and origins. The Monpas Scheduled Tribe includes people who speak languages in common with the Bhutanese Sharchop people, but also with the Dakpa people and the Brokpa people, and this is reflected in the names of their costumes and parts.

A garment not only conceals the body but may also act as a symbol to express the ethnicity, region, occupation, class, and whether the wearer is married or unmarried, among other attributes. It may also symbolize the culture and traditions of the area. On the other hand, clothing is also susceptible to change due to various factors such as "trade", "dominant culture", "contact with other groups" and "trends of the time". In the case of the Monpas, the "dominant culture" is the culture of Tibet in the past and the culture of India today, with smaller ethnic groups living adjacent to each other in the vicinity. Although there are strong Tibetan cultural influences among the mountainous Bhutanese Brokpa people who share a common Tibetan cultural influence with the adjacent Monpa people, their culture is unique. Nowadays, mainstream Bhutanese culture is the "dominant culture" for Brokpas.

The primary question I had when I first visited the land that the Monpas and the Brokpas inhabit was about the dyes and materials of the clothes worn by the women. The material of the women's tunic dresses, the *shingka* and the jacket, *tothung*, are woven from the threads of the *eri* silkworm, which in India is called *eri* silk or *endi*-silk, while in Bhutan and Tibet it is called *bura*. In Japan, it is included among the wild silks. The dye that gives the silk its various shades of red is extracted from the sticky discharge lac of the female of the insect *Kerria lacca*. Both this silk and the lac dye come from areas below 2,000 meters in the Indian plains and in Bhutan's Mongar, Trashigang and Pemagatshel districts and are not produced in the villages where the people who wear them live.

As I was conducting my research, I found out that the *shingka* and *tothung* are mainly woven in villages such as Radhi in Trashigang district of eastern Bhutan and in the villages of the Bodo and Rabha people in Assam, near the border with Bhutan, and I met people who used to trade them to the villages of Tawang and Dirang areas in Arunachal Pradesh. Some Brokpa and Monpa women have recently started weaving these items in Merak and Dirang themselves. In the weaving centers of Dirang, women from Assam and Manipur have also been weaving cloth for *shingka* and *tothung* since around 2002, after the Indian government organized dyeing and weaving workshops.

While interviewing the elderly people, I obtained the answer that women in Tawang, Sakteng and Merak originally wore woolen homespun tunics, and I was able to see the actual ones, though only in exceedingly rare cases. In many villages, women can still be seen spinning their own woolen cloth and weaving it on backstrap looms which are propped up on each house's veranda at present. It is also known that at lower elevations, clothes woven from nettle fibers were once worn. This gradually changed to white or wine-red silks, which have now become part of the common dress of many Monpa women, transcending language barriers.

The form of the tunic is also noteworthy, as tunics with a similar design were also found in Bhutan in the past and it is also found among the non-Monpa ethnic groups of West Kameng district. Not only that, the Membas of the Menchukha valley in Shi Yomi (part of what was previously West Siang) district of northeastern Arunachal Pradesh, the Monpa tribe (Mén bā zú in Chinese) of Pemakö in Tibet, who came from eastern Bhutan, and the people of the Kongpo region in Tibet to the north of the Menchukha valley also wear such tunics as their traditional costume. It shows the movement and exchange of people and the representation of each group's identity 【0-3】.

In the quarter of a century since my first visit to the border region, the people's living conditions have changed dramatically, and these changes are gradually seen in their clothing as well. Just as the woolen tunic dresses that were once worn have almost disappeared, so too have some of the things we see less and less in men's clothing. In a few years' time, if you carry this book with you and visit the same places, you may not see some of them at all.

Until around 2010, it was common to see people weaving colorful cloth for *dangnga*, commonly known as Monpa bags, in the eaves of houses and on the side of the road, but their numbers have dwindled with each visit.

In Tibet, handmade paper made from the bast of Daphne sp. was called *mon shog*, meaning 'paper from Mon' and from this it become evident that handmade paper was actively produced in eastern Bhutan and the Monpa villages. Some of these paper makers are still active today and are a valuable cultural heritage of the Himalayan region. As cheap and handy factory-made clothes, shoes, bags and papers are becoming more widely and cheaply available, the production and supply of these simple but tasteful artifacts, made entirely by hand, is diminishing. This is the reason why I felt compelled to compile this book as soon as possible.

I have learnt a lot from the people living in the border areas of India, Bhutan and China. I hope that this book can contribute to the understanding of the migration and exchange of people in the region for the readers, and in particular the local friends who helped me with my study.

For this book, I received a lot of advice from the Dutch linguist Timotheus Adrianus Bodt. I met him at the Dungyur Festival in Tawang Monastery in January 2013 and have developed a close friendship with him. I would like to thank him for his advice, and for contributing the text of chapter 8 and the column in chapter 4.

Tokyo, March 2025
Michiko Wakita

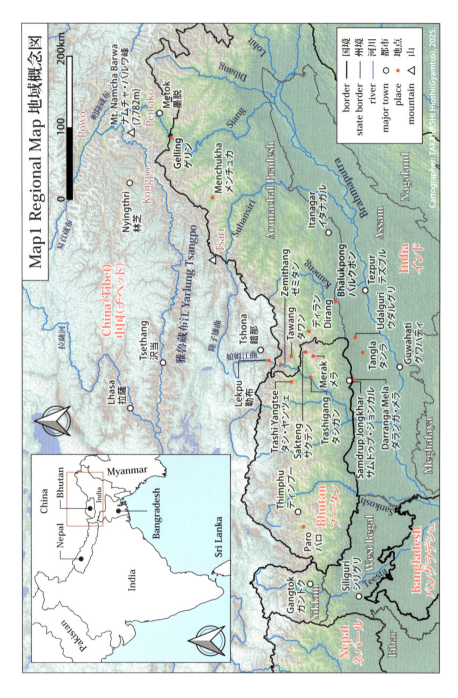

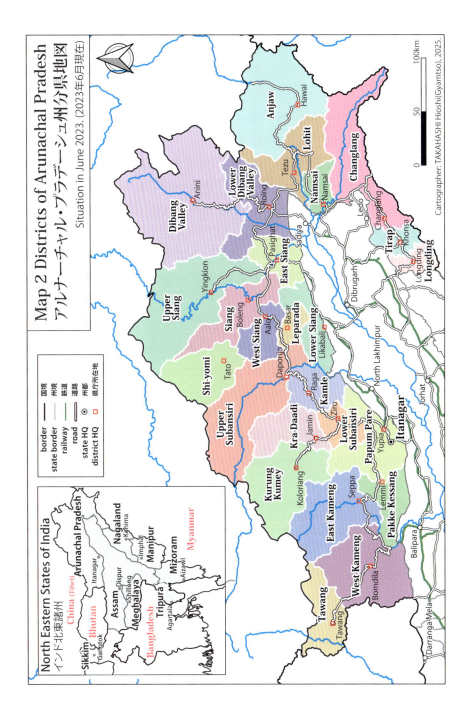

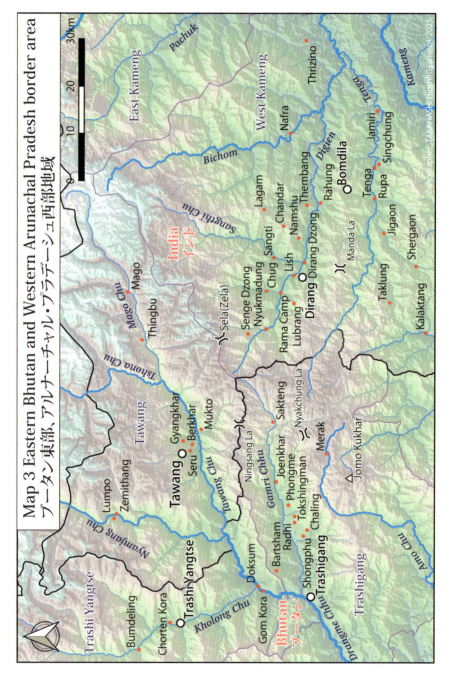

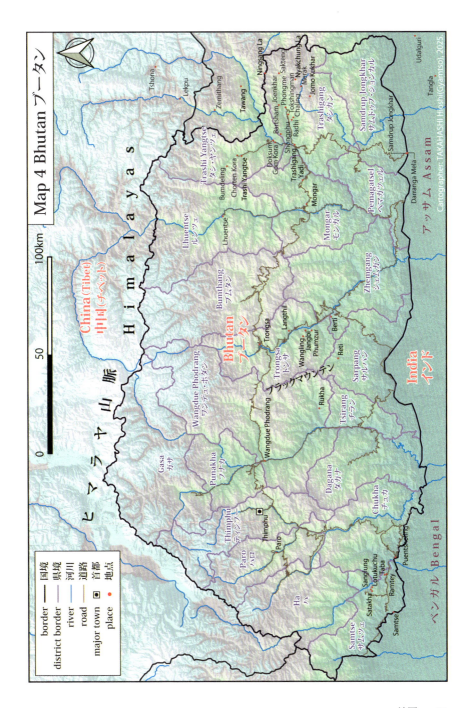

CHAPTER 1
Regional Overview

第1章 地域の概要

　本書の主たる舞台は、インドのアルナーチャル・プラデーシュ州西部の西カメン県・タワン県と、ブータン東部のタシガン県のサクテン地区・メラ地区、つまりインドとブータンの国境の東西に位置する地域である。

北東インドのアルナーチャル・プラデーシュ州

　アルナーチャル・プラデーシュ州は、19世紀前半にイギリス植民地政府によるアッサム統治が始まるまでは山岳部族が住む地帯としてしか知られていなかった。1823年にアッサムの密林で自生の茶樹が発見され、茶園経営が盛んになるにつれ、イギリス植民地政府は、インド平原部のイギリス臣民の権益が損なわれることを恐れるようになり、1873年に平原と丘陵部を隔てる内郭線（インナー・ライン）を引くことを決めた。それ以来、丘陵部は北東辺境地域として隔離されてきた。現在でもアルナーチャル・プラデーシュ州、ナガランド州、ミゾラム州、そして最近ではマニプル州の各州への入域に際しては、州外のインド国民にはインナー・ライン許可書が必要で、アルナーチャル・プラデーシュ州だけは、外国人に保護地域許可証の申請を義務付けている。

　1914年にイギリス植民地政府とチベット政府との間で調印されたインドとチベットとの国境線マクマホン・ラインは、中国が承認していないため未画定で、現在も中国が州の大部分の領有を主張する係争地である。北のマクマホン・ライン、南のインナー・ラインという二つの境界線に囲まれていることが、インドの他州にはないこの州の地政学上の特色である。

　州内には26以上の公的に認定された民族集団（指定トライブ）[1]が住み、さまざまに異なる言語集団に属している。また各集団に固有の信仰があり、たとえば多数派の集団は、ドニ・ポロ（太陽と月）と呼ばれる信仰を持つ一方、キリスト教へ改宗した者も多い。

モンユルの回廊地帯

　州西部のタワン県と西カメン県は、イギリス植民地時代からチベット南部の錯那（ツォナ）とアッサムとを結ぶモンユルの回廊地帯（Monyul Corridor）と呼ばれてきた(2)。モンユルとは、ブータンなども含むヒマラヤ山脈南麓のモンの地を指す呼称で、その住民は、モンパと呼ばれていた。現在、インドでは、タワン県と西カメン県のモンパ（Monpa）、上シアン県とシー・ヨミ県のメンバ（Memba）、そして中国（西蔵自治区）では55の少数民族の一つである門巴（メンバ）族、ブータンではトンサ県とワンデュ・ポダン県にまたがるブラック・マウンテン地域に住むモンパ（Monpa）などである。シッキムのレプチャもモンパと呼ばれていた。これらは、地域による若干の発音の違いがあるだけで、すべて「モンの住民」を意味する名称である。

　本書では、「モンユル」という用語を、ブータン東部のルンツェ、タシガン、タシ・ヤンツェ、モンガル、サムドゥプ・ジョンカル、ペマガツェルの6県と、アルナーチャル・プラデーシュ州西部のタワン県、西カメン県、そしてチベット南部のツォナ（錯那）県を含む地域を指す用語として使用している。モンパ以外には、ミジ、フルッソ（アカ）、シェルドゥクペン、ブグンなどの民族集団が主として西カメン県の低地に居住している。

　モンユルの回廊地帯は、1681年、ダライ・ラマ5世の治世にチベット仏教ゲルク派のモンユルにおける布教の拠点として建てられたタワン僧院を中心に、約300年間チベットの支配下にあった。32のツォおよびディンという行政区画が設けられ、チベット政府から税を課せられ、文化的にもチベット仏教文化の強い影響下にあった。

　数奇で悲劇的な生涯と数多くの恋愛詩で知られるダライ・ラマ6世ツァンヤン・ギャムツォ（1683-1706）は、タワンで生まれ、その両親には、歴史的にブータンとの強い絆がある。まず、父はニンマ派の在家僧で、「埋蔵宝典発掘者」としてブータンやチベットで知られた高僧ペマ・リンパ（1450-1521）の末弟ウギェン・サンポがその祖先にあたる。ダライ・ラマ6世は、ウギェン・サンポから数えて7代目の子孫である。母の家系は、チベットのティデ・ソンツェン王の長男であるツァンマ王子がその祖先だとされる。ツァンマ王子は、9世紀にブータンに追放され、彼からブータン東部の多くのクラン（血族集団）が

【1-1】2015年にダライ・ラマ6世の母の実家、クシャンナン近くに完成した新堂。
A new temple was completed in 2015 near *Kushangnang*, the family home of the mother of the 6th Dalai Lama. (Berkhar, Tawang, November 2015)

派生したが、母はそのクランの一つ、タワンのジョヲ（*Jowo*）クランに属していた(3)。母の実家は、タワンのベルカル村にあり、「母方のオジの家」の敬称であるクシャンナン（*Kushangnang*）と呼ばれ、今でもその血脈が受け継がれている。2015年には、地震で傷んだ旧居の仏間から移したウギェン・サンポと、ダライ・ラマ6世と両親などの像を納めた新堂が近くに建立された【1-1】。

　マクマホン・ラインが引かれた後もモンユルの回廊地帯の南北の往来は続き、チベットによる支配が終わり、インドの行政がタワンにまで及んだのは、インド独立後の1951年のことであった。

　1959年にダライ・ラマ法王14世がチベットからインドへ亡命した際に、モンユルの回廊地帯を経てアッサム州のテズプルに到着している。この地域は、1962年に中国がインドに侵攻した中印国境紛争の東部戦線の激戦地ともなった。この紛争後、北のチベットとの交流は途絶え、相互の往来は断絶した状態が続いている。

　独立後のインド憲法により、モンパはインドの指定トライブとなり、あいまいな総称であったモンパがそのトライブ名となった。しかし、実際にはモンパ

は10以上の言語集団からなり、そのいずれもがすべてのモンパに共通する言語ではない。また、いくつかのモンパを自称としない集団も含まれている。多くの言語は、ブータンやチベット側にも類似の言語を母語とする集団がいる。こうした言語の類似性は、この地域の人々の移住の歴史を伝えるものであるとともに、相互に往還していた時代の名残であろう(4)。

　チベット側との国境と違い、ブータンとの国境の往来は、地元民であれば身分証明書の携行が義務付けられているだけで、現在もかなり緩やかである。アルナーチャル・プラデーシュ州とブータンのタシガン県、タシ・ヤンツェ県を結ぶ国境は、すべて徒歩で越えなければならないが、そのルートは約10本ある。例外的に、最近の新型コロナウイルス流行の際には、双方の往来は厳しく制限された。ただし、これらの国境は、外国人の通行は許されていない。

ブータン東部山岳地帯のサクテン、メラ地区

　一方のブータンは、17世紀にチベット南部からブータンに亡命してきたドゥク派（ドゥクパ・カギュ派）の高僧シャプドゥン・ンガワン・ナムギェル（1594-1651）によって統一国家が誕生し、ブータン東部も1656年にはドゥク派の勢力下に入った。ブータン東部平定の戦いの際の対抗勢力の一つが、ゲルク派の僧ロデ・ギャムツォ（?-1682）で、メラに住んでいたことから現在もメラ・ラマの名で知られている(5)。彼はドゥク派との戦いに敗れてタワンに退き、後にタワン僧院を建設した。

　タシガン県のサクテン地区は、平均標高3,000 mで人口は2,059人、その南のメラ地区は、平均標高3,500 mで1,561人である(6)。両方とも高い山々に囲まれた谷である。この二つの谷の往来には途中に標高4,140 mのニャクチュン・ラ（峠）があり、険しい山道を一日かけて歩かなくてはならない。

　ダライ・ラマ2世（1475/6-1542）の時代にタワンに初めてゲルク派の寺院を建てたラマ・ロプサン・テンペイ・ドンメによって、サクテンやメラにもゲルク派の寺院が複数建てられた。人々は牧畜民を意味するブロクパと呼ばれ、ゲルク派を信奉している。言語はブロクパケである。冬は低地へ、夏は高地へと季節移動してヤクやヒツジを飼育している。ヤクの乳から作るチーズやバターをタシガン県の低地の村々やモンパの村へ運んで、農産物や日用品と物々交換するのが伝統的な暮らし方だったが、現在はすべて現金で取引される。

【1-2】魔女ハシャンの遺体が埋葬されていると伝わる「黒い仏塔」。
The Black Chorten (stupa), where the body of the demoness Hashang, is said to be buried. (Near the village of Merak, November 2008)

　希少な動植物も多く、豊かな自然に囲まれた地であることから、2003年にサクテンとメラ全域がサクテン野生保護区に指定された。文化の面では、アルナーチャル・プラデーシュ州のモンパと共通するものが多い。チベット歌舞劇で有名なカンドゥ・ドワ・サンモの物語はモンユルの回廊地帯からブータン東部が発祥の地で、メラ近くの河原に現存する黒い仏塔の下には、劇中の魔女ハシャンが王子クントレクパによって調伏され、その遺体が埋められていると伝えられている【1-2】。

　2010年9月に外国人観光客の訪問が解禁され、その後、電気が引かれ、自動車道路も少しずつ整備されつつあり、高等教育を受けた若者も年々増え、それにつれて生業である牧畜を継ぐ者が減少するなど、大きな変化の中にある。

ブータン東部からペマコへの移住とインドのメンバ

　中国の門巴族が住んでいるのは、西蔵自治区山南地区の錯那（ツォナ）県と林芝（ニンティ）地区の墨脱（メト）県であるが、現在両地域とも外国人の立ち入りは厳しく制限されている。墨脱県は、ヤルンツァンポ河がアルナーチャル・プラデーシュ州に流れ込む大彎曲部の谷に位置している。ここは8世紀にパドマサンバヴァが仏教の修行場とした隠れ里（ベユル）の一つペマコとして知られ、17世紀には、そこを「地上の楽園」とする噂がチベット圏の人々の間に流布していた(7)。

　1913年に、ペマコに住むブータン東部から移住してきた人々に会ったイギリス人情報将校ベイリーは、「彼らは、いまだに自分たちを（ブータン初代国王の以前の称号である）トンサ・ペンロップの臣民だと考えていた」と記している(8)。複数の訪問者が同様の話を伝え、この移動について考察しているが、それらを総合すると、ブータン東部のツァンラ語（シャルチョプ語）を話す人々が最初にペマコに移住したのは、17世紀の後半ではないかとされる(9)。

　ペマコの南のインド側の上シアン県には、指定トライブのメンバ（Memba）が住むが、彼らの言語もツァンラ語である。しかし、シー・ヨミ県のメンチュカのやはり指定トライブであるメンバ（Memba）の人々の言語は、チベットのコンポ地方の言語に類似している。こうした昔の人々の移動と定住が言語に多大な影響を与えていることは想像に難くない。

　本書では、現在ではインド、ブータン、中国（チベット）に暮らすモンパ／メンバ／モンバ、そしてブロクパとして知られる人々の間の移住や交流の歴史が、民族衣装にどう反映されているかを考察する。

---

(1) インド憲法第342条に基づき、各州またはその一部に指定された部族コミュニティのことで、彼らに対しては、教育・雇用・議席についての留保枠が設けられるなどの優遇政策や、所有地の指定トライブ以外への譲渡の規制などの保護政策が実施されている。
(2) [Tilman 2016(1946): 15-17]。
(3) ペマ・リンパとダライ・ラマ6世の生涯については、[Aris 1989] に詳しく書かれている。
(4) 西カメン県の人々の移住に関しては [Bodt 2014b] が参考になる。
(5) マイケル・アリスは、ブータンの史料に見えるラマ・ナクセンのことではないかと推察している [Aris 2009: 119]。
(6) 人口は、2017年の統計による。
(7) [Lazcano 2005: 46]。
(8) [ベイリイ 1968: 80-81]。
(9) [Thinley 2009: 146-147]、[Kinga 2009: 83]、[Bodt 2012: 159] など。

CHAPTER 1
Regional Overview

The primary settings of this book are the districts of West Kameng and Tawang in the western part of the Indian state of Arunachal Pradesh, and Sakteng and Merak blocks in Trashigang district in eastern Bhutan. In other words, the areas to the immediate east and west of the India-Bhutan border.

Arunachal Pradesh in North East India

Until the beginning of the British colonial government's rule over Assam in the early 19th century, Arunachal Pradesh was known only as a hilly region inhabited by tribes. With the discovery of tea plants growing wild in Assam in 1823 and the establishment and expansion of tea plantations, the British colonial government feared that the interests of its British subjects in the Indian plains would be undermined. Hence, in 1873, she decided to establish the Inner Line, an artificial border separating the hills from the plains. Since then, the hill areas have been segregated from the mainland of India as the north-east frontier region. Even today, it is compulsory for citizens of India residing outside the states of Arunachal Pradesh, Nagaland, Mizoram and Manipur to apply for an Inner Line permit to enter these states. Of these states, only Arunachal Pradesh still requires foreigners to apply for Protected Area Permit to visit the state.

The agreement concerning the border between (British) India and Tibet, known as the McMahon Line, was signed between British colonial government and Tibet in 1914. However, this border has not been demarcated as it is not recognized by China. Hence, much of Arunachal Pradesh is still a disputed area, with China claiming most of the state. Surrounded by two boundaries, the McMahon Line in the north and the Inner Line in the south, the geopolitical situation of Arunachal Pradesh is unique and not like any other state in India.

There are more than 26 officially recognized ethnic groups or 'Scheduled Tribes[1]' living in the state and the members belonging to each group speak various distinct languages. Each group has its own indigenous belief, for example the majority of the groups follow a religion commonly called *Donyi- Polo* (Sun and Moon). However, there are also many Christian converts among them.

The Monyul Corridor

Tawang and West Kameng district in the western part of the state have been known as the Monyul Corridor since British colonial times[2]. The corridor used to link Tshona in southern Tibet with the Assam plains. Monyul is the name given to the Mon region, an area in the southern foothills of the Himalayas. Its inhabitants were called "Monpa". At present, we can find "Monpa" in Tawang and West Kameng, and "Memba" in Upper Siang and Shi Yomi districts in India, "Menba" (mén bā zú), one of the 55 ethnic minorities in China (Tibet Autonomous Region), and "Monpa" of Bhutan, living in the Black Mountain region between Trongsa and Wangdue Phodrang districts. Even the Lepcha of Sikkim were known as "Monpa". All these names refer to "inhabitants of Mon", with only slight differences in local pronunciation. In this book, I use the term 'Monyul' to refer to the area that includes the six districts of Lhuentse, Trashigang, Trashi Yangtse, Mongar, Samdrup Jongkhar and Pemagatshel in eastern Bhutan; the two districts of Tawang and West Kameng in western Arunachal Pradesh; and Tshona county in southern Tibet. Other ethnic groups, such as the Miji, the Hrusso (Aka), the Sherdukpen and the Bugun, live mainly in the lower part of West Kameng district.

The area of the Monyul Corridor was under Tibetan rule for about 300 years, with the Tawang Monastery built in 1681 as a base of propagation for the Gelukpa school of Tibetan Buddhism in Monyul during the reign of the Fifth Dalai Lama. Thirty-two administrative divisions, known as *tsho* and *ding*, were established and taxed by the Tibetan government. Culturally, it was under the strong influence of Tibetan Buddhist culture.

The Sixth Dalai Lama, Tsangyang Gyamtso (1683-1706), known for his unconventional and tragic life and many love poems, was born in Tawang and his parents had close historical and family ties with Bhutan. His father was a lay monk of the Nyingmapa school, and his ancestor was Ugyen Zangpo, the youngest brother of the renowned Buddhist monk Pema Lingpa (1450-1521) who is known in Bhutan and Tibet as a *tertön* "revealer of hidden treasures". The Sixth Dalai Lama is the seventh-generation descendant of Ugyen Zangpo. His mother's lineage is said to have descended from Prince Tsangma, the eldest son of King Tride Songtsen of Tibet. Prince Tsangma was exiled to Bhutan in the 9th century, and from him many clans in eastern Bhutan were derived, and the mother of the Dalai Lama belonged to one of them, the *Jowo* clan of Tawang(3). The mother's parents' house is in the village of Berkhar, Tawang, and it is called *Kushangnang*, the honorific name for "house of the maternal uncle". The lineage is still alive today. In 2015, a new hall was built nearby the house and among others, the statues of Ugyen Zangpo and the Sixth Dalai Lama and his parents, were moved there from the earthquake-damaged alter room of the old house 【1-1】.

Even after the McMahon Line was drawn, north-south traffic in the Monyul Corridor continued. It was not until 1951, after India's independence, that the Indian administration extended to Tawang and Tibetan rule came to an end.

In 1959, His Holiness the Fourteenth Dalai Lama arrived in Tezpur, Assam through the Monyul Corridor. This area was also a battleground on the eastern front of the India-China boundary dispute in 1962 when China invaded India. After this conflict, interaction with Tibet in the north ceased and mutual traffic has remained cut off since then.

Under the post-independence Constitution of India, the Monpa became one of the Scheduled Tribes of India, and the vague generic name Monpa became its tribal name. However, the Monpa Scheduled Tribe consists of more than ten different linguistic groups. None of their languages is a common language for all the Monpas, and a few of the groups do not even call themselves Monpa. Many of the languages are related to languages spoken in Bhutan and Tibet. These linguistic similarities indicate the history of migration of the people of the region and may be a remnant of a time when people passed up and down between each other[4]. Unlike the border with Tibet, traffic on the border with Bhutan is still fairly relaxed, with locals only required to carry identity cards. All borders between Arunachal Pradesh and Trashigang and Trashi Yangtse districts of Bhutan have to be crossed on foot, and there are about ten routes. Exceptionally, during the recent Covid-19 epidemic, traffic on both sides was severely restricted. However, these borders are not open to foreigners.

Sakteng and Merak in the mountainous area of eastern Bhutan

Bhutan was unified as a single nation by Zhabdrung Ngawang Namgyel (1594-1651), in the 17th century. The Zhabdrung was a high incarnated lama of the Drukpa Kagyu school who arrived in Bhutan as an exile from southern Tibet. Eastern Bhutan came under the control of the Drukpa Kagyu in 1656. One of the forces that opposed their expansion was the Gelukpa monk Lodrö Gyamtso (?-1682), who lived in the Merak and is still known as the Merak Lama[5]. He was defeated in a battle against the Drukpa and retreated to Tawang, where he later built the Tawang Monastery.

Sakteng block in Trashigang district has a population of 2,059 and an average altitude of 3,000 m, and Merak block has a population of 1,561[6] and an average altitude of 3,500 m. Both are valleys surrounded by high mountains. The journey between the two valleys involves a day's walk along a steep rocky trail, crossing the Nyakchung La at 4,140 m.

During the reign of the Second Dalai Lama (1475/6-1542), Lama Lobsang Tenpei Drönme built the first Gelukpa temple in Tawang. He also built multiple Gelukpa temples in Sakteng and Merak. Till now, the people of Merak and Sakteng, known as Brokpa 'herdsman', are followers of the Gelukpa school. Their language is known as Brokpake. They move seasonally to the lowlands in winter and to the highlands in summer to raise their flocks of yak and sheep. Cheese and butter made from yak's milk were traditionally transported to villages in the lower valleys of Trashigang district and to the villages of the Monpa to be bartered for agricultural products and daily necessities, but nowadays everything is traded for cash.

In 2003, the whole area of Sakteng and Merak was designated as Sakteng Wildlife Sanctuary, because of its rich natural environment and rare flora and fauna. In terms of culture, the region shares much in common with the Monpas of

Arunachal Pradesh. The story of Khandro Drowa Zangmo became a famous Tibetan opera but originates from the Monyul Corridor and eastern Bhutan. The demoness Hashang from the story was subdued by the Prince Kuntu Lekpa, and her body was buried under the Black Chorten which still exists on the riverbank near Merak village [1-2]. The ban on foreign tourists to Merak and Sakteng was lifted in September 2010. Since then, the area has been undergoing major changes: electricity was installed, motorways are gradually being built, and the number of young people with higher education is increasing year by year. In the midst of all these changes, the number of successors following the traditional pastoralist livelihood is decreasing.

Pemakö migration from eastern Bhutan and the Indian Membas

China's Monpa/Menba people live in Tshona county of Shannan prefecture and Metok county of Nyingtri Prefecture in Tibet Autonomous Region. Both these areas are now strictly restricted to foreigners. Metok county is located in the valley of the great bend where the Yarlung Tsangpo River flows into Arunachal Pradesh. It is known as Pemakö, one of the Hidden Lands (Beyul) where Padmasambhava made a Buddhist asylum in the 8th century. By the 17th century there were rumours circulating in the Tibetan region that it was a 'paradise on earth'[7]. F. M. Bailey, a British intelligence officer who met the eastern Bhutanese migrants in Pemakö in 1913, wrote that they still considered themselves subjects of the Trongsa Penlop (the former title of the first king of Bhutan)[8]. Several visitors have reported similar stories and discussed the migration, which collectively suggests that the first wave of Tshangla (Sharchopkha) speakers from eastern Bhutan migrated to Pemakö in the late 17th century[9]. In Tuting of Upper Siang district on the Indian side of the border, south of Pemakö, we can also find Tshangla speakers who belong to the Memba Scheduled Tribe. But the people belonging to the Memba Scheduled Tribe of Menchukha in Shi Yomi district speak a language similar to that of Kongpo region in Tibet. It is not difficult to imagine that earlier migrations and settlements of people have had a major impact on the languages spoken at present.

This book looks at the history of migration and interaction between the people, now collectively known as the Monpa/Memba/Menba/Monba and Brokpa, who live in India, China (Tibet) and Bhutan, and how this is reflected in their traditional dress.

(1) The tribal communities designated under Article 342 of the Indian Constitution in each state or part of a state for which preferential policies, such as reserved quotas in education, employment and seats in Parliament, and protective policies, such as restrictions on the transfer of their land holdings to non-Scheduled Tribes, are in place.
(2) [Tilman 2016(1946): 15-17].
(3) For more information on the lives of Pema Lingpa and the Sixth Dalai Lama, see [Aris 1989].
(4) [Bodt 2014b] is a good reference on the migration of the people in the West Kameng district.
(5) Michael Aris assumed that Lama Nakseng in the Bhutanese record may be identified with him [Aris 2009: 119].
(6) Population figures are based on 2017 statistics.
(7) [Lazcano 2005: 46].
(8) [Bailey 1957: 72-74].
(9) [Thinley 2009: 146-147],[Kinga 2009:83],[Bodt 2012: 159] etc.

CHAPTER 2
Observing the Traditional Costumes of the Monpa

第2章 モンパの民族衣装を読む

　アルナーチャル・プラデーシュ州西部のかつてモンユルの回廊地帯と呼ばれた地域のモンパの人々の民族衣装には、次章で述べるブータンのブロクパの衣装に関する記述や写真と共通するものが多い。それは、婚姻や交易、宗教その他を通した文化伝播の結果だと考えられる。

【2-1】ディラン・ゾン（城）のある高台からディランの旧市街を望む。
A view of old Dirang from the hill where Dirang Dzong is located. (November 2003)

　「まえがき」でも述べたように、「モンパ」という名称は、もとは、現在のブータン、シッキム、ネパールの一部、さらにその先までを含むヒマラヤ山脈南麓のさまざまな言語を持つ人々に対して用いられたチベット語の総称であった。アルナーチャル・プラデーシュ州では、指定トライブとしてのモンパは、10以上の言語集団から成り、そのうちのいくつかの言語は、ブータン東部やチベット南部の人々の言語とも共通、あるいは関連性が見られる。

【2-2】西カメン県とタワン県の県境に位置するセ・ラ（峠）。
Se La Pass located on the border of West Kameng and Tawang district. (March 2009)

　中世には、アッサムとチベットの間にモンユルの回廊地帯を経由する交易ルートが開設され、イギリスがインドを統治していた時代にも継続していた。その交易品の

中には、モンユルの回廊地帯からのコメやチベットからの岩塩などの食料品だけでなく、アッサムからのシルクの布やラック染料、モンユルの回廊地帯からのアカネ染料や野生動物の毛皮、チベットからの羊毛なども含まれていた。モンパは、その交易の一端を担っていた人たちでもある。

　現在は、西カメン県、タワン県となっているモンユルの回廊地帯は、北のヒマラヤ山脈と南のアッサム平原の間の起伏に富んだ山岳地帯に広がっている。たとえば、モンパの住む西カメン県南部のカラクタンは標高1,140 mで、県庁所在地のボムディラは2,500 m、ディラン地方【2-1】は1,500 mから1,800 mで、比較的温暖で農地も多い。この地の大多数の人々は、ツァンラ語を話すが、この言語はブータン東部では、一般的に話されるシャルチョップ語とも呼ばれている。しかしながら、中には、チャンダルやルブラン、ニュクマドゥンなど、現在は指定トライブのモンパに含まれる牧畜民ブロクパの住む3,000 m前後の高地の村もある。ディランから渓谷に沿って山道を北上すると、タワン県との境、標高4,176 mのゼ・ラ（現在はセ・ラと書く）峠に達する【2-2】。

　タワン県は、タワン・チュ（川）によって形成された渓谷に東西に広がっている。タワン僧院が建つ現在の町の中心部は標高約3000 mに位置し、谷全体を俯瞰することができる【2-3】。ただし、町を取り巻く農村地帯は、タワン・チュの川岸の標高1,800 mから2,800 mほどの高さにあり、冬も温暖で雨期の

【2-3】タワンの町や周辺を見渡す高台にそびえるタワン僧院は、1681年に、メラ・ラマの愛称をもつロデ・ギャムツォによって創建された。
Perched on a hill overlooking the town of Tawang and the surrounding villages, Tawang Monastery was founded in 1681 by Lodrö Gyamtso, also known as Merak Lama. (March 2009)

【2-4】タワンの米作地帯の一つ、キトゥピ・サークルのシェルヌプ村。
Shernup village in Kitpi circle, one of the rice-producing villages of Tawang. (August 2010)

第2章　モンパの民族衣装を読む　　35

日照時間も長い【2-4】。

　タワン県北西部のゼミタンはパンチェンとも呼ばれているが、標高は1,500 mからチベット国境に近いルンポ村の2,700 mと北に向かって高くなってゆく。県東部のティンブー・サークルのティンブーやマゴウは、標高3,500 m前後の牧畜民の居住地である。

　本章では、モンパと総称される人々の衣装について観察する。衣服や帯、靴、帽子などの名前は、地域、言語によって異なるが、本書でそのすべてに言及することはできなかった。

民族衣装の素材

　モンパの男女の民族衣装の素材として使われてきたのは、イラクサ、ウール、獣皮、ヤクの毛、木綿、野生または飼育された蚕のシルク、化学繊維などである。1950年代以前は、イラクサやウール製が主流だったが、それ以降は、アッサムやブータンからもたらされたエリ蚕（学名 *Samia Cynthia ricini*）のシルクに変わってきている。エリ・シルクは、インドではエンディ・シルクとしても知られる野蚕糸のことである。エリ・シルクの名称は、アッサム語でトウゴマ、別名ヒマ（蓖麻）（学名 *Ricinus communis*）を意味する「エラ」に由来している。これは、蚕がヒマの葉を餌として育つからである【2-5】。日本でも、この蚕は、蓖麻蚕（ひまさん）と呼ばれている。

　タワンのモンパ語であるモンケットでは、エーリン、ディランのツァンラ語

【2-5】トウゴマ（ヒマ）の葉を食むエリ蚕。アッサム州ソニトプル県のミシン（ミリ）族の村にて。
Eri silkworm feeding on the leaves of the castor oil plant, in a village of the Mishing (Miri) tribe. (Sonitpur district, Assam, November 2012)

ではエリ、あるいはアリンと呼ばれる。チベット語では、ブレ（虫の布）、ブータンのゾンカ語ではブラと呼ばれる。本章では、便宜上、野蚕糸で織ったシルクをすべてエリ・シルクと表記する。

男性の民族衣装

まず、一般的なモンパの男性の上着は、大きく分けて2種類ある。第一は、ウールの赤や茶色の前合わせの上着で、タワンではチュパ（chupa）、ディラン地方ではツォラ（tshola）と呼ばれる。チベットのチュパは、裾までの長いものだが、モンパのものは、腰を覆うほどの長さである。帯は、タワンのモンケットではキチン（kichin）、ディラン地方のツァンラ語ではチュダン（chudang）と呼ばれ、幅40cmほどの手織りの布が使われる。この布は、子供や荷物を背負う時にも使われる。

現在は、モンパ男性の

【2-6】エリ・シルクのカンジャールの上からウールのチュパを着て手作りの布製のブーツを履いた男性。
A man wearing a woollen *chupa* over an *eri* silk *khanjar* and handmade cloth boots. (Tawang, March 2003)

【2-7】帽子、上着、ブーツのすべてが手作りというのは最近では珍しくなった。この上着はカンジャールではなく、チュパと呼ばれているが、チベットの影響を受けたスタイルであるという。
The hat, jacket and boots are all handmade, which is rare these days. This jacket is called a *chupa*, not a *khanjar*, and is said to be a Tibetan-influenced style. (Tawang, March 2003)

【2-8】ダライ・ラマ14世のタワン訪問時にカンジャールを着て正装した男性たち。
Men in formal dress wearing *khanjar* during the visit of the 14th Dalai Lama to Tawang. (Tawang, April 2017)

【2-9】若者たちが着ているのはエリ・シルクのカンジャール、右端の男性はその上からチュパを着ている。
The young men are wearing *eri* silk *khanjar* and the man on the right is wearing a *chupa* over it. (Tawang, April 2017)

【2-10】古いエリ・シルクの長ズボン（ドルマ）。現在は大変珍しい。
Old *eri* silk trousers (*dorma*) in Dirang. It is very rare now. (March 2004)

　チュパよりもカンジャール（*khanjar*）、あるいはケンジャール（*khenjar*）、またはアリ・フドゥン（*ali-phudung*）と呼ばれる上着のほうが正装として着られる機会が多い。斜めの前打ち合わせの上着で、襟は高めの立ち襟になっているものである。素材は、緞子でできたカラフルなもの、ウール製の黒や茶色などのもの、エリ・シルクで織られた白や、ラック染料で織られたものなどさまざまである。この上にチュパを着る人もいる【2-6, 2-7, 2-8, 2-9】。

　現在は、正装の時でも、下にズボンや、若者の場合はジーンズを着用していることが多いが、元は、タワン地方であればウール製、ディラン地方やカラクタン地方では木綿やエリ・シルクの長ズボンを穿いていた【2-10】。ズボンのことは、チベット語と同じくドルマ（*dorma*）と呼ぶ。もう一つチュパの下に穿くのは、主として牧畜民が着ける白いウール製のキュロット・スカート、カンダム（*kangdham*）、あるいはカンノム（*kangnom*）である。その下にホエジカの皮をなめしたピシュ（*pishup*）という2つの筒形のレギンスを着ける【2-11】。このカンダムの腰から円形のフェルトの携帯クッションを吊り下げていた。タワンのモンパ語（モンケット）では、このクッションは、テンタン（*tengtan*）と呼ばれる。次章にも記したが、メラやサクテンのブロクパ語（*Brokpake*）では、白いキュロット・スカートはカンゴー（*kanggo*）、円型クッションは、ク

【2-11】モンパの村では希少になったピシュを穿いた男性。当時すでに83歳の高齢だった。
A man wearing a *pishup*, which has become rare in the Monpa villages. He was already 83 years old at the time. (Mukto, August 2011)

【2-12】キュロット・スカート「カンダム」の後ろに丸い携帯クッション「テンタン」を下げている。モンパの村ではヤク・チャムの衣装（第6章）として残っている程度である。この写真はメラで撮影。
A round portable cushion "*tengtan*" is lowered on a "*kangdham*". They remain only as yak *cham* costumes (Chapter 6) in the villages of the Monpa. (Merak, Bhutan, July 2012)

プテン（*kupten*）である。

　カンダムとテンタンはモンパの地域では、ピシュはヤク・チャム（ヤクの仮面舞踏）の衣装として残っているだけで、ほぼ姿を消してしまった【2-12】。第3章、第6章を参照いただきたい。

　ディラン地方で、1980年代まで着られていた男性の膝丈の白い腰巻タネ（*tane*）【2-13, 2-14】は、元はイラクサやエリ・シルク製だったが、その後、エリ・シルクのズボンや西洋式のズボンに取って代わられてしまったという(1)。その姿が、テンバンのラーソイシェー（*lhasöshe*）やラフンのローサイボー（*lhosaibo*）など仏教以前の、主として山の神々への信仰に基づく祭りやユーミン（*yumin*）と呼ばれるシャーマンの衣装としてわずかに残されている。これらの祭りは、仏教以前の、土地の山の神々への信仰に基づいたものである。

【2-13】テンバンのユーミン（シャーマン）が腰に巻いていたエリ・シルク製のタネ。
A *tane* made of *eri* silk, which was worn around the waist by a *yumin* 'shaman' of Thembang. (Photograph by T. Bodt, April 2013)

【2-14】ラフンのローサイボー祭で。サングラスの男性が着けているのがタネである。
The man with sunglasses at the *Lhosaibo* festival in Rahung is also wearing a *tane*. (January 2020)

　実は、ラフンやその近隣のコイタム、コイナ、ジェリガオンの人々も、指定トライブのモンパとみなされてきたが、言語や来歴が異なることから、数年前からインド政府に対して、「モンパ」ではなく「サルタン（*Sartang*）」として認めるようにと要求していた。その結果、2021年8月に正式に名称の変更が認められた。サルタンの人々の衣服は、ミジやシェルドゥクペン、モンパの衣服が混ざっている。最も古い形は、女性の場合は、白いシンカに花柄のジャケット、男性の場合はウールのジャケットとタネの組み合わせである。サルタンの人々は現在、単一の言語・宗教・祭りなどと同様に、「標準化された」サルタン・ドレスを発展させている、これは独立した指定トライブとして承認されるための必要条件の一つである(2)。

　2020年1月のラフンのローサイボー祭では、男女共に、モンパと同じ衣装を着ている人もいるが、ほとんどの男性は、洋服の上から白または臙脂色のエリ・シルクの布を両肩から胸の前と背中で交差させ、腰で結んでいた。左肩だけに掛けて右腰で結ぶこともある。この布には神々への敬意を表す意味がある。腰にタネを巻いている男性もいる【2-14, 2-15】。私が見たところでは、この祭りで

【2-15】ラフンのローサイボー祭で、臙脂色あるいは白い布のエリ・シルクの布を肩から斜めに掛け、腰で結んでいるサルタンの男性たち。この布には神々への敬意を示す意味がある。
Sartang people wearing a dark red or white *eri* silk cloth draped over their shoulders and tied at the hip at the *Lhosaibo* festival in Rahung. This cloth is a sign of respect to the deities. (January 2020)

は男女ともに多くの人々が洋服を着ていたが、サルタンとして認められた結果として、彼らの標準的な衣装が、今後どのように表象されてゆくのか興味深い。

女性の貫頭衣シンカと髪飾り

現在、モンパ女性は、臙脂色に白、近年はそれに薄い青が加わった縞柄が入った貫頭衣シンカ（*shingka*）を共通の民族衣装として着用している【2-16】。この貫頭衣という形状の服は、かつては、サクテン、メラ以外のブータン中央部のブムタン地方や東部のルンツェ県のクルトェ地方などでも着られていた。それらの衣装は、ティンプーの織物博物館にも展示されている【2-17a, 2-17b】。私も、ルンツェで祭りの衣装で着られる木綿製の貫頭衣を見たことがある【2-18】。ブータンの多くの場所で、かつて女性は、ツァンラ語でノンコ（*nongko*）あるいはノンノンマ（*nongnongma*）、ゾンカ語でグツム（*gutsum*）【2-19】と呼ばれる下着や寝間着を着ていた。この寝間着は、白や時には単純な幾何

【2-16】シンカには袖はない。腰当て布と上着を着けて初めて正装となる。
The *shingka* has no sleeves. It is only with a back apron and a jacket that it becomes formal attire. (Rama Camp, Dirang, March 2009)

【2-17a】古い時代のブータン北中部と東部のウールの貫頭衣、この赤あるいは臙脂色のものは、レウシンカと呼ばれる。レウ（赤）とは、東部の織物の村で話されるザラカ語に特有の言葉である。
An old Bhutanese woollen tunic, from area of north central and eastern Bhutan, this red or maroon one is called *leushingkha*. Leu (red) is unique to the language Dzalakha in the eastern weaving villages. (Photo and caption courtesy of the Royal Textile Academy of Bhutan, Thimphu)

【2-17b】古い時代のブータンのウールの貫頭衣で、この紺色の貫頭衣は、ンガウシンカと呼ばれている。ンガウは、ブータン東部で話されているいくつかの言語の中の、青を表す言葉と似ている。
Woolen old Bhutanese tunic, from north central and eastern Bhutan. This navy blue one is called as *ngaushingkha*. Ngau is similar to the words for blue in some languages spoken in the eastern Bhutan. (Photo and caption courtesy of the Royal Textile Academy of Bhutan, Thimphu)

【2-18】ルンツェの村の祭りで使われるこの木綿の貫頭衣もシンカと呼ばれている。
This cotton tunic also called *shingka* is used during the festival in a village in Lhuentse. (Lhuentse, Bhutan, September 2008)

学模様の木綿で作られ、形状や寸法はシンカに似ていた。シャツやパジャマが持ち込まれるようになると、この寝間着は着られなくなった。ブータン東部やチベットのペマコの貫頭衣については、第8章を参照されたい。

東南アジアでは、ミャンマーのカレン族の未婚女性が着る白いくるぶし丈のワンピースと、既婚女性が着るブラウスがやはりこの形状である[3]。

シンカの素材は、1950年代から60年代以前は、イラクサやウール製だったと思われる。チベットがモンユルの回廊地帯を統治していた時代、人々はアッサムのシルクをチベットに運んでいたにもかかわらず、シルクなどのぜいたく品を身に着ける余裕はなかった。彼らが自分たちで作った米を食べることができなかったのと同じである。米は、チベット政府によって課された税であった。彼ら

【2-20a】エリ・シルクのシンカより以前に着られていたタワンのンゴウシン。
Ngoushing was worn in the Tawang area before the *eri* silk *shingka*. (Tawang, January 2020)

【2-19】パロのようなブータン西部の寒い地域では、1980年代ごろまでこのグツムと呼ばれる白い木綿の貫頭衣がキラの下、あるいは寝間着として着られていた。それは寒さを防ぐためだけでなく、キラを汚れから守るためでもあった。
In the cold regions of western Bhutan, such as Paro, this cotton white tunic called *gutsum* was worn under the *kira* or as nightclothes until around the 1980s. It was not only for keeping out the cold, but also to protect the *kira* from dirt. (This *gutsum* is from Paro in the 1960s, owned by Satoko Nishioka)

【2-20b】ンゴウシンの両脇の三角形のマチ（襠）。
The triangular gore on the sides of the *ngoushing*. (Tawang, January 2020)

　の主食は、ソバ、トウモロコシ、アワなどの雑穀であった。タワンにインドの行政官が到着し、チベット人が退去させられたのは1951年のことである。現在のエリ・シルクのシンカが着られるようになったのは、正確な年代はわからないが、おそらく1951年以降のことであろう。

　それまでは、タワンや西カメン県の一部では、ウール製のシンカ、ンゴウシン（*ngoushing*）が着られていたことがわかっている。ンゴウシンは、タワンのモンパ語で、青または紺色のシンカという意味である。現在では、着る人は皆無だが、写真【2-20a, 2-20b】は、タワンに住む1944年頃に生まれた女性が所有するもので、彼女の亡くなった母親が作ったものだという。

　サイズは縦104 cm、横79.5 cmであるから、小柄な女性ならくるぶしまで届

第2章　モンパの民族衣装を読む　　43

【2-21】オギェンリン・ラカン内部の壁画に描かれたダライ・ラマ6世の母、ツェワン・ラモ。
Tsewang Lhamo, mother of the Sixth Dalai Lama, painted on the wall inside of Ogyenling Lhakhang (October 2003).

く長さである。両脇のマチ（襠）部分を前へ折り返して帯を締める。三角形のマチの部分は、上が薄茶色、下は赤、黒、赤のウール布が接ぎ合わされている。重く、色も濃紺と、決しておしゃれで人目を引く衣服でないことは、後で述べる19世紀と20世紀の訪問者がまったく言及していないことからも推測される。

　タワンで昔のンゴウシンのことを調べていた時に、ダライ・ラマ6世ツァンヤン・ギャムツォ（1683-1706）の母ツェワン・ラモがそれを着ている絵があると、教えてくれた人がいた。その絵というのは、ダライ・ラマ6世が生まれたとされるタワンのオギェンリン（現在はウルゲリンと綴る）・ラカンの内部の左側の壁画のことを指している【2-21】。この絵では、赤と紺の縦縞の貫頭衣を着ているが、この縞柄は、後述するマゴウの女性のドレスのようにも見える。二色の布を縦に接いだンゴウシンがあったのかどうか、これ以上はわかっていない。オギェンリン・ラカンは、モンゴルのラサン・ハーンの軍隊により1714年に破壊され廃墟になった。ラサン・ハーンは、ツァンヤン・ギャムツォはダライ・ラマ5世の転生ではないと宣言し、1706年に彼を廃位させ、北京に護送した。しかしながら、ダライ・ラマ6世は、途中のクンガノールで謎の死を遂げてしまった。現存する寺は、ダライ・ラマ7世（1708-1757）によって再建されたものである[4]。残念ながら、この壁画がいつ描かれたかは不明である。

【2-22】タワンのベルカルにあるダライ・ラマ6世の母の実家、クシャンナン。
Kushangnang, the maternal uncle's house of the mother of the Sixth Dalai Lama, in Berkhar, Tawang. (March 2009)

【2-23】クシャンナンに現在も残る、ツェワン・ラモの塑像。ヘアバンドのような髪飾りを着けている。
The clay statue of Tsewang Lhamo in *Kushangnang*. She is wearing a headband-like ornament. (Berkhar, Tawang, August 2011)

　ダライ・ラマ6世の母の実家でもあるオジの家、クシャンナンは、タワンのキトゥピ・サークルのベルカル村に現存している【2-22】。それを相続して守っている現在の子孫によれば、ダライ・ラマ6世は、実家に帰った母が、オギェンリンではなく、ここで出産した可能性があるという。

　写真【2-23】は、クシャンナンにあるダライ・ラマ6世の母親の塑像である。この像は、【2-21】とは違って、青と赤の二枚重ねの前合わせの衣服を着て、ヘアバンドのような髪飾りを着けている。中央の円型部分は青く、中心が赤く描かれている。銀製のヘアバンドで、青い部分はトルコ石、赤い部分は珊瑚を表現したものだと推定される。像が作られた年代は不詳だが、ダライ・ラマ6世の没後、つまり18世紀以降のものであろう。

　同じようなヘアバンドは、モンパの地域であれば、西カメン県のテンバンのラーソイシェーの祭りで、儀礼の一端を担う少女ブローモ（*bro-mo*）が着けている【2-24】。この祭りは、仏教がこの地に伝わる以前からあった、周囲の山に住む土地神に捧げる祭りで、テンバンでは6年に1度行われる。ブータンのクルテ地方の山の神々に奉献する祭りの際の女性の踊り子たちは、貫頭衣を着て、頭にも同様の金属製のヘアバンドを着けている(5)。このことから、ヘアバンドとこうした山の神々などに対する土俗的な信仰とを結び付ける考察もある

【2-24】テンバンのラーソイシェーの祭りでブローモを演じる少女たちも同様のヘアバンドを着けている。
Young girls, *bromo*, at the festival of *Lhasöshe* in Thembang also wearing same type of headband. (Photograph by Kazuharu Mizuno, February 2011)

が(6)、それらの各地での古くからの伝統衣装の一部であった可能性もあり、断定はできない。なぜならば、類似のヘアバンドは西カメン県のミジ、フルッソ（アカ）、ブグンなどのトライブにも見られるからである。西カメン県のモンパ以外のトライブの服装については、第9章で紹介する。

　現在のシンカはエリ・シルクの平織りで、色は、染めていない白い生地のままのものと、ラック・カイガラムシ(学名*Kerria lacca*)の分泌液で染めた臙脂色があるが、染料の濃度、媒染剤などによってピンクがかったもの、赤に近いものなどさまざまである。白い生地のままのシンカの方が安価であるが、現在、正装として着用されるのはラック染料で染められたものである。これらは、初期にはブータンから、後にアッサムの商人が運んでくるようになった。もともとモンパはシルクを織ってはいなかったが、ディランに、2人だけ例外的に織る女性がいた。2002年頃にインド政府が主催した染織講習会が行われ、ボムディラやディランに数カ所のモンパ所有の工房が開かれたが、織り手は、アッサムやマニプルから雇われてきた少女たちである。モンパの衣服を織る人々、商う人々に関しては、第4章で述べる。

　現在見られる一般的なシンカは、アッサム製の高機で織られたものは、幅80cmから90 cm、長さ2～3 mの一枚布であるが【2-25】、腰帯機で織られたものは、その半分の幅の2枚の布を接ぎ合わせたものである。それを二つ折りにして、

【2-25】エリ・シルクのシンカを広げたもの。幅広の織機で織ったものは、一枚布で、二つ折りにして頭の部分と腕の部分だけ開けている。このシンカは、ラック染料をふんだんに使って染められたディラン・シンカと呼ばれる高級品である。
An unfolded *shingka* of *eri* silk. Woven on a wide loom, it is a single piece of cloth, folded in two and opened only at the head and arms. This *shingka* is a luxury item called the Dirang *shingka* and dyed with a lot of lac dye. (Dirang, March 2009)

【2-26】シンカの両側を前に寄せて後ろの腰当て布を押さえるようにして帯を締める。
Both sides of the *shingka* are gathered at the front of the body, and the belt is fastened with the back apron. (【2-26】-【2-28】, Rama Camp, March 2009)

【2-27】腰当て布をして、上着のトトゥンを着る。
With the back apron in place, the *tothung* (jacket) is put on.

輪の部分の中央に頭が楽に入るほどの穴を開け、両脇を腕の部分だけたっぷりと開けて縫い閉じる。形状はごく単純な貫頭衣であるが、中南米のポンチョのような両脇の開いた上着ではない。全体を身体の前方に寄せてギャザーを作り、後ろのエプロンのような腰当て布を押さえるようにして帯を締める【2-26, 2-27】。この腰当て布は、帯の一部のようなもので、シンカには欠かせないものである。この腰当て布については、第5章で述べる。

　一枚布の場合は、頭を入れる部分を

【2-28】この女性はスカーフをしているように見えるが、正装用に白いトトゥンを下に着て折り返している。This lady appears to be wearing a scarf, but for formal wear, she wears a white *tothung* underneath and folds outwards in front.

【2-29】ブータンのブロクパ女性のトトゥン【3-5】に比べると、モンパのトトゥンの特に星のような柄は大きめである。Compared to the *tothung* of the Bhutanese Brokpa women 【3-5】, the *tothung*'s pattern of the Monpa, especially the star-like pattern, is larger. (Dirang, March 2009)

ハサミで切り、その布端がほつれないように、別布で作ったバイアス・テープで布端を包んで玉縁にする。2枚の布を接ぎ合わせる場合も同様である。玉縁用の布は多くは緑色で、稀に銀色もあるが、元は地元で作られていたが、今は他州から持ち込まれたナンブと呼ばれるウールの幅広の布である。

　形状は、袖なしのワンピース・ドレスであるが、横幅がたっぷりしていて運動しても着崩れしにくいことから、農耕や牧畜に適している。

上着トトゥンとその模様・東南アジアとの関係・首飾り

　チベット語でトトゥンは、シャツ、ブラウス、上着を意味するが、モンパは、シンカの上に着る上着をトトゥン、あるいはトゥトゥンと呼んでいる。トトゥンもシンカ同様に、ラック染料で染めたものが大半だが、白無地のものもある。素材は、エリ・シルクだが、下着のように着る白いトトゥンは、木綿や化学繊維が多い。それを前で折り返すので、白いスカーフを着けているように見えることもあるが、これは正装のときだけで、普段着には着けない【2-28】。模様が

前後に織り込まれたものが大半だが【2-29, 2-30】、裾に少しだけ織り込みがあるシンプルなものもある。

　トトゥンには、黒いウール製のものもあり、チベット語やブロクパ語ではウールはバー（bal）であるが、タワンではバイ（bai）で、ウール製の上着はバイ・トトゥン（bai tothung）と呼ばれる【2-31】。だがこのトトゥンには模様はなく、一般的に正装として着用されることはない。

　ブータンのブロクパは、シンカはエリ・シルクだが、トトゥンは、化学繊維のものが多くなっている。しかし、モンパのシンカ、トトゥンは必ずエリ・シルクである。エリ・シルクは、短い糸を紡いでいるため、つるつるとした光沢はないので、麻や木綿と間違われることがある。その特性は、シルクとしては安価であるばかりか、大変丈夫で、普段着や野良着にも適して、何度も洗ううちに柔らかくなってくる。意外に保温性があり、アッサムでは、冬の衣服や夜具として使われていた(7)。

　トトゥンの柄には、星・花・矢・万字（卍）などの他に、馬・象・鳥などの動物や、その上に乗った人物などをモチーフにした幾何学模様が、カラフルな糸で織り込まれている。模様入りのトトゥンと強調する場合には、タワンでは、トトゥン・キャンチャン、ディラン地方のチュグ村では、トトゥン・モムナンなどと呼ぶ。しかし、トトゥンと言えば多くの場合は、模様入りである。

【2-30】細かい柄が織り込まれた白いトトゥンは、珍しくなった。
White *tothung* with fine woven patterns have become rare. (Dirang, March 1999)

【2-31】ウール製の上着バイ・トトゥンを着ているモンパ女性。
A Monpa woman wearing a *bai tothung* made of wool. (Tawang, December 2011)

【2-32】ブータン北東部の古い貫頭衣（クシュン）の絵柄。下の方に、人間のようなものを運んでいる動物のデザインが見える。
The design of an old tunic (*kushung*) from north-eastern Bhutan. You can see animal designs carrying something that looks like human beings at the bottom. (Photo courtesy of the Royal Textile Academy of Bhutan, Thimphu)

トトゥンに織り込まれた絵柄のデザインで興味深いのは、動物の上に乗る人物像が、古い時代のブータンの織物【2-32】や、現在のラオスなど東南アジアの少数民族の織物にも見られることである。例えば、【2-33】は、タワンのモンパのトトゥンの柄である。1970年代から80年代に織られたものだという。基本的なデザインは現在も大きくは変わっていない。このトトゥンに織り込まれた大きな星型のモチーフは、ラオスの織物の中の星とも大変似ているが、ラオスでは星は、豊穣や子宮（子孫繁栄）を象徴しているという【2-34】(8)。

ラオスの場合には、国の中東部のシェンクアンに住んでいたプアン族や北部のサムヌアやルアン・ナムター周辺に住むタイ・デン（赤タイ族Tai Daeng）、タイ・ダム（黒タイ族Tai Dam）などの布にも、トトゥンの柄

【2-33】1970年代から80年代のタワンのモンパのトトゥンの図柄。どこで織られたものかは不明である。
The design of the *tothung* which was woven in the 1970s or 1980s. It is not clear where the weaving took place. (Tawang, March 2004)

【2-34】ラオスの星の模様。ラオスでは、星は豊穣と子宮、つまり子孫繁栄を象徴しているという。
In Laos, the stars symbolise fertility and the womb, indicating the prosperity of offspring. (Photo courtesy of Chanthasone Inthavong)

【2-35】ラオスのタイ・デン（赤タイ族）のシャーマンが儀礼に用いる布の図柄。下の黒い部分に、手を挙げた動物に乗った人物が織り込まれている。
A pattern on a cloth used by shamans of the Tai Daeng (Red Thai) tribe in Laos for rituals. A figure is woven into the black area at the bottom, riding on the animal with its hands raised. (Photo courtesy of Chanthasone Inthavong)

【2-36】ラオスのルアン・ナムター近くで入手したタイ・ダム（黒タイ族）が織った布。
A cloth woven by the Tai Dam (Black Thai) tribe near Luang Namtha, Laos. (January 2011)

にある動物の上に人が乗っている図柄によく似たデザインが織り込まれている。写真【2-35】はタイ・デン族のシャーマンが儀礼に使う布の図柄だが、赤タイの名前の由来でもある女性の赤いターバンやタイ・ダム族の葬儀に使う旗などの柄にも、動物の上に乗る人物の絵柄が見られる。神話上の動物の上に両手を挙げて立つ人物は、祖霊を表しているという(9)。

　写真【2-36】は、私が、2011年にラオス北部のルアン・ナムター近くの赤タイ族の村で入手したものである。織ったのは黒タイ族で、黒地に白の絵柄は、動物の上に乗った人の姿で、人の姿をしたものは、精霊だという。東南アジアのタイ、ビルマ、ラオスと同種のデザインとの類似に関しては、マイヤーズ

【2-37】アルナーチャル・プラデーシュ州東部のナムサイ県ナムサイに住むタイ・カムティ族の人々。高僧の葬儀で遺骸が納められた山車を引いている。既婚者は緑色の布を腰に巻いている。
The Tai Khamti tribes live in Namsai, Namsai district, eastern Arunachal Pradesh. The people are pulling a float containing the remains of a high priest at his funeral. The married women wear a green cloth around their waists. (Namsai, January 2020)

【2-38a】このネックレスは、タワンの有力者の縁者が着けていたもので、大きな珊瑚、金製のビーズ、トルコ石、中央のズィー（縞瑪瑙）など、見るからにかなりの高級品である。
This necklace was worn by a relative of a prominent person in Tawang. It is quite luxurious with several large corals, turquoise, gold beads and a zi stone (striped agate) in the centre. (Tawang, July 2010)

【2-38b】この女性は、小さな淡水真珠をつないだ銀のペンダントや大きな銀製のブローチやチェーン、珊瑚や銀のビーズのネックレス、そして四角いお守りと、持てるアクセサリーをすべて身に着けているように見える。
This woman appears to be wearing all the accessories she has: a silver pendant with small freshwater pearls strung together, a large silver brooch and chain, a necklace of coral and silver beads, and a square amulet. (Zemithang, March 2009)

（Diana K. Myers）とポマレ（Françoise Pommaret）が、メラとサクテンのブロクパのトトゥンの柄とを比較し、チベットに近いブータンが遠く離れた東南アジアと共通点を持つことに注目している(10)。

モンパやブロクパには、これらのデザインについて説明する伝承などは伝わっていない。その代わりに、タワンのある女性は、ラオス人の言う星と精霊を「輪」、馬の上に立っているのは「人物」だと語っていた。アッサムに13世紀から約600年続いたアホム王国を建国したのは、シャンと呼ばれたタイ系の民族であった(11)。このことから彼らがブータンやモンユルの回廊地

帯の織物に影響を与えた可能性もある。アホム時代の古い織物の中にこうしたデザインが残されている可能性も考えられるが、今のところその手掛かりはつかめていない。アルナーチャル・プラデーシュ州には、タイ系のトライブであるタイ・カムティ（Tai Khamti）がいる。彼らは、ビルマのイラワディ川源流付近からアッサムのサディヤ付近に移住したと考えられている(12)。現在は、アルナーチャル・プラデーシュ州東部のナムサイ県が主たる居住地となっている【2-37】。リーチ（Edmund R. Leach）は、彼らのアッサムへの移住の時期を1795年頃としている(13)。しかし、タイ・カムティの現在の織物の中には、鳥をモチーフにしたものは見られるが、モンパやブロクパの鳥とは異なるデザインである。

　女性の正装には首飾りは欠かせない。その多くは、珊瑚やトルコ石、銀細工、真珠などを組み合わせたものである。伝統的なモンパ社会は、男性が親の不動資産を相続するが、これらのアクセサリーや女性の衣類や織物、台所用品などの可動資産は、母から娘たちへと受け継がれてゆくものである【2-38a, 2-38b】。

女性の肩掛けの役割

　女性の四角い肩掛け【2-39】は、タワンでは、ウール製の赤い色のものが多いが、これをレンバ（lhemba）、カラフルなチベットの布を縫い合わせて作ったものをディンガ（dhin-nga）あるいはディンガ・レンバ（dhin-nga lhemba）と呼んでいる。ディラン地方でも同様だが、ウールやヤクの毛で織ったものをナムシュ村やチュグ村では、ヘムバクタン（hembaktang）と呼んでいる。雨具あるいは防寒具として使われるが、タワンの

【2-39】タワン僧院のトルギャ祭で肩掛けをしていたのは、一部の中高年者だけであった。
Only a few elderly women wore a shoulder cape at the *Torgya* festival in Tawang Monastery. (January 2017)

第2章　モンパの民族衣装を読む　53

【2-40a】ディラン地方のナムシュ村のラーソイシェー祭のブローモは、この少女1人だった。ゴイチェン・ジャムを被り、肩掛けをしている。
This girl was the only *bro-mo* at the *Lhasöshe* festival in Namshu village. She wears a *goychen zhamu* and a shoulder cape. (Namshu, January 2020)

【2-40b】ブローモの肩掛けディンガ・レンバは、鮮やかなチベット布で作られている。
The *bro-mo*'s shoulder cape *dhin-nga lhemba* is made of bright Tibetan cloth. (Namshu, January 2020)

1950年代生まれの女性の話では、元々は普段でも身に着けたもので、例えば、朝、この肩掛けをしていない女性に会うと縁起が悪いと言われるほどだったという。特に、正装には欠かせないものだったが、近年はそのことを知らない人が多く、寺院での法要や祭りなどで着用しているのは年配者ばかりで、若い人は誰一人着けていない。

ディラン地方のテンバン村やナムシュ村の土地の神々に捧げる祭

【2-41】ナムシュのラーソイシェー祭に参加した女性たちが祭礼の場所に供え物を運んでいる。肩掛けは誰もしていなかった。
Women at the *Lhasöshe* festival in Namshu carrying offerings to the festival site. No one was wearing a shoulder cape. (January 2020)

り、ラーソイシェーでは、ブローモと呼ばれる少女たちが、色鮮やかなチベット布で作ったディンガ・レンバを着けている【2-40a, 2-40b】。私が見学した2020年のナムシュ村のラーソイシェーでは、村人は、男女ともに正装して参加していたが、肩掛けを着けている女性は皆無だった【2-41】。かつては、一般の人々も礼装として肩掛けを着けていた習慣が次第に失われ、ブローモの儀礼用衣装として残ったのではないだろうか。

2種類の帽子

モンパの帽子には、錦織（にしきおり）の布製のものと、ヤクの毛をフェルト状にしたものの2種類がある。前者は、タワンではゴチェン・ジャム（*gochen zhamu*）、ディランでは、ゴイチェン・ジャム（*goychen zhamu*）、チュグ村では、ジャラベンダン・コートン（*jalabengdang khothong*）と呼ぶ【2-40a, 2-42】。チベット語のゴチェン（*gochen*）は、シルクなどで織られた錦織のことで、花模様などの刺繍が施されているものが多い。この帽子は、チベット南部のロカ地区やコンポ地区の人々の帽子とほぼ同じである。タワンやボムディラのチベッ

【2-42】ディラン地方の帽子ゴイチェン・ジャムと、布製ブーツのツァンズム。
Hat, *goychen zhamu*, and cloth boots, *tsangzum*, in the Dirang region. (Durang, December 2004)

【2-43a】メラやサクテンの帽子の房と比べるとモンパの帽子の房は太い。
The tassels of the Monpa hat are thicker than those of the hat of Merak and Sakteng (Zemithang, March 2009).

【2-43b】帽子を頭の後ろから押さえるように被る女性もいて、なかなかおしゃれ。モンパのイヤリングは男女ともにユーと呼ばれるトルコ石である。
Some women wear their hats as if they were pushed from the back of the head, which is quite fashionable. Monpa's earrings for both men and women are made of the turquoise, locally called *yu*. (Tawang, December 2010)

第2章 モンパの民族衣装を読む 55

【2-44a】モクトウの帽子づくり。作っているのは、【2-11】の男性と同一人物である。
Hat making in Mukto. This is the same person as the man in 【2-11】. (August 2011)

【2-44b】ニュクマドゥンでのヤクの毛の帽子作り。
Making a hat of yak hair in Nyukmadung. (March 2004)

ト人が経営する店で作られ、売られている。これらは、以前は、西カメン県のサンティ谷でも作られていた。

　後者は、ヤクの毛をフェルト状にしたもので、5本の房があることは共通しているが、その房が太かったり、頭の部分が小さかったり、形状も被り方もさまざまである【2-43a, 2-43b】。ブータンのメラやサクテンの人々も同じような帽子を被っているが、最近は、頭頂部が平たく房が細いなど、モンパの帽子との違いが強調されてきている。作り方など、詳細については、第3章を参照されたい。シェルドゥクペンの人々も似たような帽子を被っているが、房は4本だけである。このヤクの毛の帽子は、タワンではンガム・ジャム（ngam zhamu）、ディランではツィパ・ジャム（tsitpa zhamu）と呼ばれている。タワン県のモクトウや西カメン県のニュクマドゥンなどで作っているのを見たことがあるが【2-44a, 2-44b】、被っているのはほとんどが年配者である。ヤクの毛で頭皮がチクチクするからと、若い女性たちは、布製の帽子を好んで被っている。今の若い人々には、ヤクの毛の帽子は、おしゃれには見えないのであろう。

　タワン県のマゴウとゼミタンの人々の帽子は、これらとは異なるものだが、

【2-45】女性が履いている手作りのブーツ、ツェム・ラム。
Handmade boots *tsem lham* worn by a woman. (Tawang, November 2012)

【2-46】布製のブーツに皮の底を縫い付けている。
He sews leather soles onto cloth boots. (Seru village of Tawang, January 2013)

このことについては本章で後述する。

布製のブーツ

　2000年代初頭までは、モンパの人々が、メラやサクテンの人々が現在も履いているような、ヤクやウシの皮を靴底にした手作りの布製ブーツを履いているのをよく見かけた。ただし、履いていたのは、やはりほとんどが60歳以上の年配者であった【2-6, 2-7, 2-45】。次章に書いたように、メラやサクテンでは、男性用ブーツの甲は赤、女性用ブーツの甲は青と決まっていて、モンパの場合も原則は同じだが、それほど厳格ではない。皮の靴底のある手作りのブーツは、タワンではツェム・ラム（*tsem lham*）と呼ばれるが、それを作れる人は次第に減っている【2-46】。

　近年は、布製のブーツを履く人はごく稀で、寺院での法要などで民族衣装を身に着ける場合には、チベット製の布製ブーツを履いている場合がある。イベントのショーでダンサーが履いているものもチベット製で、甲から膝にかけては赤と緑色のフェルト、筒の部分は黒いフェルトが使われ、刺繍

【2-47】1950年代にラサで買ってきたというツァンゾムを履いている女性。
A woman wearing a pair of *tsangzom* bought in Lhasa in the 1950s. (Tawang, October 2012)

が施されている。靴底は革製で、縫い目の部分は編まれた木綿糸で囲まれている。この靴は、タワンのモンケットではツァンゾム（tsangzom）、ディランのツァンラ語ではツァンズム（tsangzum）という【2-42】。1962年の中印国境紛争以前には、チベットとの交易があった。例えば、写真【2-47】のタワンの女性が履いているブーツは、1940年生まれの彼女が1950年代に家族や隣人とラサへ巡礼に出かけた時に購入したものだという。現在は、ほとんどが西ベンガル州のカリンポンで作られているものである。

初期の訪問者の記録から

　以下は、イギリス植民地政府がモンユルの回廊地帯に関心を持ち始めた19世紀から20世紀にかけて、そしてインド独立前にこの地方を訪れた人々、あるいはこの地について聞いた人々が語ったモンパの衣服に関する報告の一部である。

（1）　ワイズ・コレクションの絵

一人のチベット人僧侶により描かれた、タワンのモンパの男性の服装が興味深い絵がある【2-48】。これは、ワイズ（Thomas Alexander Wise 1802-1889）のコレクションの中にある絵で、元の持ち主である東インド会社の退役軍人であったW. E. ヘイ（William Edmund Hay 1805-1879）が、ラサからヒマ

【2-48】このイラストのキャプションは、「モン地方のタワンの人々」である。左の人物には、「家の守り神を入れた箱を下げている」と手書きの説明が書かれているが、この丸いものは、携帯クッションであろう。右の人物には、「仏教僧あるいは宗教的な熟達者」と書かれている。
This illustration is captioned 'The People of Mon Tawang'. The handwriting explanation for the figure on the left says that he is 'carrying the guardian deity of his house in a box suspended', but this round object is probably a portable cushion. The right figure is described as 'a Buddhist monk or adept'.
(From the Wise Collection [Lange 2020: 51])

ーチャル・プラデーシュのナガールに旅してきた僧侶に描かせた地図や絵の中のもので、描かれた時期は、1857年7、8月から翌年6月の間であったと推察されている(14)。

　この絵の左側の男性は、赤いジャケットに白いスカートのようなものを着けて、布製のブーツを履いている。ヘルメットのような黒い帽子を被り、腰から丸いバッグのようなものを下げ、長いパイプでタバコを吸っている。この丸いバッグのようなものは、モン地方のタワンの地図上に描かれた人びとに共通していることから、ブロクパの人々が腰から下げている携帯用座布団のことで、これがモンパのトレード・マークであった可能性がある。赤いジャケットは、現在でも見られるウール製のチュパ、黒い帽子は、ヤクの毛をフェルト状にしたものであろう。白いスカートのように見えるものは、モンパがカンダムと呼ぶキュロット・スカートか、ディラン地方のシャーマンや祭りで男性が履いているタネ【2-13, 2-14】の可能性もあるが、この絵からでは断定はできない。

　この絵や地図を描いた僧侶の名や、彼が実際にタワンを訪れたことがあるのかどうかは書かれていない。もし彼が伝聞に基づいてこの絵を描いたのなら、その服装は正確ではないかもしれない。

（2）　ナイン・シン（1830?-1882?）

　タワンを訪れた外来者によるもっとも古い英語の記録は、ナイン・シン（Nain Singh）の報告であろう。彼は、現在のインド北部のウッタラーカンド州クマーオン地方の出身で、英国植民地政府のインド測量局に雇われた「パンディット」であった。パンディットの本来の意味は、「ヒンドゥー教徒の学者」であったが、実際には測量技術を習得した密偵で、チベットを経て、1874年12月24日にタワンに到着した。彼はタワン地方の住民を、モンパ、あるいはタワンパと呼び、「チベット人とは言語・衣服・風習・容貌が異なり、西側のブータン人と似通っている。チベット人は髪を長くして三つ編みにしているが、モンパは、丸く頭を囲むように髪を切り揃えて、小さなウール地またはフェルト地で作った帽子を被っている。チベット人の長いガウンの代わりに、膝丈の短い上着を着て、ウールの帯を締め、長い刀をそこに差している」と報告している(15)。これは明らかに男性の服装であるが、女性の服装については記述がない。

(3) F. M. ベイリー（1882-1967）

　イギリス人の情報将校フレデリック・マーシュマン・ベイリー（Frederic Marshman Bailey）は、1913年10月16日にタワンに着いた。彼の旅行は、翌年のシムラー会議でのインドとチベットの国境画定のための情報収集が目的だった。彼は、タワンのモンパについて、「チベット人とは異なり、ブータン人やシッキム人に、より似ている」「髪を短く切り、フェルトの縁なし帽を被り、赤く染めた衣服を着ている」と記述している(16)。それ以外の服装に関する唯一の記述は、ディランからタワンに向かう途中のニュクマドゥンでのもので、「ここの人々の服装は下の谷の人々とは違っている。女たちの衣服は、木綿やアッサム・シルクの代わりに毛織物で、男たちは、小さな携帯用の座布団といってもよい奇妙なパッドを腰から吊り下げていた。彼らのほとんどがチベット語を話し、モンパよりもチベット人に近いように見えた」という内容である(17)。ニュクマドゥンの人々の言語は、牧畜民の言語ブロクパケで、西カメン県のセンゲ・ゾンやルブラン、タワン県のルンタン、ブータンのメラやサクテンのブロクパと呼ばれる人々とほぼ共通している。ここに書かれている小さな座布団については、先にも述べたが、ブロクパの男性が腰から吊り下げて座布団代わりにしている円型のクッションである【2-12】。

　ベイリーは、タワン県のマゴウやゼミタンの服装についても記述しているが、それについては後で述べる。

(4) R. E. クーパー（1890-1962）

　タワン県の西部に住むダクパ（Dakpa）は、現在はモンパの下位集団であるが、ブータンのタシガン県とタシ・ヤンツェ県にも住んでいる。ブータン東部のツァンラ語（シャルチョプ語）話者の人々は、タワンのモンパをブラーミ（Brami）と呼ぶが、ダクパと呼ぶ人々もいる。そのダクパをタシガンの人々が「尻尾のある人々」（Tailed People）と呼んでいたという記述がある。これを書いたのは、1915年に東ブータンのタシガンを訪れた植物学者のクーパー（Roland Edgar Cooper）で、この報告書は、1933年の『Man』誌に写真入りで掲載されている【2-49】(18)。だが、クーパーはこの報告の中で、彼らを「ダクタ」（Dakta）と呼んでいる。しかし、ダクタと呼ばれる民族集団は存在しないことから、これはクーパーがダクパを聞き間違えたのであろうと思う。男性

【2-49】R. E. クーパーが1915年にタシガンで撮影した「尻尾のある人々」。
'Tailed People', photographed by R.E. Cooper in Trashigang in 1915. (From *Man*, August,1933)

は、ウールの上着を着ていて、腰のところでたくし上げてポケットのようにしているが、ブータンのゴと比べると袖の折り返しがないという。右の写真の男性の後ろ姿をよく見ると、大きな円型のクッションの上部に尻尾のようなものが見える。クーパーによると、「タシガンの人々の間では、タワンの東の渓谷に尻尾のある人びとが住んでいる」という話が信じられているという。ブータン人が、彼らを「粗暴、粗野」な人々とみなしていて、その服装の特徴からそう見えたのだろうとクーパーは推測している。

　この尻尾は、モンパやブロクパ男性が着る、動物の毛皮を2枚、前後に合わせて作るパクツァというベストの後ろの尻尾が垂れ下がっていたことからきているのであろう。2枚の毛皮を合わせると尻尾が前後に垂れ下がる形になるからである【2-50a, 2-50b】。ベイリーも記述している円型のクッションは、次章の写真【3-17】のサイズは、直径14 cmほどであるが、クーパーの説明では約23 cm（9インチ）もある。写真の男性の説明では、腰から下げたこのパッドは、若い時に着けてから一度も外していないという。そして、重いものを運んだ後の休憩用に使うものだが、それを使用しているのを見たことはないと書いている(19)。

　男性の帽子に関して、クーパーは、「ヤクかヤギの毛のフェルトで作られ、長さ2インチ、指の太さの5本の房があり、毛で編んだあご紐がある」と書いている。そして、この房を、多雨地域の植物の葉の先端が雨水を素早く排水する

ようにドリップ・チップと呼ばれる尖った形をしていることになぞらえている(20)。これは、彼の植物学者としての職業が表れた表現である。

　この帽子は、モンパやブータンのブロクパが被っている帽子と変わらないが、現在のものは形が整っていてデザインも洗練されていて、あご紐はない。
女性の帽子は、現在のモンパ女性のものと異なっているようだが、クーパーは写真の二人の女性の帽子について、下記のように記述している（原文のまま）。

【2-50a】毛皮のベストを作る場合には、2頭分の皮を前後に合わせて作るので、前後に尻尾が垂れ下がる。
When a waistcoat is made of animal hides, two skins are put together front and back, so that the tail hangs down both sides. (Merak, July 2019)

【2-50b】この毛皮は、雄牛と雌ヤクの交配種から生まれた子牛のもの。
These hides are from two calves born from a cross between a bull and a female yak. (Merak, July 2019)

　女性の帽子は濃い色の布で、青の無地か茶と赤の縞模様で、幅2インチの小さなつばには縫い目があり、紐の房が付いている。頭頂部は、つばの内側の円と同じくらいの大きさの丸いトップピースに、高さ2〜3インチの直立した帯がついていて、つばとつながっており、外径は約5インチある。雨の日には何の役にも立たないので、単なるファッションでしかないようだ。明らかに、乾燥した気候のためのもので、雨除けのためのものではなく、単なる衣服の必須アイテムの一つのようだ(21)。

　この説明と写真【2-49】（左の写真の中の右端）の女性の帽子は、現在のモンパの帽子とは異なっているが、ラフン村のサルタンの人々の祭りで、儀式に携

【2-51】ラフン村のローサイボー祭で儀礼を担当する少女たち。
Girls participating in the rituals at the *Lhosaibo* festival in Rahung village. (January 2020)

わる二人の少女が被っている帽子のうち、左側の少女の帽子がよく似ているのではないかと思う【2-51】。二つの帽子は古いもののようだが、昔のものを保存して祭りなどの特別な時に使用しているのかもしれない。

　クーパーの写真の右端の女性の衣服は、現在のシンカとよく似ていて、幅広の帯に腰当て布を着けている。靴もモンパやブロクパの手作りのブーツと同じである。説明によると、2枚の布を縫い合わせて頭と腕の部分を開けた筒形の貫頭衣であることがわかる。普通より粗い木綿でできていて、縞模様が入っているものもあると書かれている。この、より粗い木綿というのは、イラクサのことかもしれない。衣服の名称や色に関する記述はない。

　この写真が、現在までに確認できたもっとも古いモンパのシンカに近い衣服の写真である。だが、この4人が実際には、どこから来たのかは書かれていない。

マゴウとゼミタンの例外的で独特な衣装

　タワン県東部のティンブー・サークルのマゴウ（Mago）は、タワンの町からだと途中まで車、そこから東へ徒歩2日を要する標高3,500 m 以上の山岳地

【2-53】マゴウのワンピース、リゴーのスカート部分は、赤と黒のウール布を縦に交互に縫い合わせて、全体がたっぷりと広がるようになっている。
The skirt part of the dress of Mago, the *rigo*, is made of red and black wool cloth sewn together alternately lengthwise, so that the whole piece spreads out generously. (Tawang, August 2005)

【2-52】マゴウの女性の衣装一式を身に着けている人はなかなかいないので、著者が着てみた。
It is not easy to find someone wearing a complete set of Mago women's costumes, so the author put them on. (Tawang, August 2005)

【2-54a】マゴウ女性のヤクの毛の帽子は、ンガシャとよぶ。この白い帽子は深さ10cmで、18本の房がある。
The yak-hair hats of the Mago women are called *ngazha*. This white hat is 10 cm deep and has 18 tassels. (Nyukmadung, March 2004)

【2-54b】この黒いンガシャは深さ17センチ、房は20本である。
This black *ngazha* is 17 cm deep and has 20 assels. (Tawang, Ausust 2005)

帯にある牧畜民の村である。言語は、ブータンのメラやサクテンの人々などと同じブロクパ語である。だが、彼らも現在は、指定トライブのモンパの一員である。

マゴウの女性の衣服は、一般のモンパ女性が着るシンカやトトゥンではなく、ウールのリゴー（rigo）という膝丈のワンピース型の衣服である【2-52】。赤と黒の二色の厚手のウール地を互い違いに接ぎ合わせて作られたスカート部分を広げると4m以上もある【2-53】。前開きになっていて日本の和服の着物のように右前に

【2-55】タワン僧院のトルギャ祭に来ていたマゴウの女性。ンガシャの代わりに毛糸の帽子を被っている。
A Mago woman at the *Torgya* festival in Tawang Monastery. She is wearing a hat knitted from yarn instead of a *ngazha*. (January 2011)

【2-56】ダライ・ラマ法王14世の法要に参加するためにやって来たマゴウの女性。彼女もンガシャは被っていなかった。
A Mago woman who came to attend the public teaching of His Holiness the 14th Dalai Lama. She was also not wearing a *ngazha*. (Tawang, April 2017)

して合わせ帯をする。ヤクの毛をフェルト状にした帽子は、深さが10〜17cmあり、18〜20本の細い房が垂れ下がっている【2-54a, 2-54b】。また、20個ほどの大きな琥珀や紅玉髄の玉をつないだ紐を頭に掛け、その長さはウエストあたりまで達する【2-55, 2-56】。帯は17cmほどの幅があり、その上から日本の帯留めのような金属の飾り帯を締めている。タワンで開かれるイベント祭などで、若い人たちが舞台衣装としてこの服と帽子にブーツを履いた姿はなかなかファッショナブルではあるが、実際には、この衣服を着る人は年々減っていて、タワンの町で見かけることもごく稀になっている。彼らの地元の村でも女性たちは、シンカやトトゥンを着始めている。

先述のベイリーは、1913年にマゴウを訪れ、マゴウの女性たちが赤と青の縦縞のウールのスカートを穿いていたと書いている。私が先に述べた現在のリ

ゴーのように、おそらく、二色の布を接ぎ合わせたものが、縞柄に見えたのであろう。ベイリーは、そのスカートの下にウール製のニッカーボッカーズを履いていたと書いている。彼女たちが、これを今でも履いているかどうかはわからない。ベイリーは、さらに、装飾品について、「大きな琥珀玉が頭の上の銀の板から耳の前までぶら下がり、真鍮の飾り帯で留めてあった。そしてそれでも足りずに頭の上の銀の板から紅玉髄が額までぶら下がっていた」と書いている。現在のアクセサリーと1世紀前のベイリーの記述とを比べると、当時のマゴウのアクセサリーは、さらに豪華だったことがうかがえる。

　男性の服装に関して、ベイリーは「チベット人と同じような長い赤のコートを着ているが、チベット人が剣を前に下げるのに対し、彼らは後ろに下げていた。縁に房の付いたフェルトの帽子はどちらかと言えばモンパの帽子に似ていた」と記している(22)。

　タワン県北西部のゼミタン・サークルのゼミタンの人々の自称はパンチェンパで、彼らも指定トライブのモンパの一員である。彼らの言語は、パンチェンパ語（Panchengpa 'mat）と呼ばれ、タワンのモンパ語ともダクパ語とも著しく異なっている(23)。彼らの民族衣装も独特である。

【2-57】高僧の法要に集まったゼミタンの人々。
People of Zemithang gathered for the special prayers of a high lama. (Zemithang, March 2009)

男性の赤いウールの上着は、ふくらはぎまでの長さのものもあるが、多くは、それを腰でたくし上げて帯を締め、最終的な長さは膝下程度にする着方である。前から見るとブータンの男性のゴに似ているが、横幅が狭いため後ろの折り返しはほんの少しである【2-57】。

　女性は、現在は、タワンのモンパと同じシンカやトトゥンを着ている人が多いが、元はウールの膝丈の貫頭衣を着ていた。ホームスパンの厚手の40 cm幅のウール布を2枚縦に縫い合わせ、頭を入れる輪の部分だけ縫わずに残す。貫頭衣の脇を縫い合わせる時には、カラフルな縞柄のチベットのウール布が「三角形の襠（まち）」として用いられている。この「襠」の部分を前に

【2-59a】赤いウールの貫頭衣はブータンの古い時代の赤いウールの貫頭衣【2-17a】と同じくレウシンカと呼ばれている。
The red woollen tunic is called a *leushingka*, as is the old Bhutanese red woollen tunic 【2-17a】. (Lumpo village, August 2005)

【2-58】ゼミタンの女性たちは、現在のシンカが普及する前は、このウールの貫頭衣を着ていたという。筆者と。
The women of Zemithang used to wear woollen tunics before they accepted the current *shingka*. On the right is the author. (Lumpo village, August 2005)

【2-59b】茶褐色の貫頭衣はゲナシンカと呼ばれる。
The brownish tunic is called a *genashingka* (Lumpo village, August 2005)

第2章　モンパの民族衣装を読む

【2-60】ルンポ村のカップル。
A couple from Lumpo village.
(Zemithang, March 2009)

倒して見えるようにして帯を締める【2-58, 2-59a, 2-59b】。タワンのンゴウシンと似ているが、長さが膝丈であることが異なっている。この貫頭衣のうち赤色のものをレウシンカ（leushingka）、茶褐色のものをゲナシンカ(genashingka)と呼ぶ。パンチェンパの言語は、東ブータンのタシ・ヤンツェ県のザラカ（Dzalakha）やルンツェ県のコマカ（Khomakha）と呼ばれる言語と近いと言われている(24)。そのことで思い出すのは、ブータン北中部と東部の古いウールの貫頭衣のうち、赤色のものを同じくレウシンカ（leushingka）と呼ぶことである【2-17a】(25)。

もともとゼミタンの女性たちは、四季を通じてこのウールの貫頭衣を着ていたが、1962年の中印国境紛争以後、国境警備のために道路が整備されたおかげで、ゼミタンの人々もタワン僧院の法要やトルギャ祭やドンギュル祭などに出かけるチャンスが増えた。タワンの女性が臙脂色のシンカを着ているのを見て、パンチェンパの女性たちもシンカを着るようになったという。

現在、このウール製のシンカを着る人は、ゼミタンの中心地の北西にあるルンポ（Lumpo）村の年配者である【2-60】。このウールの貫頭衣を着たときには、腰当て布は着けないが、子牛一頭分の皮を背中に掛けている【2-61, 2-62】。この子牛の皮は、フィウ（phiu）あるいはフェウ（pheu）と呼ばれる。この地域のマクマホン・ラインのすぐ北側の西蔵自治区錯那県勒布（レブ）谷（中国語では勒布溝）に住む門巴族も、全く同じように子牛の皮を背負っているのが中国の研究者による資料とその写真からわかる。彼女たちは、腰に白いウールの布を巻いている。説明によると、この子牛の皮にはいくつかの伝説があり、その一つが唐からチベットの王に嫁いだ文成公主が、門巴族の女性たちに耕作の仕方を教えた際に、魔除けのために子牛の皮を背負っていた。それを門巴族に贈ったものが踏襲され、習慣化したものだという内容である(26)。複数の中国の研

【2-61】右側の女性は、小牛の皮を背中から掛けている。男女ともに、この地方特有の帽子シャルジャを被っている。
The woman on the right is wearing a small calfskin over her back. Both the man and the woman are wearing *sharja*, a hat unique to this region. (Zemithang, March 2009)

【2-62】シンカを着ているが腰当て布はせず、代わりに子牛の皮を背中から腰にかけて掛けている。
The woman is wearing a *shingka*, but without a back apron, and instead she is wearing a calf skin hung-over her back. (Zemithang, March 2009)

究者による資料から、勒布谷の男性が、パンチェンパと同じような長い赤い上着を着ていることがわかる(27)。

　先述のベイリーは、1913年10月20日に現在のゼミタン・サークルのシャクティを通り、翌日チベット側の勒布谷のレ(Le) 村に到着している。レ村の人々の服装については、男女どちらのものかはっきりしない。

　　このあたりの人々は、パンチェンより下の地域の人々とは異なる服装をしている。フェルト帽には孔雀の羽根がねじって巻き付けられていた。コートは赤色ではなく白色で、背中に動物の皮をぶら下げていた(28)。

　中国の資料によると、勒布谷の女性も男性も白い上着は着ていない。だが、中国の門巴族女性は、白い布を腰に巻き、動物の皮を背中に掛けている。つま

【2-63a】ヤクの毛を円筒形に固め、孔雀の羽根を飾り付けた帽子ドゥイジュ・マプジャ。
Duiju-mapja, a hat made of yak hair in the shape of a cylinder and decorated with peacock feathers (Zemithang, November 2003)

【2-63b】ドゥイジュ・マプジャを被ったゼミタンのパンチェンパの男性。
A Pangchenpa man wearing a *duiju-mapja* (March 2009)

り、勒布谷の門巴族もゼミタンのパンチェンパも、動物の皮を背中に垂らしているのは女性であるようだ(29)。

さらに現在のパンチェンパの人々の服装を特徴づけるものに2種類の帽子がある。一つは、浅い円筒形をしており、外側に折り返された部分にはオレンジ色の起毛ウールが使われているシャルジャ（*sharja*）またはシルジャ（*siruja*）という帽子で、多くの男女が被っているものである【2-57, 2-58, 2-61】。これは、勒布谷の門巴族が被っているものと非常に似ているが、パンチェンパの帽子は頭頂部が平らであるが、門巴族のものは円錐形に盛り上がっている。門巴族の女性の帽子はセルシャ、男性の帽子はバルシャというという(30)。もう一つは、ヤクの毛を浅い円筒形に固め、クジャクの日本の羽根を周囲に飾ったドゥイジュ・マプジャ（*duiju-mapja*）である【2-60, 2-63a, 2-63b】。孔雀（マブジャ）は再生のシンボルであるという。ベイリーもレ村でこの孔雀の羽根を巻き付けた帽子について記述していることは、先述の通りである。だが、最近の勒布谷の門巴族に関する記録に、この帽子についての記述が見当たらないことから、今では姿を消してしまったのではないだろうか。

日常着からハレ着へ

モンパの人々の民族衣装は、少しずつ日常着から祭りや寺院での法要、公的な行事の際のハレ着に変わってきている【2-64, 2-65】。50代以下の若い世代は、洋服を日常着にしている人が圧倒的に多い。それ以上の年代でジーンズを着用

【2-64】着飾って祭りに参加したナムシュ村の少女たち。
Girls dressed up for the festival in Namshu. (January 2020)

【2-65】タワン僧院で行われた、ダラムサラから招かれた高僧の法要に正装して集まった人々。
Local people gathered in formal dress for the public teaching of a high lama from Dharamsala at Tawang Monastery. (October 2013)

第2章　モンパの民族衣装を読む　　71

【2-66】最前列にブルーのシャルワール・カミーズを着た女性と、ピンクのガレを着けた女性の姿が見える。インド独立記念日のイベントを見学しているところだが、寺院での法要に比べ民族衣装を着ている人は少ない。A woman is seen wearing a blue *shalwar kameez* and a woman in pink *gale* in the front row. They are observing the Indian Independence Day event, but fewer people are wearing traditional dress than at the monastery. (Tawang, 15th August 2015)

することを好まない女性は、一枚布の腰巻スカート、ガレ（*gale*）を着ることが多い。ガレは、アルナーチャル・プラデーシュ州のアディ（Adi）、ガロ（Galo）など複数の民族集団の女性が着けている手織布で、さまざまな色やデザインを楽しむことができる。また、インドの他地域で着られているシャルワール・カミーズを着る女性もいるが、サリーを着る人は稀である。この傾向は、町で暮らす人々に顕著である【2-66】。

【2-67】制服がない学校では、2000年代初期には民族衣装や洋服などまちまちな服装で通学していた。
In schools without uniforms, in the early 2000s, students attended school in a variety of clothes, including traditional costumes and western clothes. (On the roadside near Rama Camp, March 2004)

【2-68】タワン県モクトウの公立学校の中学生の制服。
Uniforms of junior high school students at a public school in Mukto, Tawang district. (Mukto, October 2012)

　モンパの子どもたちが通う学校には、2000年代の初頭は、ある者は民族衣装、ある者は洋服あるいはガレを着ていて、制服がなかった【2-67】。最近は、多くの学校が洋服を制服にしている【2-68】。女子のみシャルワール・カミーズという学校もある。モンパ固有の文化を奨励するために、モンパの居住地のいくつかの学校では、毎週1回、民族衣装を着ることが求められている。

　州外の工場で大量生産された衣服は、民族衣装に比べかなり安価で、色やデザインなども豊富である。こうしたことが、民族衣装の将来にも強い影響を与えるだろうことは否めない。

(1) [Bodt 2020: 199]。
(2) [Bodt 2021]。
(3) [Fraser-Lu: 1988: 94-95]。
(4) [Aris 1989: 121, 165]。
(5) [Myers 1994: 115]。
(6) [Huber 2020a: 480-482]。
(7) [Ghosh & Ghosh 2000: 10]。
(8) [インタヴォン 2006: 81]。
(9) [Brittig & Fajcsák 2016: 161-163, 175, 178-185]、[インタヴォン 2006: 48-49]。
(10) [Myers & Pommaret 1994: 67-69]。
(11) [ゲイト1945: 96]。
(12) [Chowdhury 1983: 32]。
(13) [リーチ 1987: 41]。
(14) [Lange 2020]。
(15) [Trotter 1877: 119-121]。
(16) [Bailey 1914: 358]。
(17) [ベイリイ 1968: 258]。
(18) [Cooper 1933: 125-128]、クーパーのタシガン訪問年については、[Aris 1994: 149-150] より。
(19) [Cooper 1933: 127]。
(20) [Cooper 1933: 126-127]。
(21) [Cooper 1933: 127-128]。
(22) マゴウに関する記述は、[ベイリイ 1968: 248-253] を参照。
(23) [Bodt 2014a: 208]。
(24) [Bodt 2014a: 208-209]。
(25) [Myers 1994: 114-115]。
(26) [于 1995: 438-439] および、写真ページの33-40頁。[陈・张 2014: 66-69]
(27) [于 1995]、[陈・张 2014: 66]。
(28) [ベイリイ 1968: 270]。
(29) ベイリーが訪れた頃には、男性が白い上着を着て女性と同じように動物の皮を背中に掛けていた可能性もあり、断定はできない。
(30) [陈・张 2014: 69-70]。

CHAPTER 2
Observing the Traditional Costumes of the Monpa

The traditional dress of the Monpa people of the region that was once known as Monyul Corridor in western Arunachal Pradesh, India, has much in common with the dress of the Brokpas of Bhutan, which will be discussed in the next chapter. This is most likely the result of cultural diffusion through matrimonial, trade, religious and other contacts and exchanges. As mentioned in the preface, the name Monpa was originally used as a generic Tibetan term for various ethnolinguistic groups living on the southern slopes of the Himalayas, including in present-day Bhutan, in Sikkim, and in some areas in Nepal and even beyond. In Arunachal Pradesh, the Monpa Scheduled Tribe includes people speaking more than ten languages, some of which are also spoken by, or related to, the languages of the people of eastern Bhutan and southern Tibet. In medieval times, a trade route was established between Assam and Tibet through Monyul Corridor, and this continued to be a trade route during the British rule in India. Its trade goods included not only food items such as rice from Monyul Corridor and rock salt from Tibet, but also clothing items, such as silk cloth and lac dye from Assam, madder and skins of wild animals from Monyul Corridor and wool from Tibet. The Monpa people also participated in this trade. The Monyul Corridor area now comprises of West Kameng and Tawang districts and stretches across the rugged mountainous terrain between the Himalayas in the north and the Assam plains in the south. Examples of areas where Monpa people live are: Kalaktang in the southern part of West Kameng, at an altitude of 1,140 m; Bomdila, the capital of the district, at 2,500 m high; and the Dirang region 【2-1】, located between 1,500 m and 1,800 m. The majority of these people speak Tshangla, which is more commonly spoken in eastern Bhutan, where it is known as Sharchopkha. However, there are some villages at higher altitudes of around 3,000 m such as Chandar, Lubrang and Nyukmadung that are inhabited by the pastoralist Brokpa, who also belong to the Monpa Scheduled Tribe. From Dirang, a mountain road leads north through the valley to the Ze La (now written Se La) Pass at an altitude of 4,176 m, which forms the border with Tawang 【2-2】. Tawang is a district that stretches from east to west in a valley formed by the Tawang Chu river. The present centre of the town where the Tawang Monastery is built lies at about 3,000 m above sea level and offers a bird's eye view of the whole valley 【2-3】. However, the altitude of the rural area surrounding the town is about 1,800 to 2,800 m above sea level on the banks of the Tawang Chu, with mild winters and long sunshine hours in the rainy season 【2-4】. Zemithang, also called Pangchen, in the north-west of Tawang, rises from 1,500 m to 2,700 m in the village of Lumpo, near the Tibetan border. In the eastern part of the district, Thingbu and Mago in the Thingbu circle are pastoralist settlements at altitudes of around 3,500 m.

This chapter describes the costumes of the people that are generally referred to as the Monpa. The names of garments, sashes, shoes, hats, etc. vary according to region and language. But it was not possible to include all of them in this book.

Materials used for traditional dress

Nettles, wool, animal skins, yak hair, cotton, silk from wild and cultivated silkworms and synthetic fibres have been the materials used for the traditional dress of the Monpa men and women. Before the 1950s, most of the garments were made from nettles and wool, but since then, the Monpa people have adapted garments woven from *eri* silkworm (*Samia cynthia ricini*) from Assam and Bhutan. Eri silk, also known as *endi* silk or *errandi* silk in India, is a wild silk. The name of *eri* silk comes from the Assamese word "*era*" which means "castor-oil plant (*Ricinus communis*)". This is because the *eri* silkworm feeds on the leaves of the castor-oil plant 【2-5】. Even in Japan, this silkworm is called hima-san (hima is castor-oil plant, san is silkworm).

In Monket, the Monpa language of Tawang, wild silk is called *erin*. In Tshangla, the language of the Dirang and Kalaktang areas, it is called *eri* or *arin*. In Tibetan it is called *bure* (insect cloth), and in Bhutanese Dzongkha it is called *bura*. For the sake of convenience, all silks made from wild silkworm yarn will be referred to as *eri* silk in this chapter.

Men's traditional dress

There are two main types of Monpa men's jackets. The first one is called *chupa* (in Tawang) or *tsola* (in Dirang area), a red or brown colour woollen garment with the right side of the front tucked under the left. The Tibetan *chupa* is long enough to reach the hem, while the Monpa's version is shorter and covers only the waist. The sash or belt, called a *kichin* in Monket of Tawang and a *chudang* in Tshangla of Dirang, is a hand-woven cloth about 40 cm wide. This cloth is also used to carry babies or luggage. Nowadays, Monpa men wear the *khanjar* (or *khenjar*) or *ali-phudung* jacket more commonly as formal wear than the *chupa*. This khanjar or *ali-phudung* jacket has an oblique front with a high stand-up collar. It can be made of a variety of materials, including colourful brocade silk, black or brown wool, and white or lac-dyed *eri* silk. Some people wear a *chupa* over this 【2-6, 2-7, 2-8, 2-9】.

Nowadays, even for formal occasions, people often wear trousers underneath, and younger people wear jeans. But in the past, men wore long trousers made of wool in Tawang, and of cotton or *eri* silk in Dirang and Kalaktang 【2-10】. The trousers are called *dorma*, as in Tibetan. Another traditional dress worn under the *chupa* is the *kangdham* or *kangnom*, a white woollen culotte skirt worn mainly by pastoralists. Underneath are two cylindrical leggings called *pishup*, made of tanned barking-deer skin 【2-11】. From the waist of this *kangdham* people used to hang a circular portable felt cushion 【2-12】. In the Monpa language of Tawang (Monket), this cushion is called a *tengtan*. As mentioned in the next chapter, in the Brokpa language, the white culotte skirt is called *kanggo* and the circular cushion is called *kupten*.

The *kangdam* and *tengtan* only survive in the Monpa region as yak cham (yak masked dance) costumes, while the *pishup* has almost disappeared. See chapters 3 and 6.

The men's knee-length loin cloth, wrapped around the waist, is called *tane* and was worn in the Dirang region until the 1980s. The *tane* was originally made of nettle, cotton, or *eri* silk but has since been replaced by *eri* silk trousers or Western-style trousers (1). There are only a few surviving examples of *tane* in the costumes of festivals such as *Lhasöshe* in Thembang and *Lhosaibo* in Rahung in West Kameng district, and in the costume of shamans called *yumin* 【2-13, 2-14】. These festivals are pre-Buddhist and mainly based on the belief in the local mountain deities.

In fact, the people of Rahung and the nearby villages of Khoitam, Khoina and Jerigaon were considered a part of the Monpa Scheduled Tribe, too. For several years they have been demanding the Indian Government to recognize them as Sartang, instead of Monpa, because of their distinct language and history. This separate status was officially granted in August 2021. The Sartang dress combines elements of Miji, Sherdukpen and Monpa dress. The oldest forms are a white *shingka* and a flowery tothung jacket for woman and a *tane* and woollen *chupa* for men. The Sartang people have now developed a 'standardised' Sartang dress, as, like a single language, religion, festival etc., this is one of the requirements for recognition as a separate Scheduled Tribe (2).

At the *Lhosaibo* Festival in Rahung in January 2020, some men and women wore the same clothes as the Monpas, but most men tied a dark red or white eri silk cloth over their western dress. It is crossed over the shoulders, in front of the chest and back, and tied at the hip. Sometimes it is worn over the left shoulder only and tied at the right hip. This cloth is meant to show respect. Some men wore a *tane* around their lower back 【2-14, 2-15】. At the festival I observed that many people, both men and women, wore western clothes but it will be interesting to see how their standard dress will be represented as a result of being recognised as Sartang.

Women's shingka and hair ornaments

At present, Monpa women wear the *shingka*, a dark red or pinkish tunic with white or, more recently, pale blue stripes, as their traditional dress 【2-16】. This tunic-style dress was once worn in the Bumthang region of central Bhutan and the Kurtö region of Lhuentse district in eastern Bhutan. Those costumes are also on display at the Textile Museum in Thimphu 【2-17a, 2-17b】. I have also seen tunic dresses worn as festival costumes in Lhuentse 【2-18】. In some areas in Bhutan, women also used to wear an undergarment and night gown called *nongko* or *nongnongma* in the Tshangla language and *gutsum* in Dzongkha 【2-19】. This gown was made of plain white cotton, sometimes with simple geometric designs, and in shape and dimension it closely resembled the shingka. This gown ceased to be worn when shirts and pyjama pants started to be imported. More information about the tunic-style dress in eastern Bhutan and Pemakö in Tibet can be found in Chapter 8.

In Southeast Asia, the white ankle-length dress worn by unmarried Karen women in Myanmar and the blouse worn by married women also have this shape (3).

Before the 1950s and 1960s, the *shingka* was probably made of nettle, cotton, or wool. In the days when Tibetans ruled Monyul Corridor, the Monpa people could not afford to wear luxury items such as silk, even though they carried Assam silk to Tibet. Similarly, the people in Tawang were hardly able to eat the rice that they produced themselves, because it had to be given to the Tibetan government as tax. The Monpa staple food consisted of miscellaneous other cereals such as buckwheat, maize, and millet. It was not until 1951 that Indian officials arrived in Tawang and the Tibetans were expelled. The Monpa women probably started to wear the present day eri silk shingka after 1951, although the exact date is not known.

Until then, we know that a dress called the *ngoushing*, a woollen *shingka*, was worn in Tawang and some parts of West Kameng district. The *Ngoushing* is the Monpa word for 'blue shingka'. Nowadays, no one wears it, but the dress in photo 【2-20a, 2-20b】 belongs to a woman born around 1944 in Tawang, who says that her late mother made it. It measures 104 cm in length and 79.5 cm in width, making it long enough for a short woman to reach the ankles. The gores at the sides are folded forward to fasten the belt. The upper part of the triangular gore is light brown, and the lower part is made of red, black, and again red wool cloth. The fact that the garment is heavy, navy blue in colour and not particularly fashionable or eye-catching is inferred from the fact that it is not mentioned at all by 19th and 20th century visitors, who will be discussed later.

When I was researching the old *ngoushing* in Tawang, someone told me that there is a painting of Tsewang Lhamo, mother of the Sixth Dalai Lama Tsangyang Gyamtso (1683-1706), wearing it. The painting refers to a wall painting on the left side of the interior of the Ogyenling (now spelled Urgeling) Lhakhang in Tawang, where the Sixth Dalai Lama is said to have been born 【2-21】. In this painting, she is wearing a red and dark blue vertically striped tunic dress, which looks like the dress of a Mago woman as described later. It is not known whether there were any *ngoushing* made of two colours of cloth joined vertically. Ogyenling Lhakhang was destroyed in 1714 by the Mongolian troops of Lajang Khan. He made a public declaration that Tsangyang Gyamtso was not the true incarnation of the Fifth Dalai Lama and dethroned and removed him to Peking in 1706. However, the Sixth Dalai Lama passed away mysteriously at Kunganor on the way (4). The existing temple was rebuilt by the Seventh Dalai Lama (1708-1757). Unfortunately, it is not known when this wall painting was created.

The maternal uncle's house, *Kushangnang*, which is also the family home of the Sixth Dalai Lama's mother still exists in the village of Berkhar of Kitpi circle in Tawang. According to the current descendants who inherited and preserve the house, it is possible that the Sixth Dalai Lama was not born in Ogyenling but in this house after his mother returned to her parents' home 【2-22】. Photo 【2-23】, taken in Kushangnang is a statue of the mother of the Sixth Dalai Lama. Unlike the wall painting, this statue wears two layers of garments, one red and one blue, one on top of the other, as well as a headband. The central circle of the headband has a red centre with blue around it. This is a silver headband, the blue part presumably representing turquoise and the red part coral. The date of the statue is not known, but it must have been made after the death of the Sixth Dalai Lama, i.e., after the 18th century.

A similar headband is worn by young girls, *bro-mo*, who play a part in the rituals at the festival of *Lhasöshe* in Thembang village in West Kameng district 【2-24】. This festival is dedicated to the local deities of the surrounding mountains, which probably existed before Buddhism was introduced to the region and is held once every six years.

The female dancers during the festival of consecration to the mountain deity of the Kurtö region of Bhutan wear a woollen and cotton tunic dress and silver headbands with a small round central ornament on their heads (5). There is said to be a link between the headband and the local belief in mountain deities (6), but this cannot be confirmed as the headband may have been part of the traditional costume of the region. Similar headbands are found among the Miji, Hruso (Aka) and Bugun tribes of West Kameng district. The dress of these tribes in West Kameng is described in Chapter 9.

Today's shingkas are made of plain weave *eri* silk cloth and come in white (undyed) and dark red (dyed with the sticky discharge lac of the female of the insect (*Kerria lacca*). Although the white *shingka* is cheaper, it is the lac-dyed *shingka* that is now worn as formal wear. These lac-dyed shingkas were brought from Bhutan in the early days, and later they were brought by traders from Assam. Originally, the Monpas did not weave silk, except for two women in Dirang, and around 2002, the Government of India organised a dyeing and weaving workshop. After this, several Monpa weaving centres were opened in Bomdila and Dirang, but the weavers were girls hired from Assam and Manipur. The weavers and traders of the Monpa garment are discussed in Chapter 4.

When the common *shingka* that we see today is woven on Assamese horizontal frame loom, it is a single piece of cloth 80 to 90 cm wide and 2 to 3 m long. But when it is woven on a backstrap loom, the width of the cloth is so narrow that two pieces of cloth are joined together. The cloth is then folded in half, a hole is made in the middle of the crease so that the head can fit through easily, and the cloth is sewn closed at the sides, leaving just enough space for the arms 【2-25】. The shape of the garment is very simple, but it is not an open-armed jacket like a Latin American poncho. The left and right sides of the shingka are gathered at the front of the body, and the belt is fastened with the apron-like waist cloth 【2-26, 2-27】. This back apron is like a part of the belt and is an essential part of the *shingka*. It will be discussed in Chapter 5.

In the case of a single piece of cloth, the part for the head is cut with scissors, and the edge of the cloth is wrapped with bias strip made from another piece of cloth to prevent it from fraying. The same applies when two pieces of cloth are to be stitched together. Most of the cloth used for this bias tape is green, and rarely silver, but it is made of *nambu* 'woollen broadcloth', which was originally made locally, but is now imported from other states.

The shape of the garment is that of a one-piece dress without sleeves, but the wide width of the garment makes it suitable for farming and herding, as it does not come loose during movement.

Upper garment *tothung*, its pattern and its relation to Southeast Asia

In Tibetan, *tothung* can mean both shirt, blouse, or jacket, but the Monpa call only the jacket worn over the *shingka* as *tothung* or *totung*. Like the *shingka*, the tothung is mostly dyed with lac dye, but some are plain white. The material used is eri silk, but the white *tothung*, worn like an under blouse, is often made of cotton or synthetic fibre. This under *tothung* is folded outwards in front so that it looks like a white scarf 【2-28】 and is only worn on formal occasions and not for everyday wear. The *tothung* is generally woven with colourful patterns on the front and back 【2-29, 2-30】, although some have simple patterns or even no pattern at all. Some *tothungs* are made of black wool. In Tibetan and Brokpake, wool is called *bal*, and in Tawang, a woollen *tothung* is called *bai* (wool) *tothung* 【2-31】. However, they are not patterned and are not generally worn as formal attire.

In Bhutan, the Brokpa women's *shingka* is made of *eri* silk, but the *tothung* is made more and more commonly of synthetic fibres. However, the *shingka* and *tothung* of the Monpas are always made of *eri* silk. *Eri* silk is sometimes mistaken for linen or cotton because it is spun from short yarns, which are coarse to the touch and lack a smooth sheen. Its characteristics are not only that it is inexpensive for silk, but also that it is very durable, suitable for everyday and field wear, and that it softens with repeated washing. *Eri* silk is also surprisingly warm, and it was used in Assam for winter clothing and bedclothes (7).

The pattern on the *tothung* is woven in colourful threads with geometrical patterns of stars, flowers, arrows, swastikas, animals such as horses, elephants, birds, and figures riding on them. To distinguish the patterned *tothung* from the plain one, the patterned one is called *tothung kyanchan* in Tawang and *tothung momnang* in the villages of Dirang region. However, in many cases, the *tothung* is patterned.

What is interesting about the design of the patterns woven into the *tothung* is that similar images of human figures standing on animals can be seen in the textiles of Bhutan in the olden days 【2-32】 and in the textiles of Laos and other ethnic minorities in Southeast Asia today. For example, 【2-33】 is a pattern of a *tothung* from Monpa in Tawang, woven in the 1970s or 1980s. The basic design has not changed much. The large star-shaped motifs on the *tothung* are very similar to the stars on Lao textiles, and in Laos the stars symbolise fertility and the womb (prosperity of offspring) 【2-34】(8).

Designs similar to the pattern of the *tothung* with a human figure on top of an animal are also woven into the cloth of the Phuang people who live in Xieng Khouang in the central-eastern part of Laos, and of the Tai Daeng (Red Tai) and Tai Dam (Black Tai) people who live around Xamunuea and Luang Namtha in the north of the country. Picture 【2-35】 shows a pattern on a cloth used by the Tai Daeng shamans for rituals, the pattern of a woman's red turban cloth, which is the origin of the name "Red Tai", and a banner used at funerals by the Tai Dam people that also show the design of human figures riding on animals. The human figures standing on top of animals with their hands up represent ancestral spirits (9).

The photo 【2-36】 shows a piece of cloth which I got in 2011 in a village of the Tai Daeng near Luang Namtha. The weaving was done by the Tai Dam people and the human figures standing on animals are their spirits. Regarding similarities with designs from Thailand, Burma and Laos in Southeast Asia, Diana K. Myers and Françoise Pommaret also compared them with the *tothung* patterns of the Brokpas in Merak and Sakteng. They note that despite Bhutan's proximity to Tibet, its textiles have much more in common with distant Southeast Asia (10).

The Monpa and Brokpa have no oral tradition that explains these designs. Instead, a Monpa woman in Tawang described the Lao people's pattern of stars and sprits as wheels (*kholo*) or human figures on horses. Since a Tai tribe called the Shan founded the Ahom kingdom which lasted from the 13th century for about 600 years in Assam (11), it is possible that the Shan people brought textile designs to Assam that influenced the design of the Bhutanese and Monyul Corridor textiles. While some of these designs may have survived in the old textiles of the Ahom period, so far there are no clues to this. In Arunachal Pradesh there is a tribe of Tai descent, the Tai Khamti (or Khampti) people. They are thought to have migrated from the source of the Irrawaddy River in Burma to around Sadiya in Assam(12). Nowadays, Namsai district in eastern Arunachal Pradesh is their main settlement 【2-37】. Edmund R. Leach dates their migration to Assam to around 1795 (13). Although bird motifs can be seen in the present textiles of the Tai Khamti, the designs are different from those of the birds of the Monpa and the Brokpa.

A necklace is an essential part of the woman's formal dress. Many of them are made of coral, turquoise, silverwork, and pearls. In traditional Monpa society, where men inherit their parents' immobile property, these dress accessories and other movable property, like women's clothing and weaving and kitchen implements, are passed on from mother to daughter 【2-38a, 2-38b】.

The role of the woman's shoulder cape

In Tawang, women's square shoulder capes, often made of wool and red in colour, are called *lhemba*, while those made of colourful Tibetan cloth sewn together are called *dhing-nga* or *dhing- nga lhemba*. These names are also used in Dirang, but the shoulder cape made of wool or yak hair is called *hembaktang* in the villages of Namshu and Chug. These various shoulder capes are used for rain or cold protection, but according to a woman born in Tawang in the 1950s, it was originally worn daily, for example, it was said to be bad luck to see a woman without it in the morning. The shoulder cape was especially essential for formal wear, but in recent years, many people do not know about it. While only the elderly wear it at Buddhist ceremonies and festivals at the monastery, none of the young people wear it 【2-39】.

At *Lhasöshe*, a festival dedicated to the local deities in the villages of Thembang and Namshu in the Dirang region, girls called *bro-mo* wear *dhing-nga lhembas* made of brightly coloured Tibetan cloth 【2-21, 2-40a, 2-40b】. When I visited Namshu village in 2020, villagers, both men and women, were dressed in formal attire, but no one wore a shoulder cape 【2-41】. It is likely that the custom of wearing the shoulder cape as formal dress, which was once worn by the public, gradually disappeared, and remained only as a ceremonial costume for the *bro-mo*.

Two types of hats

Monpa hats come in two types, one made of brocade cloth and the other made of felted yak hair. The former is called *gochen zhamu* in Tawang, *goychen zhamu* in Dirang and *jalabengdang khothong* in Chug village. The Tibetan word gochen means a silk brocade, and the material is often embroidered with floral or other patterns 【2-40a, 2-42】. These hats are like those worn by the people of the Lhoka and Kongpo regions of southern Tibet. They are made and sold in Tibetan-owned shops in Tawang and Bomdila. They were formerly also stitched in Sangthi valley in West Kameng district.

The later type of hats are made of felted yak hair, and these commonly have five tassels, but some of them are thicker, some are thinner, the head part can be smaller or bigger, and the general shape and wearing style varies 【2-43a, 2-43b】. The Merak and Sakteng people of Bhutan also wear similar hats, but recently the differences between their hats and those of the Monpa have been emphasised, with the Brokpa hats having become flatter with thinner tassels. See the next chapter for details of how these hats are made. The Sherdukpen people also wear similar hats, though only with four tassels. The yak hair hat is called *ngam zhamu* in Tawang and *tsitpa zhamu* in Dirang. I have seen them being made in Mukto village of Tawang

and Nyukmadung of West Kameng 【2-44a, 2-44b】, but most of them are worn by elderly people. Young women prefer to wear cloth hats because the yak hair stings their scalps. Today, for young people, yak hair hats may not seem so fashionable.
The hats of the people of Mago and Zemithang in Tawang are different from these, but this will be discussed later.

Boots made of cloth

Until the early 2000s, it was common to see the Monpa people wearing handmade cloth boots with a yak or cow leather sole like those still worn by the people of Merak and Sakteng. However, most of the people who wear them were over 60 years old 【2-6, 2-7, 2-45】. As described in the next chapter, in Merak and Sakteng, men's boots must have a red instep and women's boots must have a blue instep. In the Monpa area, the rule is the same but less strict. These handmade boots with leather sole are called *tsem lham* in Tawang and the number of people who can make them is gradually decreasing 【2-46】.

In recent years, it has become very rare to see people wearing cloth boots, but some Tibetan cloth boots can be seen when people wear their traditional dress for a festival and a ceremony at the monastery. The boots worn by the dancers of the cultural shows are also Tibetan, they are made ofred and green felt from the instep to the knee, and black felt for the tube, which is embroidered. The soles are made of leather and the seams are surrounded by woven cotton thread. These shoes are called *tsangzom* in Monket of Tawang and *tsangzum* in Tshangla of Dirang 【2-42】. Before the Sino-Indian border dispute in 1962, there was trade with Tibet. For example, the boots worn by the Tawang woman in the photo 【2-47】who was born in 1940 were bought in the 1950s when she went on a pilgrimage to Lhasa with her family and neighbours. Nowadays, most of them are made in Kalimpong in West Bengal.

From the records of early visitors

Here follow some of the reports regarding Monpa clothing as described by those people who visited or heard about the Monyul Corridor area during the 19th and 20th century, when the British colonial government began to take an interest in the area, and before India's independence.

(1) Pictures from the Wise Collection
There is an interesting painting by a Tibetan monk depicting the male dress of the Monpa of Tawang 【2-48】. It is in the collection of Thomas Alexander Wise (1802-1889). This painting was on one of the maps and drawings that the original owner, William Edmund Hay (1805-1879), a veteran of the East India Company, ordered from a monk who travelled from Lhasa to Nagar in Himachal Pradesh. It is believed to have been painted between July and August 1857 and June of the following year (14).

The man in the painting is wearing a red jacket and white skirt, cloth boots, a helmet-like black hat, a round bag from his waist and a long pipe which he smokes. The round bag-like object, common to all the people depicted on the Mon Tawang map, may have been the same portable cushion worn around the waist by the Brokpa people and may have been a Brokpa and Monpa trademark. The red jacket is the woollen *chupa* still seen today, and the black hat is probably made of felted yak hair. What appears to be a white skirt may be a culotte skirt, called *kangdam* by the Monpas or a *tane*【2-13, 2-14】which is still worn by shaman and men at the festival in the Dirang region, but it cannot be determined from this painting.

There is no mention of the name of this monk and whether this monk had ever been to Tawang himself. If he painted this picture based on hearsay, the clothes depicted may not be accurate.

(2) Nain Singh (1830?-1882?)

The earliest English record of an outsider visiting Tawang is probably the report of Nain Singh. He was a "pundit" employed by the British colonial government's Survey of India, originally from the Kumaon division of present-day Uttarakhand state in northern India. The original meaning of pundit was 'Hindu scholar', but in reality, he was a spy who had mastered the surveying technology and arrived in Tawang on 24 December 1874, after passing through Tibet.

He referred to the inhabitants of Tawang as Monpa or Tawangpa and wrote, "Monpas are not like Tibetans. They differ from the Tibetans in language, clothing, customs, and appearance, and are similar to the Bhutanese in the west. The Tibetans keep their hair long and braided, while the Monpas keep their hair cropped round their heads and wear small woollen or felt headgear. Instead of the long Tibetan gown, they wear a short knee-length jacket, a woollen belt, and a long sword attached to it" [15]. This is clearly the dress of the men, but there is no description of the dress of the women.

(3) F. M. Bailey (1882-1967)

Frederic Marshman Bailey, a British intelligence officer, arrived in Tawang on the 16th of October 1913. The purpose of his trip was to gather information for the Indo-Tibetan border demarcation at the Simla Conference the following year. He described the Monpas of Tawang as "different from Tibetans, more like Bhutanese or Sikkimese", and "they cut their hair short, wearing felt rimless caps and red dyed clothes"[16]. The only other description of their dress is from Nyukmadung, on the way from Dirang to Tawang: "The people here dressed differently from those further down the valley. The women wore woollen clothes instead of cottons and Assam silk; and the men carried a curious pad hanging from the waist behind, a sort of portable cushion to sit on. Most of them could speak Tibetan and they appeared more Tibetan than Mönba (Monpa)" [17]. The language of the people of Nyukmadung is Brokpake, the language of the pastoralists, and it is identical to that of the people of the Senge Dzong of West Kameng district, the language of the people of Lungtang in Tawang district, and the language of Lubrang in West Kameng district and of Merak and Sakteng in Bhutan. The small cushions described here are as I wrote already, the circular pads that are hung from the waist by Brokpa men as portable cushions 【2-12】.

He also reported on the dress of the people of Mago and Zemithang in Tawang district, as I shall describe later in this chapter.

(4) R. E. Cooper (1890-1962)

The Dakpa, who live in the western part of Tawang district, are now a sub-group of the Monpa, and they also live in Trashigang and Trashi Yangtse districts of Bhutan. The Tshangla (Sharchopkha) speaking people of eastern Bhutan call the Dakpa and Monpa of Tawang as Brami, while some call them the Dakpa too. There is an account of the Dakpa being called 'Tailed People' by the people of Trashigang. This was written by Roland Edgar Cooper, a British botanist who visited Trashigang in eastern Bhutan in 1915, and his report was published with photographs in *Man* magazine in 1933 【2-49】(18). However, Cooper called them "Dakta" in this report. However, since there is no ethnic group called Dakta, I suspect that this is a mishearing by Cooper. The man is wearing a woollen jacket, which is folded up at the waist to form a pocket, and has no folded sleeves compared to the Bhutanese *go*. If you look closely at the back of the man on the right, you can see what looks like a tail on the surface of a large circular cushion. According to Cooper, there is a rumour among the people of Trashigang that "people with tails live in an eastern valley of the Tawang district". He surmises that the Bhutanese regarded them as a "rough, coarse" people, and that they appeared so because of the character of their dress.

The tails probably refer to the hanging tail at the back of the *paktsa*, a waistcoat made of two animal hides joined together front and back, worn by the Monpa and the Brokpa men. This is because when the two hides are put together, the tails hang down from the front and back 【2-50a, 2-50b】. The circular mat, also described by Bailey, is about 14 cm in diameter in the photograph 【3-17】 in the next chapter, but according to Cooper's description it is about 23 cm (9 inches) in diameter. According to the man in the photograph who was wearing the pad, it was put on in their youth and never removed. Cooper also wrote that it was said to be used as a resting pad when loads were carried, but he never saw one in use (19).

With regard to the men's hats, Cooper writes that they are 'made of felted yak or goat hair, two inches long, with five tassels the thickness of a finger, and a chinstrap woven from hair'. He then compares the tassels to the pointed tips of leaves on plants in high rainfall areas, called drip tips, which allow rainwater to drain away quickly (20). This is an expression of his profession as a botanist.

It is still the same as the hat worn by the Monpas and the Bhutanese Brokpas, but the present one is more shaped and refined in design, and the present ones have no chin-strings.

The women's hats seem to be different from those of the present-day Monpa women. Cooper describes the hats of the two women in the photograph as follows (quoted in the original):

> "The women's hats were of dark cloth, plain blue or striped brown and red, with a small brim two inches wide stiffened with stitching and a tassel of strings. The crown appears to be made of a round top piece as big as the inner circle of the brim with an upright strip two to three inches high, connecting it with the brim, the outside diameter of which is about five inches. Their use is merely a vanity tribute as they cannot possibly be of any service in rainy weather; obviously a dainty shower proof of a dryish climate rather than a weatherproof that a climate of rainstorm would make an essential dress feature "(21).

The hat of the woman in this description and photograph is not the same as the current hat of the Monpas, but I think it is very similar to the hat worn by the ceremonial girl on the left at the *Lhosaibo* festival in Rahung village 【2-51】. The two hats appear to be old, but perhaps the old ones have been preserved and are used for special occasions such as festivals.

The garment of the woman on the far right in Cooper's picture is very similar to the present-day *shingka*, with a wide sash and back apron. The shoes are also like the handmade boots of the Monpa and the Brokpa people. It is a monochrome, and the description confirms that the garment is a vertically striped tunic dress, like the present-day *shingka*, but the material is described as "coarser cotton". This coarser cotton may mean nettle. There is no description of the name or colour of the garment. This photograph is the earliest known photograph of a garment similar to the *shingka*. However, it does not say where the four people actually came from.

Exceptional and unique costumes of Mago and Zemithang

Mago in Thingbu circle located in the eastern part of Tawang is a pastoralist village located in the mountains at an altitude of 3,500 m or above. The language is Brokpake, similar to that of the Merak and Sakteng people of Bhutan. But they are also a member of the Monpa Scheduled Tribe now. The clothing of the Mago women is not the shingka and tothung but a woollen rigo, a knee-length one-piece garment 【2-52】. This garment is made of two colours of thick wool, red and black, sown together, and when the skirt is opened and spread, it is more than 4 m wide 【2-53】. It has a front opening, which is worn on the right front like a Japanese *kimono*. The hat, made of felt yak hair, is 10 to 17 cm deep and has about 18 to 20 thin tassels hanging from it 【2-54a, 2-54b】. A long string of around 20 large amber and red carnelian balls, hanging from the head on either side and reaches around the waist. The sash is about 17 cm wide and is fastened with a metal accessory like a Japanese *obidome* (sash band with decorative ornament) 【2-55,2-56】. It is fashionable to see young people wearing this dress, hat, and boots as a stage costume at the events in Tawang, but the number of people wearing this dress in daily life has been decreasing over the years and it is very rare to see it in Tawang nowadays. Even in their own villages, the women of Mago started to wear *shingka* and *tothung*.

Bailey, mentioned earlier visited Mago in 1913 and wrote that the women of Mago wore woollen skirts with broad red and blue longitudinal stripes. As I wrote about the present-day *rigo* earlier, the dress was made by sowing two different colour cloths together, but perhaps to Bailey it looked striped. Bailey also wrote that underneath the skirts, the women wore woollen knickerbockers. I don't know whether they are still wearing it or not. Bailey continues to write that as ornaments, the women wore large amber beads hung from a silver plate on the head to the front of the ears which was fastened with a brass band. And if this was not finery enough, they had long carnelians dangling from the silver plate on to their foreheads. Comparing the contemporary ornaments to these descriptions by Bailey of a century ago, we can imagine that the ornaments of the Mago women were even more luxurious back then than they are now.

As for the men's dress, Bailey writes "They wore long red coats like the Tibetans, but they had their swords behind them, whereas the Tibetans had theirs in front. Their felt hats with tassels on the rim were more like those of the Monpa(22) ".
The people of Zemithang Circle in north-western Tawang district call themselves Pangchenpa, and they are also a member of the Monpa Schedule Tribe. Their language is called Pangchenpa 'mat, which is markedly different from the Monpa and Dakpa languages of Tawang (23). Their traditional dress is unique too.

The men's jackets are made of red wool, some are as long as the calf, but most are pulled up to the waist or below the knee and tied with a sash at the waist. From the front it resembles the Bhutanese man's go, but the width is narrower and there is only a small fold at the back 【2-57】.

Most women now wear a shingka or *tothung*, the same as other Monpas but originally, they wore a knee-length woollen tunic dress. These tunics are made of two pieces of homespun, thick, 40 cm wide woollen cloth sewn together, with only the head part left open without sewing. Tibetan woollen cloth with colourful stripes is used to sew the sides of the robe together as a "triangle gore". Both sides of the gore are folded in front of the body so that the pattern can be seen, and the belt is fastened over it 【2-58, 2-59a, 2-59b】. It resembles the Tawang's ngoushing but differs in that it is knee-length. The red robe is called leushingka. The brownish one is called genashingka. It is said that the language of the Pangchenpa is closely related to the language called Dzalakha of Trashi Yangtse district and Khomakha spoken in Lhuntse district in eastern Bhutan (24). This reminds me of the old, red coloured woollen tunic from north central and eastern Bhutan, which is also called leushingka 【2-17a】(25).

Originally, Zemithang women wore this woollen tunic dress throughout the year, but after the Sino-Indian border dispute in 1962, when roads were built to protect the border, the Zemithang people had more opportunities to go to Tawang Monastery for Buddhist ceremonies and the Torgya and Dungyur festivals. Seeing the Tawang women wearing *eri*-silk *shingka*, the Pangchen women also began to wear them.

Today, those who wear this woollen *shingka* are the older generation from Lumpo village, northwest of the centre of Zemithang 【2-60】. They wear this leushingka without back apron but with a calfskin over their backs 【2-61, 2-62】. This calfskin is called phiu or pheu. From Chinese documents and photographs, we can see that the Menba (Ménbāzú) people living in Lekpu valley (Lèbùgōu in Chinese) in Tshona County of Tibet Autonomous Region, just north of the McMahon Line, also carry a calfskin on their backs in the same way. They are also wearing a white woollen cloth around their waists. According to Chinese scholars, there are several legends about the calfskin, one of which is that the Tang Dynasty Princess Wencheng who married a Tibetan king in the 7th century, carried a calfskin on her back to ward off evil spirits when she taught the women of the Menba tribe how to cultivate the land. The story goes that the calfskin was given to the Menbas as a gift, which then became a custom (26). It can also be seen from several Chinese sources that the men of the Lekpu Valley wear long red jackets similar to those of the Pangchen people (27).

Bailey, mentioned earlier, passed through Shakti in the present Zemithang circle on 20 October 1913 and arrived at Le village located in Lekpu valley on the Tibetan side the following day. The following original text on the costumes of Le villagers is unclear as to whether they are male or female. He writes as follows:

> "The people in this part dressed differently from those below Pangchen. Round their felt hats they all wore a twisted peacock's feather. Their coats were white, not red, and hanging down their backs they had an animal skin (28)".

Chinese sources do not mention that both men and women in Lekpu valley wear white jackets. But in the picture of Chinese Menba tribe, the women have a white cloth around their waists and calfskin draped over their shoulders. In other words, it is the women, not the men, who wear the animal skins hanging down their backs in both the Menba in Lekpu valley and Pangchenpa in Zemithang (29).

There are also two types of hats that characterise the Pangchenpa people. One is the *sharja* or *siruja*, a shallow cylindrical hat with an outer fold made of raised orange wool, worn by many men and women 【2-57, 2-58, 2-61】. This hat is very similar to the Menba's hat in the Lekpu valley, but the Pangchenpa's hat has a flat top, whereas the Menba's hat is raised in a conical shape. The women's hats are called *sersha* and the men's hats are called *barsha* ⑳. The other hat of Pangchenpa is the *duiju-mapja*, which is a shallow cylinder of yak hair, with peacock feathers around it 【2-60, 2-63a, 2-63b】. The peacock, or *mapja*, is said to be a symbol of rebirth. As I already mentioned, Bailey also describes this hat with a peacock feather in Le village. However, there is no mention of this hat in the more recent records of the Menba of Lekpu valley and it is thought to have disappeared there.

From daily wear to formal wear

The traditional dress of the Monpa people is gradually being replaced by a more formal dress for festivals, Buddhist ceremonies and public events 【2-64, 2-65】. The younger generation, under 50 years old, tends to wear western clothes on a daily basis, while middle aged women, who do not like to wear pants, tend to wear *gale*, a single piece of cloth wrapped the entire body from the waist down. The *gale* is a hand-woven cloth worn by women of various ethnic groups, including the Adi and Galo of Arunachal Pradesh, and is available in a variety of colours and designs. Some women wear the shalwar kameez, also known as the Punjabi suit, which is a one-piece upper garment and trouser combination worn by many women throughout India, but saris are rarely worn. This trend is more pronounced among the urban dwellers 【2-66】.

The school uniforms for the Monpa children were also different in the early 2000s, when some students wore traditional dress, some wore western or *gale*, but no uniforms 【2-67】. Recently many schools have adapted western cloths as their uniform 【2-68】. Some schools are using shalwar kameez for girls only.

To promote the indigenous Monpa culture, some schools in the Monpa area now require students to wear Monpa dress once a week.

Clothes mass-produced in factories outside the state are much cheaper than ethnic costumes and come in a wide variety of colours and designs. It is undeniable that this will have an impact on the future of traditional costume.

(1) [Bodt 2020: 199].
(2) [Bodt 2021].
(3) [Fraser-Lu 1988: 94-95].
(4) [Aris 1989: 121, 165].
(5) [Myers 1994: 115].
(6) [Huber 2020a:480-482].
(7) [Ghosh & Ghosh 2000: 10].
(8) [Inthavong 2006: 81].
(9) [Brittig & Fajcsák 2016: 161-163, 175, 178-185], [Inthavong 2006: 48-49].
(10) [Myers & Pommaret 1994: 67-69].
(11) [Gait 1926: 76-77].
(12) [Chowdhury 1983: 32].
(13) [Leach 1954: 35].
(14) [Lange 2020].
(15) [Trotter 1877: 119-121].
(16) [Bailey 1914: 358].
(17) [Bailey 1957: 234-235].
(18) [Cooper 1933: 125-128]; for the year of Cooper's visit to Trashigang, see [Aris 1994b: 149-150].
(19) [Cooper 1933: 127].
(20) [Cooper 1933: 126-127].

(21) [Cooper 1933: 127-128].
(22) For an account of Mago, see [Baily 1957: 225-230].
(23) [Bodt 2014a: 208].
(24) [Bodt 2014a: 208-209].
(25) [Myers 1994: 114-115].
(26) [Yu 1995: 438] See also the colour photos of the Menba people on pages 33 to 40 of the photo pages. [Chen & Zhang 2014: 66-69].
(27) [Yu 1995], [Chen & Zhang 2014: 66].
(28) [Baily 1957: 245].
(29) It is not definite, as it is possible that at the time of Bailey's visit the men were wearing white jackets and had animal skins draped over their back, just like the women.
(30) [Chen & Zhang 2014: 69-70]

CHAPTER 3
The Herder(Brokpa)'s Valleys, Merak and Sakteng

第3章 牧畜民ブロクパの谷、メラとサクテン

　ブータン東部のタシガン県の山岳地帯にあるメラ(1)【3-1】とサクテン(2)【3-2】の二つの谷は、1991年に一時的に外国人観光客に開かれたが、すぐに閉じられ、再び2010年9月1日に正式に開放された(3)。サクテンは標高約3,000m、メラは3,500mの高地に位置している。季節によりヤクやヒツジなどを、夏は高地へ、冬は低地へと牧草地を移動する移牧によって生活している。人々は、牧畜という生業から「遊牧民」や「牧畜民」を意味するブロクパ（Brokpa）と呼ばれ、言語はブロクパ語である。ブータンの公用語のゾンカ語とも東ブータンの多数派言語であるツァンラ語（シャルチョプ語）とも異なっている。同じ言語は、アルナーチャル・プラデーシュ州の西カメン県のセンゲ・ゾンやニュクマドゥン、ルブラン、そしてタワン県のルンタンなどでも話されている。メラとサクテンがある地域は、豊かな森林に囲まれ、希少な動植物の宝庫であることから、2003年にサクテン野生保護区に指定された。

　私は、観光解禁前の2006年に初めてこの地域を訪問した。政府のゲストという立場であったが、当時は、自動車道路も電気も携帯電話のネットワークもなかった。だが、2010

【3-1】メラは、ニェラ・アマ・チュの上流にあるパンザム・チュ(川)の谷間に広がる村で、サクテンへは、標高4,100 mのニャクチュン・ラ(峠)を越えて徒歩で1日の行程である。
Merak is a village lies in the valley of the Pangzam Chu (river), which is located upstream from the Nyera Ama Chu. The journey to Sakteng is a day's walk over the 4,100 m high Nyakchung la (pass). (Merak, November 2015)

【3-2】サクテン谷の中心地。中央の赤い屋根の建物がサクテン・ナクツァンと呼ばれる建物。2019年までは、サクテンとメラの二つの郡（ゲオ）を管轄するサクテン・ドゥンカクの役所と裁判所があったが、現在、その機能は、サクテンの他の場所に移転している。
The heart of the Sakteng valley. The red-roofed building in the middle is called Sakteng Nagtshang. Until 2019, this was the office and court of the Sakteng drungkhag, which had jurisdiction over the two gewogs of Sakteng and Merak. However, apart from the building, they have now been moved to another location within Sakteng.(Sakteng, August 2007)

年以降、劇的な変化が起きている。2011年には携帯電話が通じるようになり、電気も引かれ、テレビも見られるようになった。それだけでなく、現在はメラまで至る舗装された自動車道路ができ、サクテンまでの道路も一部未舗装ながら完成している。これらの急激な道路や通信などのインフラの発達は、長年隔絶されてきたこの地に、今後10年の間に、大きな変化をもたらすことだろう。

ブロクパ独特の民族衣装

ブロクパの人々の民族衣装は、アルナーチャル・プラデーシュ州のモンパのものと共通点が多いが、言語の違いからいくつかの呼称が異なっている。形状や柄などにも、小さな違いがいくつかある。同じ民族衣装を着ていたことから、しばしばタシガン県のトンロン、チャリン、トクシンマン、ションフーなど、メラやサクテンよりも川の流域に近い村に住むダクパ（Dakpa）と混同さ

第3章　牧畜民ブロクパの谷、メラとサクテン　　91

れる。これらのダクパは、アルナーチャル・プラデーシュ州のタワン地方のダクパ（モンパの下位集団）と同じである。ブータンのダクパは、タワンから交易や婚姻などの機会に移住してきた人びとで、元は牧畜に携わっていた人びともいる。彼らの言語は、タワンのモンパ語に近いが全く同じ言語というわけではない。私が2006年に初めてチャリンの村を訪ねた時には、ブロクパと同じ衣服を着ている人が複数人いたが、現在はほとんどの人々がゴやキラを着るようになっている。

　ブータンでは、1989年1月6日に公布された国王の勅令により、宗教施設・宗教行事・公官庁・学校・公的集会における民族衣装着用が義務化された。男性は「ゴ」（go）、女性は「キラ」（kira）が正式な民族衣装である。例外は、メラ、サクテンの人々、サムツェ県のロップ（Lhop）と、プナカ県北部のラヤの牧畜民ラヤップ（Layap）、トンサ県ランテル郡に住むモンパ（Monpa）である。ブラック・マウンテンのモンパとも呼ばれ、ブータンに古くから住む先住民と考えられるが、彼らとアルナーチャル・プラデーシュ州のモンパと明らかなつながりはないとされる(4)。いずれも独自の伝統的な衣装を持っているが、それを保護するために、彼らには自分たち独自の民族衣装の着用が許され、かつ推奨されている。ロップとブラ

【3-3】メラの小学校。当時の生徒数は198人だった。
Primary school in Merak, at the time there were 198 pupils enrolled. (Merak, August 2007)

【3-4】ブロクパ女性は、日常的にシンカ、トトゥンを着用している。
Brokpa women wear *shingka* and *tothung* every day. (Near the village of Merak, November 2015)

【3-5】ブロクパのトトゥンの多くは、柄が細かく、色彩も鮮やかである。
Many of the Brokpa *tothung* are finely decorated and brightly coloured. (Merak, July 2012)

【3-6】バー（ウール）・トトゥンは、普通のトトゥンの上に重ね着されることが多い。ヨーコルという紡錘車を使って糸を紡いでいる男女の姿もよく見かける。
A *ba* (wool) *tothung* is often worn over the regular *tothung*. It is also common to see men and women spinning yarn with *yokkor*. (Merak, September 2008)

【3-7】小学生の女児は、トトゥンの上から帯（ケラ）を締めている。
The schoolgirls wear their *kera* over their *tothung*. (Merak, September 2008)

ック・マウンテンのモンパの衣装については、第9章に記述した。

　メラに一つだけある1987年創立の小学校【3-3】では、多くの生徒たちがブロクパの民族衣装を着ているが、6年生までのクラスしかなく、それ以上は、他の村の寄宿舎付きの学校で学ばなければならない。その場合、他の生徒と同じようにキラやゴを着る必要があるが、その着用に慣れるために、6年生は週1回、ゴとキラで登校する規則があった(5)。

女性の民族衣装

　モンパと同じく、女性の貫頭衣はシンカと呼ばれ、帯で腰当て布を後ろに挟み、その上にトトゥンを羽織る【3-4】。シンカは、ブロクパの人々がエリン（タ

ワンのエリ・シルクと同じもの）と呼ぶ野蚕糸で織られ、白あるいはラック・カイガラムシで染められたピンクがかった臙脂色に白い縞柄が織り込まれている。どちらも裾に水平な矢模様がぐるりと織り込まれている。ブロクパのシンカは、山道を歩くことが多いので、モンパのものより短めでひざ丈ほどである。

トトゥンは、インド製の化学繊維を化学染料で染めたものが増えている。トトゥンのうち、模様が織り込まれているものをズクテン・トトゥンと呼ぶ。その模様は、幾何学模様・星・花・馬・象・鳥などと、その上に立つ人物像などで、モンパのものよりも細かいデザインで、色も多く使われている【3-5】。黒いウール製のトトゥンもあり、これはバー・トトゥンと呼ばれる【3-6】。

シンカをウエストで結ぶ帯はチベット語やゾンカ語と同様にケラと呼ばれ、元は幅広の布だったが、最近はキラの帯と同じような細い帯に変わってきている。小学校に通う少女たちは、トトゥンを右手が入るように合わせ、その上から帯を締める【3-7】。こうすれば、前がはだけることはない。右胸にポケットのようなスペースのあるキラに似せるという意図もあるのではないだろうか。この着方は、モンパの少女たちにはないものである。ブロクパ語でメーキム（*me-kim*）と呼ばれる腰当て布はすべて黒いウール製で、他の色を着ける人はいない。以前は、モンパと同じように、赤いウールの腰当て布を着ける人もいたが、次第に黒に統一されていった。

しばしば、このメーキムの右後ろに金属のチェーンを垂らし、その先に小さな小刀（バレーあるいはンガゾール）や鍵（ディミ）が結ばれているのを見かける【3-8】。縫い針のケース、カブシュを付ける場合もある。これらは、仕事に出かける時の必須アイテムでもある。盛装する際には、フレンガと呼ばれる珊瑚（ジュル）やトルコ石（ユー）、猫目石（ズィ）などの重い首飾りを着け

【3-8】この金属製のチェーンは「タクパ」と呼ばれ、いくつかのコインをつなぎ、先端に折り畳みナイフ（「バレー」または「ンガゾール」）、あるいは鍵（ディミ）を付けている。
This metal cord is called a *thakpa*, it is made up of several coins joined together and a folding small knife (*baree* or *ngazor*) or key (*dimi*) attached to the end. (Merak, August 2007)

【3-9】普段着でも首飾りを着けている女性は多い。イヤリングはトルコ石が多い。
Many women wear neck ornaments even with everyday clothes. Their earrings are usually made of turquoise. (Merak, September 2008)

【3-10】2008年の初の民主化選挙の前年に、説明会と模擬選挙が行われた。その会場に集まった女性の多くは、レンバを着けていた。
The year before the first democratic elections in 2008, a mock election was also held in Merak. Many of the women who gathered at that venue wore *lhemba*. (Merak, August 2007)

る【3-9】。これらの多くは、母から娘へと代々受け継がれてきたものである。

　以前は、ガムリ川流域のラディなどの村で織られたシンカやトトゥンをチーズやバターと交換していたが、現在は、現金で購入している。最近では自分たちで織る人も少しずつ増えてきている。野蚕糸、ラック染料のいずれもメラやサクテンにはないので、ガムリ川流域地帯の村やインドとの国境の町サムドップ・ジョンカルのインド側のメラ・バザール(6)で入手している。ブロクパのシンカは野蚕糸で織られているが、トトゥンは化学繊維の布から作られていることもある。特に、子供のトトゥンの多くは化学繊維で、染料もインド製の化学染料の粉末を使っている。

　ブロクパ女性は、しばしば雨や雪、寒さを防ぐためにウール製のレンバ（またはヘンバ）と呼ばれる肩掛けをする。この肩掛けは、公の集まりや、外部からの賓客を迎えるときにも身に着けるものでもある【3-10】。しかしながら、若い女性たちがこれを着けているのを見るのは稀なことである。

これまでのところ、メラやサクテンの女性にとって民族衣装は日常着である。

男性の民族衣装は変化が速い

男性は、厚手のウール製で、尻を隠す長さの上着チュバ（またはチュパ）を着る。色は多くは赤だが、黒や灰褐色のものもある(7)。灰褐色のチュバは、ヤクの毛から織られ、プー・チュバと呼ばれる。メラでは、チュバは、ワンポイント刺繍が施されているが、これはサクテンでは一般的ではない【3-11, 3-12】。

下半身は、太ももから足首まである筒状の左右に分かれた皮のレギンス、ピシュ（*pishup*または*pishub*）【3-13】を穿き、その上からカンゴー（*kanggo*）と呼ばれる白いウールの半ズボンを着け、ピシュを腰の位置で結ぶ【3-14, 3-15】。ピシュは、なめしたホエジカ（barking dear）（学名*Muntiacus muntjak*）の皮から作られるが、最近では、これを着る人は極めて稀である。サクテン谷とメラ谷は野生動物保護区内であることから、ホエジカなどの野生動物の捕獲が禁止されているからである。その代わりにほとんどの男性は、運動用のナイロン素材のスウェットパンツを穿いている。このズボンは、1980年代初頭に、タ

【3-11】 ワンポイント刺繍が施されたチュバとスウェットパンツを着た男性たち。
The men are wearing *chubas* with one point embroidery and sweat pants. (Merak, March 2006)

【3-12】小学生の男児のチュバ。
The *chubas* of schoolboys. (Merak, August 2007)

【3-13】ピシュは左右に分かれている。足首を紐で締める。
The *pishup* is separated into left and right. The ankle is fastened with laces. (Sakteng, March 2006)

【3-14】ピシュの上の紐をカンゴーの上から締めたベルトに結ぶ。
The string above the *pishup* is tied to the belt that is fastened over the *kanggo*. (Sakteng, March 2006)

【3-15】キュロットスカートのようなカンゴーの前後には、四角い布が縫い付けられている。
A square piece of cloth is stitched to the front and back of the *kanggo*, which is shaped like a culotte skirt. (Merak, September 2008)

【3-16】動物の毛皮のベスト、パクツァ。
Animal skin fur waistcoat, *paktsa*. (Near Chaling, September 2008)

【3-18】現在の野蚕糸で織られたシンカの前には、このウールのンゴウシンが着られていた。
Before the present day *shingka* that is woven from wild silk yarn, this woollen *ngoushing* was worn. (Reproduced by Sang Tshomo and Dema Yangzom in Merak in 2013)

【3-17】クプテンはフェルトで作られた携帯用座布団。最近は稀にしか見かけなくなった。
The *Kupten* is a portable cushion made of felt. It is rarely seen these days. (Merak, March 2006).

シガンの町へ商売に出かけた男性が持ち帰ったのを皆が真似て購入し、穿くようになったという。

　チュバの上から野生ヤギの一種であるゴーラル（学名*Naemorhedud goral*）やヤギの毛皮2枚から作ったベスト、パクツァ（*paktsa*）を着る人もいる。前後に動物の尻尾が垂れていて、まるで尻尾がある人のように見える【2-50a】【2-50b】

【3-16】。円形のフェルトで作られた携帯座布団クプテン（*kupten*）（またはクブテン*kubteng*）を腰から着けていたが、現在は日常生活でこれを着けている人はほとんど見られなくなった【3-17】。

衣服はヤクやヒツジの毛から

　現在は、シルクや木綿、化学繊維などで作られた衣服を着るようになっているメラやサクテンの人々も、これまで身近な家畜であるヒツジやヤクの毛やウシの皮などから、衣服・帽子・ブーツ・テント・毛布・バッグなど、さまざまな生活用品を作ってきた。

　例えば、女性のシンカやトトゥンは、1960年頃からのもので、それまでは

【3-19】慣れた手つきでヒツジの毛を刈っている。
Shearing sheep with an experienced hand. (Merak, July 2012)

【3-20】村の近くで放牧されているヤク。
Yaks grazing near the village. (Merak, August 2007)

メラやサクテンで羊毛を紡いで織り仕立てた厚手の貫頭衣であったという。メラの70歳代の女性たちに頼んで再現してもらったのが写真【3-18】であり、ンゴウシンと呼ばれる。「ンゴウ」は青色のことで、藍を使って染める。この藍は、ラディ周辺で栽培されている。ンゴウシンを再現した女性の一人が子供の頃、エリン・シルクの白や臙脂色のシンカやトトゥンが、ラディ村からもたらされたが、臙脂色のものを買えたのは一部の金持ちだけで、それでも初めて白い染めていないシンカを買ってもらった時はとても嬉しかったという。ンゴウシンが重く、あまり見栄えのするものではなかったため、女性たちはエリン・シルクのシンカを好み、そのうちにンゴウシンは忘れられてしまったという。ラック染めのエリン・シルクは寒冷地には合わない素材ではあるが、色もデザインもよりおしゃれで、ウールの物より軽い。そのころには、インド製の下着や防寒用の上着なども簡単に入手できるようになっていただろう。

現在でも男性のチュバや女性のメーキム、レンバ、毛布などは、彼らが育てているヒツジやヤクの

【3-21】下から熱を当てて、織ったウール布をフェルト状にする作業。
The process of felting woven woollen cloth by applying heat from below. (Merak, August 2007)

【3-22】チュバを裁断し、縫製するのは難しい。この作業ができる女性は少なくなってきている。
It is difficult to cut and sew a *chuba*. The number of women who can do this work is decreasing.
(Merak, August 2007)

【3-23】男性用のブーツ、プー・ラム。
Men's boots, *pu-lham*. (Merak, March 2006)

【3-24】女性用のブーツ、モ・ラム。
Women's boots, *mo-lham*. (Merak, September 2008)

【3-25】ヤクの毛の長さや剛柔によって、部位ごとに用途が異なる。
Depending on the length and stiffness of the yak's hair, it has different uses. (Illustrated by Yoko Ishigami)

毛から織られている【3-19, 3-20】。村の中で、歩きながら木製のヨーコル (*yokkor*) と呼ばれる紡錘車で糸を紡いでいる人たちの姿もよく見かける【3-6】。ウール織の布を下から熱を当て、こすってフェルト状にし【3-21】、化学染料を使って赤や黒に染める。長方形の布を縫い合わせた腰当て布や肩掛けに比べると、チュバの裁断と縫製は難しく、メラではそれができるのは4〜5人の年配の女性だけである【3-22】。ブロクパ男性のシンボルでもあるチュバがなくならないためには、若い後継者が育つ必要があるだろう。

　長靴は、男性用はプー・ラム (*pu-lham*)、女性用はモ・ラム (*mo-lham*) と呼ばれる。男性用のプー・ラムの筒状のふくらはぎ部分は、ヤクの毛、プー (*pu*) で作られ、甲の部分はウールで作られている。女性のモ・ラムは、全体をウー

ルで作るが、灰褐色のヤクの毛が使われることもある。男女用ともに、靴底は獣皮をなめしたもので作られる。多くの長靴には、幾何学模様の刺繍が施されている。それをラムロク・ケラ (*lhamrok kera*) と呼ばれる細いベルトで締める。意外なのは、甲の部分が赤いものが男性用で、青が女性用であるということである【3-23, 3-24】。子供のころから赤やピンクは女子、青は男子と刷り込まれて育った日本人や西洋人には意外に感じるが、考えてみるとブロクパ男性のチュバも基本的には赤で、女性のかつてのンゴウシンも青であったから、それにはマッチしている。

　ヤクの毛もブロクパの生活には欠かせないものである。さまざまなものがヤクの毛から作られるが、その部位によって3つの名称と異なる用途が決まっている【3-25】。たとえば、ヤクの身体の両側の最も柔らかい部分の毛プー (*pu*) は、男性のチュバ（プー・チュバ）【3-26】や、雨具のツァムズィ (*tsamzhi*)【3-27】、毛布などを作る際に使われ、下腹部の毛ツィッパ (*tsid-pa*) は、テントや防水用布リウ (*liu*)【3-28】やバッグなどさまざまな物に利用される。しかし、雌雄両方のヤクから作られるツィッパは、特に帽子に使われ、0才のヤクの毛ダブ

【3-26】ヤクの毛、プーで織ったプー・チュバを着た男性。ブロクパの民族衣装一式をすべて身に着けている男性は珍しくなった。
A man wearing a *pu-chuba* woven from *pu*, the hair of the yak. It is rare to see a man wearing a complete set of Brokpa traditional dress. (Merak, August 2007)

【3-27】雨具のツァムズィ。現在はほぼ姿を消してしまった。
Tsamzhi is rain gear. They are now rarely seen. (Sakteng, March 2006)

【3-28】馬やヤクで荷物を運ぶ際には、防水用布リウで覆う。手前のヤクの荷物の下に見えている黒いロープはナンダ。
When carrying goods by horse or yak, they are covered with waterproof cloth *liu*. The black rope you see under the yak's load in the front is called *nan-da*. (Merak, September 2008)

【3-29】ヤクの尻尾の固い毛で織った袋、パー・チュン。大変丈夫で長持ちする。
Pha-chung is a bag woven from the hard hair of a yak's tail. It is very strong and long lasting. (Joenkhar, Sakteng, August 2007)

【3-30】子供のヤクの後ろにいる雌ヤクの前脚は、搾乳のためにギダというロープで縛られている。
The front legs of the female yak behind the calf are tied with a rope called a *gida* for milking. (Merak, August 2007)

(*drab*) は糸（クッパ*kud-pa*）や、馬やヤクなどに荷物を括り付ける時のロープ、ナンダ（*nan-da*）【3-28】を作るのに使われる。ヤクの毛の中で最も長く粗いのは、尻尾の部分に生えているンガマ（*nga-ma*）で、パー・チュン（*pha-chung*）と呼ばれる袋【3-29】や、搾乳時に雌ヤクの前足を縛るロープ（ギダ*gida*）に使われる(8)【3-30】。

ツィッパで作るブロクパの5本の房のある帽子のツィッパ・ジャモ（*tsid-pa zhamo*）の作り方は、次頁の写真【3-31】–【3-36】のキャプションに記した。ブロクパの帽子は、1980年代に撮られた写真(9)では、モンパのものと同じように頭頂部が丸く頭を包み、5本の房も太めだが、最近は平たい頭頂部で房も細くな

［帽子ツィッパ・ジャモの作り方］

【3-31】ヤクの毛を、先がとがった金属を張り付けた2枚の木板（プルクシェ）に挟んで梳く。
Yak hair is carded between two wooden *prukshe* covered with pointed metal. (【3-31】-【3-36】: Merak, March 2006)

【3-32】長方形の木製のボウルの中に、大麦から作る酒（バンチャン）、あるいはチーズを作ったあとの乳清（チュルク）を入れて、その中に漬けて毛を柔らかくする。
The hair is softened in a rectangular wooden bowl filled with barley wine (*bangchang*), or the whey (*churkhu*) from making cheese.

【3-33】針を使って周囲の5か所から毛を引き出し、それに別のほぐした毛を混ぜて帽子に縫い込み、よじって、房を作る。
Using a needle, the hair is pulled out from five places on the rim of the hat, mixed with another bunch of carded hair, sewn into the hat and twisted to make 5 tassels.

【3-34】別の梳いた毛で約1.5mの糸を作り、それを針に通して帽子の縁に沿って縫い、糸を引っ張って縮め、帽子の縁を内側に曲げる。
A thread of about 1.5 m length is made from another bunch of carded hair, passed through a needle, and then sew along the rim of the hat, pulling the thread to crop the hat and fold the rim of the hat to the inside.

【3-35】形を整えながらこぶしで押し付ける作業を繰り返し、フェルト状にする。
The hat is felted by pressing it repeatedly with the fist while shaping it.

【3-36】2〜3日、天日で干し、仕上げに、余分な細かい毛を木片の先に点けた火で焼いて取り除く。
The hat is dried in the sun for a couple of days, then it is finished by burning off any excess short hairs with a piece of firelit wood.

っている。メラでは、形を整えた後に、表面のぼさぼさした短い毛を、先端に火を点けた木片で焼いて取り除く。

カブネの代わりにニャリを
ラチュの代わりにレンバを

ブータンでは一般的に、役所と僧院のある城（ゾン）に入る場合や公式の行事の際には、男性は「ゴ」の上から「カブネ」（*kabne*）と呼ばれるスカーフをまとい、女性は「キラ」の左肩から赤系の色の帯状の布「ラチュ」（*rachu*）を着用する義務がある【3-37】。カブネとラチュには、その場に、敬意を示す意味が込められている。

メラとサクテンの人々は異なる民族衣装を着ているため、その義務はないが、その代わりをするのが男性のニャリ（*nyari*）【3-38】と、女性のレンバ（*lhemba*）

【3-37】ブータンでは、役所など公的な場所では、女性のキラにはラチュ、男性のゴにはカブネの着用が義務付けられている。
In Bhutan, it is compulsory to wear a *rachu* with the women's *kira* and a *kabne* with the men's *go* in government offices and other public places. (Photograph by Kitsho Wangchuk, Thimphu, May 2021)

【3-38】サクテンから来たサクテン・ドゥンカクの長（ドゥンパ）を出迎えるために、ニャリを着けて待つメラの村役人たち。
Merak village officials wait, wearing *nyari*, to welcome the head of Sakteng drungkhag (*Drungpa*) from Sakteng. (Merak, July 2012)

【3-39】ブータンの軍人や警察関係者がカブネの代わりに身に着けるニャレ。階級別に色や肩章の数やデザインが異なる。
The *nyare* is worn by Bhutanese military and police personnel in place of the *kabne*. Different ranks have different colours, number of shoulder patches and designs. (Illustrated by Yoko Ishigami)

【3-40】雨具のツァムズィ【3-27】を後ろから撮影したもの。ニャリが使われる前にはカムニの代わりに礼装用に着用された。襟下のスモッキングの縫い方を「ツァムズィ」と呼ぶことからきた名称だという。
The *tsamzhi* 【3-27】, a raincoat, was worn for formal wear in place of the *kabne* before the use of the *nyari*. This picture shows the back of the garment, and the name comes from the way the smocking under the collar is sewn, which is called '*tsamzhi*'. (Sakteng, March 2006)

【3-41】僧侶が着るマントもツァムズィと同じ形状だが、こちらはチベット語と同じくダガムと呼ぶ。
The cloaks worn by monks are the same shape as the *tsamzhi*, but it is called *dagam*. (Photo courtesy of Lama Tashi Wangdi, Merak, May 2021)

【3-10】である。ニャリは、ヤクの白と黒の毛を編んで作ったロープ状の紐で、それを輪にして左肩から右の腰あたりまで掛けたたすきのようなものである。ブータンの軍人や警察関係者が、カブネの代わりにする布製のニャレ（*nyare*）と用途は同じである【3-39】。だが、1990年代初頭ぐらいまでは、男性は、ニャリではなく、ツァムズィと呼ばれるマントをカブネ代わりに着ていた【3-40】。僧侶が着るマントも同じ形状だが、こちらはダガム（*dagam*）と呼ばれる【3-41】。ダガムは現在でも僧侶によって着られているが、ツァムズィはほとんど姿を消してしまった。

　女性のレンバは、防寒用、あるいは雨具としても用いられる四角い厚手のウールの肩掛けである。他人への敬意を示すための正装の一部であった。メラの女性たちは、その上に男性のチュバと同じように、さま

ざまなワンポイントの刺繡を施している【3-10】。

サクテンには、2019年までサクテン郡（ゲオ）とメラ郡の二つを管轄するサクテン・ドゥンカクの役所や裁判所として使われていた建物、ナクツァンがあった（現在その機能はサクテンの別の場所に移転している）。そこを訪問する際や公の集会などでは、ニャリまたはレンバの着用が以前からの決まりであったが、守らない人がいたため、2017年夏にタシガン県から規則遵守の通達が出され、郡の役場へ行く場合にも適用されることになるなど厳しくなった。インドのモンパの場合には男女ともこうした規定はなく、現在帰属している国の違いが明確に表れている。

結婚式の衣装

2008年9月にメラに

【3-42】サクテンから花嫁がメラに到着。前から6人目（左から2人目）のカラフルな布で顔を隠しているのが花嫁。
The bride arrives in Merak from Sakteng. The bride is the second from the left, her face covered by a colourful cloth. (Merak, September 2008)

【3-43】メラに到着した後も、一行は数カ所で村人の接待を受ける。若い新郎は、新婦の隣の女性の右手に座っている。全員がパンケップを首に掛けている。
After arriving at Merak, the group was entertained by the villagers at several places. The young groom is sitting to the right of the woman next to the bride. All of them are wearing *pangkheb* around their necks. (Merak, September 2008)

第3章　牧畜民ブロクパの谷、メラとサクテン　107

滞在していた間に、結婚式に参列する機会があった【3-42, 3-43】。サクテンへ花嫁を迎えに行き、メラで近所の人々が祝いの席を各所に設けて出迎え、花婿の自宅まで送り届けるという儀式だった。ブロクパの社会では、女性が男性の家に嫁ぐのが9割、女性の家に男子がいない場合には、男性が女性の家に婿に入るのが1割くらいだという。

　ブロクパの家族の中には、2人、あるいは3人の兄弟と結婚する一妻多夫婚が見られることに留意すべきである。これは家畜や土地などの相続財産を分散させないためと、放牧のために長期間家を離れる夫の代わりに、他の夫が家事や交易を担当する必要があったためである。だが、この慣習も若い世代には見られなくなっている。

　結婚式に話を戻すと、花嫁は、五色の布で頭を覆い、終始うつむいているので、顔は家の中に入るまでほとんど見られなかったが、衣装は新しいシンカとトトゥンを着ていた。花婿は、新しいチュバに伸縮素材のスポーツ用ズボンであった。村人は、全員が新しい衣服を着ている。普段と異なるのは、参加者がほぼ全員パンケップと呼ばれる木綿の儀礼用の布を首に掛けていることである。この布は、贈答品として使われるが、子供や荷物を背負う布として、あるいはテーブルクロスとして使われるなど多目的である。織っているのは、ラディやポンメなどガムリ川流域の村の人々で、結婚式の前に花婿・花嫁双方の親族が何十枚もまとめて注文し、親戚や結婚式の参加者に配るものである。

　布は、ブータンではさまざまなシーンでの贈答品として欠かせないものだが、ブロクパ社会でも同様で、たとえば、男性から女性の親戚へは相手が女性ならトトゥン用の布、男性ならカンゴー用の布を贈る。

　結婚式に付き添う人たちや手伝いの人への現金での謝礼も必要で、経済的に豊かな家以外は、こうした結婚式は行われていない。

　ブロクパの結婚の慣習に関しては、ダショー・テンジン・ドルジが、小冊子にまとめた興味深い記述がある(10)。この本は、2002年に古典チベット語で書かれた原著を後に英訳したものだが、著者は、「ブロクパの結婚の伝統と慣習は、変化しつつある」と書いている。私が見たような結婚式も、すでに変化しているかもしれない。

メラの三大イベントの装束と衣服

メラには、毎年行われる3つの主要な宗教行事がある。いずれも多くの人々が、放牧地や学校から村へ戻ってくる夏に行われる。

(1) チョエコルのアルファの装束が伝える英雄叙事詩『リン・ケサル大王伝』

1つ目は、メラとゲンゴーの村中総出のチョエコル（Choekor）である。この祭りは、仏陀の教え、つまり仏法（ダルマ）を回すという意味で、サクテンやインドのモンパの居住地でも行われる行事である。メラの場合は、ブータン暦5月の12日から21日の間の一日に行われる。村人が、メラのサムテンフェリン寺（通称メラ・ラカン）【3-44】とゲンゴーのタシチョリン寺（通称ゲンゴー・ラカン）【3-45】や各自の家の仏壇にある経典を担いで、2つの村の外周を一日かけて歩いて回る儀礼である。担いでいるのは主として女性や子供たちで、西暦の7月で学校も夏休みに当たるため、多くの男女の若者たちも里帰りして、普段は静かなメラも活気で溢れてい

【3-44】メラのサムテンフェリン寺（通称メラ・ラカン）。1902年頃、チベットのスンバという僧によって建てられたと伝わる。アマ・ジョモがチベットから持ってきたと言われる手書きと木版の経典合計18巻が収められている。
Samtenpheling Lhakhang (also known as Merak Lhakhang) in Merak was built around 1902 by a Tibetan monk named Sumba. It contains a total of 18 volumes of handwritten and woodblock printed scriptures, said to have been brought from Tibet by Ama Jomo. (July 2019)

【3-45】ゲンゴーのタシチョリン寺（通称ゲンゴー・ラカン）。1445年にタントン・ギェルポと彼の（霊的な）息子であるブチュン・ギェワ（またはキョワ）・サンポが建てた寺と言い伝えられている。
The Trashicholing Lhakhang (popularly known as the Gengo Lhakhang) is said to have been built in 1445 by Thangtong Gyalpo and his 'spiritual' son, Buchung Gyelwa (or Kyoba) Zangpo. (Gengo, July 2012)

【3-46】サムテンフェリン寺を出発したチョエコルの一行。大事な経典には、防水用の布や衣類を掛けている。
The *Choekor* group leaving Samtenpheling Lhakhang. The important sacred texts are covered with waterproof cloth and clothes. (Merak, July 2012)

【3-47】メラとゲンゴーの村の周囲を、重い経典を担いで一日かけて歩く。
Participants spend a day walking around the villages of Merak and Gengo, carrying heavy sacred texts. (Near Gengo, July 2019)

る。雨期に当たるため、傘は必需品だが、さまざまな布をお経に被せて濡らさないようにしている【3-46, 3-47】。

　チョエコルを行うことによって、恵みの雨が降り、周辺地域に豊作がもたらされ、家畜が健やかに成長し、村人の間の病気や争い、誤解が取り除かれるなどの恩恵が得られる。

　メラのチョエコルでユニークなのは、アルファ（*arpha*）またはアルパ（*arpa*）と呼ばれる兵士の格好をした5人の男たちである【3-48, 3-49】。彼らは、メラとゲンゴーの5つのトカ（*tokhag*）と呼ばれるグループの代表で、経典を運ぶ人々を先導し護衛する役目をする。トカはグループを意味する言葉である。それぞれのトカの休憩所で、そのトカに属する女性たちが、僧侶やゴムチェン[11]、

【3-48】出発前の5人のアルファたち。その装束は、『リン・ケサル大王伝』に由来しているという。
Five *arpha* before departure. The costume is said to have originated from *the Epic of King Gesar of Ling*. (Merak, July 2012)

役人などの客を、お茶や酒類、スナック菓子などで接待し、その間にアルファたちは、詩を吟じて舞う【3-50, 3-51】。

興味深いのは、この5人のアルファは、有名なチベットの英雄叙事詩『リン・ケサル大王伝』のケサル王とその4人の将軍であり、そのヘルメットやカラフルな布を網目のように結んだ鎧、刀などの衣装や持ち物も、この物語に由来するという説明である。アルファたちの役目は、仏敵から仏法を守ることである。実際には、もともとアルファは2人だったが、後にトカが5つになったのでそれに合わせ増えたものだと

【3-49】アルファたちの胸と背中には、カラフルな布が網目のように編み込まれていて、鎖帷子や鎧のように見える。背中に刀と大きな鈴を背負っている。
On their chests and backs, the *arpha* have colourful cloth tied into mesh-like form, which looks like habergeon or armour. They carry a sword and large bells on their backs. (Merak, July 2012)

いう。アルファ役は世襲ではなく、『リン・ケサル大王伝』の詩を暗唱して踊りのステップを習った人たちの中から選ばれる。彼らが吟じる詩は、「成就の歌」コンル（konglu）と呼ばれ、すべて土地の神々を誉め讃える内容になっている(12)。このアルファの装束を見て思い出すのは、タワン僧院のトルギャ祭、ドンギュル祭で、「邪悪なトルマ」を運ぶ兵士アルポ（またはアルファ）の装束【7-12】

【3-50】僧侶や来賓は、各休憩場所でお茶などの接待を受ける。
Monks and guests will be served tea and other refreshments at each resting place. (Merek, July 2019)

【3-51】詩を吟じながら舞うアルファたち。
The *arpha* are reciting poetry and dancing. (Merak, July 2019)

【3-52】チョエコルに随行する髑髏の仮面を着けた2人のケンパ。
Two *kengpa* are wearing skull masks accompany the *Choekor* group. (Merak, July 2019)

だが、メラのものの方が、タワンのものより精巧にできている。チベット語のアルパ（*arpa*）には、「泥棒、強盗、酒場の経営者、レンガ職人」などの意味があるが、アルポ（*arpo*）は、状況によって、「（肉体）労働者、アシスタント、護衛隊」などの意味にもなり、時には、ボン教の祭司のアシスタントを指すこともある(13)。トルギャ祭やドンギュル祭のアルポやチョエコルのアルファは、「護衛隊」とするのが最も適切な説明であろう。

アルファは、サクテンの年に2回のチョエコル(14)や、3年に1度村を挙げて行われるサクテンのマン・クリム（*Mang Kurim*）という村人総出の悪霊払いの儀礼にも登場する。このマン・クリムの祭りで最も有名なのは、全裸の仮面舞踊テル・チャム（テルコン・チャムとも呼ぶ）である。

メラのチョエコルの行列には、アルファとは別に、髑髏の面を着けた2人のケンパが随行する【3-46, 3-52】。彼らは、独別な装束は身に着けておらず、洋服の上着とズボン、ゴム長靴姿で、ブータン中で行われているツェチュ祭で見られる道化役のアツァラと同じような役割を果たしている。サクテンのテルチャムの踊り手も髑髏の面を着けているが、頭を入れる穴の開いた飾り襟【3-53】を着けている以外は、全裸である(15)。この襟は、ツェル・

【3-53】サクテンのテルチャムでは、ケンパは全裸に髑髏の面を着け、首の周りにはこのツェル・ンガという襟だけを着けている。
In Sakteng's *tercham*, *kengpas* are naked and wear a skull mask and only this collar called *tser nga* around their neck. (Photograph by Karma Tshering, Thimphu, May 2022)

第3章　牧畜民ブロクパの谷、メラとサクテン

【3-54】ニュンネの最終日に行われるワン（灌頂）の儀式に参加するため集まった人々。People gathered for the *wang* (empowerment) ceremony on the last day of *Nyungne*. (Merak, August 2007)

【3-55】朝晩2回行われるワンの間に舞われるヤク・チャム（ヤクの仮面舞踏）。
The yak *cham* is performed between the *wang* which is held twice a day, one in the morning and one in the evening. (Merak, August 2008)

ンガ（*tser nga*）と呼ばれる。ツェルは、「上」で、ンガは「5」を意味する。この名は、4つの方角と上方向で5つの方角を象徴している(16)。ゾンカ語では、ドルジ・ゴン（*dorji gong*）と呼ばれ、4つの金剛杵（ドルジ）でできた襟（ゴン）となっている(17)。

　メラのケンパは衣服を身に着けているが、もとは、全裸で木製の男根を腰から吊り下げていたのではないかと考えられる(18)。全裸のケンパは、ブータン各

地の村、特に東ブータンのタシ・ヤンツェ県やタシガン県のダンメ川、ガムリ川流域の村で見られるという。それは、モンユルの回廊地帯の村の儀礼や祭りでも観察されてきた(19)。ディラン地方のチュグ村では、毎年恒例のチョスコル祭（チョエコルと同じ）では、ケンパは、近年まで全裸だったが、現在は半ズボンを着け、肩の周りに布を巻き、木製の男根をベルトから下げているという(20)。

(2) ニュンネで舞われるヤク・チャム

2つ目は、ブータン暦6月11日から7月1日の間の、ニュンネ（*Nyungne*）と呼ばれる断食と無言の行を行う仏教行事である。この儀礼自体は、参加する在家の女性信者たちがメラのサムテンフェリン寺とゲンゴーのタシチョリン寺に籠もるのが主であるが、その最終日に護摩が焚かれ、僧侶による早朝と夕方の2回の灌頂の儀式（ワン）の間にヤク・チャム（ヤクの仮面舞踏）が披露される【3-54, 3-55】。その時には、子供の玩具などを売る出店が出て、人々も着飾って僧侶による2回の灌頂を受け、家族ぐるみでヤク・チャムを楽しんで一日を過ごす。ヤク・チャムに関しては、第8章を参照されたい。

【3-56】 サクテンの小さな祠堂に祀られていた忿怒形のアマ・ジョモの像。
A wrathful Ama Jomo statue in a small shrine at Sakteng. (Sakteng, May 2016)

(3) ジョモ・コラ

3つめは、アマ・ジョモへの奉献祭である。アマ・ジョモ（Ama Jomo）【3-56】とは、ブータンの他の地域の人々やモンユルの回廊地帯の人々も崇拝する「山に住む女神」である。メラ、サクテンの人びとには独自の伝説があり、アマ・ジョモを、救い主・守護神として畏怖の念を持って信仰している。アマ・ジョモは、かつてブロクパの人々が、チベット南部のツォナ（錯那）の領主の圧政下にあったのを、現在の地へ導いたと信じられている(21)。仏教以前からの信仰

【3-57】中央の右手にやや高く見える山がアマ・ジョモの宮殿のあるジョモ・クカルまたはジョモ・フォダン。メラの村からの遠望。
The slightly higher mountain to the right of the centre is Jomo Kukhar or Jomo Phodrang, where Ama Jomo's palace is located. This is a distant view from the village of Merak. (Merak, November 2015)

に基づくものだと推察されるが、現在では、メラやサクテンの人びとは、護法尊パルデン・ラモ（Palden lhamo）の別の姿であるジョモ・レマティ（Jomo Remati）とアマ・ジョモとを同一視している。伝説の中では幼子を背負った少女として語られるが、寺院の中の壁画や像としては、多くの場合、忿怒尊の形をとっている。

　メラの村から眺められるアマ・ジョモの宮殿があるとされる標高4,383mのジョモ・クカル（Jomo Kukhar）またはジョモ・フォダン（Jomo Phodrang）【3-57】は聖山である。巡礼はジョモ・コラ（Jomo Kora）と呼ばれ、ブータン暦8月14日と15日に行われるが、7月に行う人も何人かいる。

　複数の家族がジンダと呼ばれる出資者となって、グループを組んで2泊3日かけて巡礼する。参加者は、新品の衣服を着るのが望ましいが、標高が高く寒い場所なので、シンカを二枚重ねにして着る女性も多い。

　ジョモ・コラには「死」「血」「食物」「喫煙」に関わる厳しい禁忌がある。死者が出た家は、1年間巡礼に参加できず、その家からは参詣に必要なチーズやバターなどの供物の提供を受けてはならず、馬を借りることもできない。も

【3-58】女性が登ることが許されるのは、対岸に見えるジョモ・クカル直下のこの湖ラツォ（Lhatso）まで。
Women are only allowed to climb up to this lake, Lhatso just below Jomo Kukhar, which can be seen on the other side of the lake. (Merak, September 2008)

【3-59】女性たちが、ジョモ・クカルに向かって、バターやチーズ、果物や野菜を供えて礼拝の準備をする。
The women prepare for their prayers by offering butter, cheese, fruit and vegetables in the direction of Jomo Kukhar. (Merak, September 2008)

し、村内に死者が出た場合と出産があった場合、3日間は誰もこの山に入山することができない。つまり、出発予定日の3日前から出発日までに死者が出た場合は入山は中止となる。死に関する忌みはメラの普段の生活にも存在する。たとえば、サクテンでは遺体を百八つに切り刻んで川に流す慣習があり、現在はその処理場の近くに火葬施設が設置され、火葬が中心となっている。しかし、アマ・ジョモの宮殿のお膝元のメラの場合には、そのいずれも厳しく禁じられ

【3-60】女性たちは何度も地面にひれ伏してアマ・ジョモに祈りを捧げる。
The women offer prostrations to the ground to pray to Ama Jomo. (Merak, September 2008)

ているため、ガムリ川流域のランジュンまで遺体を運び火葬することが習慣となっている。

　また、月経中の女性は巡礼には参加できず、そうでない女性も、「魂の湖」を意味するラツォ（Lhatso）という湖【3-58】までしか行くことができない。湖は頂上直下にあり、標高は4,150mである。つまり、頂上は女人禁制となっている。私が2008年に参加した時には、用意した経文旗や線香を男性に託して頂上で供えてもらった。男性たちが戻ってくるまで、女性たちは湖のほとりでアマ・ジョモへの供えをする。最初に五体投地を繰り返し、それから家畜がうまく繁殖するように願いを込めたバターで象った動物を湖に投げ入れる【3-59, 3-60】。

【3-61】メラで演じられるアチェ・ラモの衣装。
Costumes of *Ache Lhamo* played in Merak. (Merak, September 2008)

参加予定の村人は、前日から下山まで豚肉・鶏肉・鶏卵・ニンニク・タマネギは食すことが禁じられている。これらの食材を持ち込むことも禁止されている。そのため、私も持参したインスタント食品の成分を注意深くチェックしなければならなかった。喫煙も厳禁である。過去に、あるインド人女性ジャーナリストが頂上に登ることを主張したことがあった。村人が拒否したので登頂はあきらめたが、彼女が登山中に喫煙したため悪天に見舞われ、その年のコラは散々だったという話が語り種になっている。

アチェ・ラモの衣装

　アチェ・ラモ（*Ache Lhamo*）は、アルナーチャル・プラデーシュ州のモンパやシェルドゥクペンの村でも見られるが、メラとサクテンでも演じられている。しかしながら、ヤク・チャム同様に、しばしば来賓や役人、観光客などに見せる短縮されたものである。写真【3-61】は、メラで演じられた時のものである。

　アチェ・ラモについては、第8章を参照されたい。

---

(1) メラの地名は、ブロクパ語で「焼く」を意味するメレ（mereg）から来ている。ブロクパがチベットからこの地に来た時に、調理の火で周囲が焼けたという伝説がある。
(2) ブロクパ語で、土地の一番高い場所を意味するサテン（sateng）に由来する。
(3) その理由は、村からいくつかの骨董品が失われたからだという（2004年3月メラの村長の話）。
(4) [Pommaret 1999: 53]。
(5) 2008年9月、当時の校長より。
(6) アッサム州バクサ県ダランガ・メラ村にある。
(7) チュバ用の布の染色については、第4章で説明する。
(8) このヤクの毛についての説明は [Karchung 2011: 33-34] によるが、ブロクパの友人に確認して訂正した。
(9) [Edmunds 1988: 150-155]。
(10) [Dorji 2008]。
(11) ゴムチェン（*Gomchen*）は、宗教者であるが妻帯し、農業に従事することができる。メラとサクテンでは、僧侶の数が十分でないため、日々の生活の中で重要な役割を果たしている。
(12) メラのチョエコルについての基本情報は、2019年7月23日の、ラマ・タシ・ワンディからの教示による。
(13) [Huber 2020a: 397]。
(14) サクテンの1回目のチョエコルは、ブータン暦3月15日、2回目は同7月15日である。
(15) 私は、サクテンのテルチャムを見たことがないが、写真は [Choden 2014: 36] に掲載されている。
(16) 2021年5月のラマ・タシ・ワンディからの個人的な教示による。
(17) ドルジ、あるいはサンスクリット語のヴァジラは、金剛杵と和訳される法具で、密教（金剛乗仏教）のシンボルである。
(18) メラの92歳の男性は「ケンパが全裸だった記憶はない」と言うが、ゴムチェンのジャンバ氏は、「昔は全裸だったかもしれない」と語っていた（2021年5月31日）。
(19) [Huber 2015: 220]。
(20) T. A. Bodtからの個人的な教示（2021年5月）と [Bodt 2020: 97] による。
(21) アマ・ジョモの伝説は、口承、あるいは数種類のチベット語の伝記の他に、[Wangmo 1990]、[Wangchuck 2006]、[Chand 2004]、[Bodt 2012] などの英語の著作の中で紹介されている。

CHAPTER 3
The Herder(Brokpa)'s Valleys, Merak and Sakteng

The Merak(1) 【3-1】 and Sakteng(2) 【3-2】valleys, located in the mountainous region of Trashigang district in eastern Bhutan were once opened to foreign tourist in 1991, but were soon closed and officially reopened on 1st September 2010(3) . Sakteng is located at an altitude of about 3,000 m above sea level, and Merak at 3,500 m above sea level. Many people in these valleys make their living by shifting their yaks and sheep from one pasture to another, depending on the season, moving from the lowlands in winter to the highlands in summer. Because of their occupation as pastoralists, the people are called Brokpa, meaning 'nomad' or 'herder/pastoralist' and their language is called Brokpake. It is a different language than Dzongkha, the official language of Bhutan, and Tshangla (Sharchopkha), the language of the majority in eastern Bhutan. Brokpake is also spoken in Senge Dzong, Nyukmadung and Lubrang in West Kameng district and Lungthang in Tawang district of Arunachal Pradesh. The area of Sakteng and Merak was designated as the Sakteng Wildlife Sanctuary in 2003 because these valleys are surrounded by rich forests that are home to rare flora and fauna. I first visited the region in 2006, before tourism started. I was a guest of the government, but at that time there were no motorways, no electricity, and no mobile phone network. However, since 2010, dramatic changes have taken place. In 2011, mobile phones, electricity and television became available. Not only that, but there is now a paved motorable road to Merak, and the road to Sakteng has been completed, albeit partially unpaved. These rapid infrastructural and communication developments will, in the next ten years, bring about greater changes in this long–isolated region.

Unique traditional costumes of the Brokpas

The traditional dress of the Brokpa people has much in common with that of the Monpas of Arunachal Pradesh, but some of the names are differ because the languages are different. There are also some minor differences in shapes and patterns. Because they used to wear the same dress, the Brokpa were often confused with the Dakpa people, who live in villages in the valley closer to the rivers than Merak and Sakteng, such as Thongrong, Phongme, Chaling, Tokshingman and Shongphu in Trashigang district. These Dakpa people are the same as the Dakpa people (i.e., a subgroup of the Monpas) of Tawang district in Arunachal Pradesh. Many of Bhutan's Dakpa people migrated from the Tawang area for trade and marriage, and some of them were formerly engaged in cattle herding. Their language is similar to the Monpa language of Tawang, although not exactly the same. When I first visited the village of Chaling in 2006, there were several people wearing the same clothes as the Brokpas, but now most people there wear *go* and *kira*.

In Bhutan, a royal edict issued on the 6th of January 1989 made it compulsory to wear the national dress in religious institutions, during religious events, in public offices, in schools and at official gatherings. The national dress is the *go* for men and the *kira* for women. The exceptions are the Merak and Sakteng people, the Lhop of Samtse district and the Layap pastralists of Laya in northern part of Punakha district, and the Monpa, living in Langthel gewog of Trongsa district. The Monpa are also known as the Monpa of Black Mountain and they are believed to be an indigenous people of Bhutan, and there is no obvious link with Monpa of Arunachal Pradesh(4). All these groups have their own traditional costumes, and in order to protect them, they are allowed and even encouraged to wear their own traditional clothing. The costumes of the Lops and the Monpa of Black Mountain are described in Chapter 9.

At the only primary school in Merak, founded in 1987, many students wear the Brokpa costume, but they can only attend school there up to class 6 【3-3】. Beyond that, they have to study in boarding schools in other villages. There, they have to wear kira and go like the other students. To get used to wearing the national dress, the students in class 6 in Merak primary school have to come to school once a week in *go* and *kira* (5).

Women's traditional dress

Like the Monpa, the Brokpa call the women's tunic dress a *shingka*. Furthermore, they wear a back apron tucked behind the sash and a *tothung* (or *totung* /*todung*) over it 【3-4】. The *shingka* is woven from wild silkworm yarn, called *erin* (same as *eri* silk in Tawang) by the Brokpa, and is either white or a pinkish-red rouge colour dyed with lac and woven with white stripes. Both have a horizontal arrow pattern woven around the hem. The Brokpa shingka is shorter than the Monpa one, about knee length, as it is often worn while walking on mountain paths.

The *tothung* is increasingly made in India from synthetic fibres and dyed with chemical dyes. The *tothung* with different patterns woven into it is called *zukten tothung*. The patterns include geometric patterns, stars, flowers, horses, elephants, birds and figures standing on top of them, and are more detailed and colourful than those of the Monpas 【3-5】. There is also a black wool *tothung*, called a *ba- tothung* 【3-6】.

The belt that ties the *shingka* at the waist is called a *kera*, as in Tibetan and Dzongkha, and was originally a wide piece of cloth, but has recently been replaced by a narrower one, similar to the belt for *kira*. Girls attending primary school adjust the front of their *tothung* so that their right hand can enter, and then fasten the *kera* tightly over it. In this way, the *tothung* does not open sloppily. This may be also an attempt to make it look more like a *kira* which has a pocket-like space on the right side of the chest 【3-7】. This way of wearing is not seen among the Monpa girls. The back apron, *me-kim* in Brokpake, is mainly made of black wool but sometimes made of yak hair or wool and yak blends. The colour is always black, and no one wears any other colour. In the past, some women wore a red wool *me-kim* like the Monpa do, but gradually they became uniformly black.

I often see women hanging a metal chain with a folding knife (*baree* or *ngazor*) or key (*dimi*) on the end, right behind this *me-kim* 【3-8】. Sometimes, a *khap-shup*, a case for sewing needles is attached to the end of the chain. These are also an essential item when going out for work. The women wear *phrenga*, heavy necklaces with coral (*juru*), turquoise (*yu*), cat's eye onyx (*zi*) etc. when in full dress 【3-9】. Many of these are handed down from mother to daughter.

In the past, the Brokpa used to trade their cheese and butter for *shingka* and *tothung* woven in Radhi and other villages in the Gamri river valley, but now they buy them with cash. Recently, some of the young women of Merak have learnt how to weave and they are now weaving themselves. Both wild silk and lac dye are not available in Merak and Sakteng, so they get them in the villages in the Gamri river valley or in Mela Bazar(6) in India, located just outside the border gate at Samdrup Jongkhar. The *shingka* worn by the Brokpa women are made from wild silk, while the *tothung* is sometimes made of synthetic fibre. In particular, most children's jackets are made of synthetic fibres and dyed with Indian chemical dyes.

The Brokpa women often wear a woollen shoulder cover, called a *lhemba* (or *hemba*), to protect themselves from rain, snow and cold. This cover is also worn at public gatherings and when receiving guests from outside 【3-10】. However, it is rare to see young women wearing it.

So far, for women in Merak and Sakteng, their traditional dress is a garment that they wear every day.

Men's dress is changing fast

Men wear a *chuba* (or *chupa*), a thick woollen jacket long enough to cover the hips. The colour is often red, but some are black or greyish brown(7). The greyish brown colour chuba is woven from yak hair and called a *pu-chuba*. In Merak, the chuba is decorated with one-point embroidery, although this is less common in Sakteng 【3-11, 3-12】.

The lower part of the body is covered with a pair of leather leg guards, pishup (or *pishub*) which are cylindrical, groin to ankle length. Over this, a pair of white short woollen trousers, *kanggo*, are worn, and the top of the *pishup* is tied to the *kanggo* at the waist 【3-13, 3-14, 3-15】. The *pishup* is made from the tanned skin of the barking deer (*Muntiacus muntjak*), but it is very rarely worn these days. This is because Sakteng and Merak valleys are within a wildlife sanctuary and hunting of wild animals such as the barking deer is prohibited. Instead, most men wear long nylon exercise trousers ('sweat pants'). The trousers were first bought in the early 1980s by a man who went to the town of Trashigang for business. When other people saw it, they started to buy and wear similar trousers one after another.

Some people wear a *paktsa*, a waistcoat made of the hide of two gorals (wild goat, *Naemorhedus goral*) or domestic goats, over the chuba. The tail of the animal hangs down in the front and back, making it look like a person with a tail 【2-50a, 2-50b】【3-16】. The round, portable felt cushion *kupten* (or *kubten*), which many Brokpa men used to wear hanging around their waists, is now rarely worn by anyone on a daily basis 【3-17】.

Clothing made from yak hair and sheep's wool

The Merak and Sakteng people, who now wear clothes made from silk, cotton, and synthetic fibres, have also made clothes, hats, boots, tents, blankets, bags, and many other household items from the hair of sheep and yaks and the hides of cattle.

For example, the women's *shingka* and *tothung* as we know them today were brought in from outside in the late 1960s. Before that, Brokpa women wore a tunic made from thick wool spun at Sakteng and Merak itself. I asked some women in their 70s in Merak to recreate it for me 【3-18】. It is called *ngoushing*. *Ngou* means blue, and indigo is used as the dye. This indigo is grown around Radhi. When one of the ladies who recreated *ngoushing* was a child, white and lac dyed *shingka* and *tothung* made of wild silk were brought from the village of Radhi. Since only a few rich people could afford the lac dyed *shingka*, she was very happy when she was given her first plain *erin shingka*. The women preferred *erin shingka*, as the *ngoushing* was heavy and not very presentable, and the *ngoushing* was soon forgotten. The lac dyed *erin* silk is thin and unsuitable for the high-altitude area, but it is more fashionable in colour and design and lighter than wool. By that time, it was probably easier to get Indian undergarments and winter jackets to wear against the cold.

Even today, the men's *chuba*, the women's *me-kim* and *lhemba* and blankets are woven from the wool of the sheep and the hair of the yak they raise 【3-19, 3-20】. It is a common sight to see people walking around the village spinning wool yarns on wooden drop spindles called *yokkor* 【3-6】. Woven wool cloth is heated from below, rubbed and felted, then dyed red or black with chemical dyes 【3-21】. Compared to the back apron and shoulder cape, which are rectangular pieces of cloth sewn together, the cutting and sewing of the chuba is more difficult and in Merak, only four or five older women can do it 【3-22】. However, as the chuba is a symbol of the Brokpa man, I hope that the method will somehow be passed on to the younger generation.

The pair of boots is called *pu-lham* for men and *mo-lham* for women. In the men's *pu-lham*, the calf part of the tube is made of yak hair (*pu*) and the instep part is made of wool. The women's *mo-lham*, on the other hand, is made entirely of wool, but sometimes using greyish-brown yak hair too. The soles of both the men's and women's boots are made of tanned leather. Many of these boots are embroidered with geometric patterns. They are fastened with a narrow belt called *lhamrok kera*. Surprisingly, the red woollen boots are for men and the blue ones for women 【3-23,3-24】. This may seem surprising to Japanese and Western people, who have been taught from childhood that red or pink is for girls and blue for boys, but when you think about it, it is no surprise since the *chuba* of Brokpa men is also basically red, and the female former *ngoushing* was blue, so the colour of the boots matches them.

Yak hair is an essential part of Brokpa life. A variety of things are made from yak hair, and three different types of yak hair have three names and different uses【3-25】. For example, the softest *pu* on both sides of the yak's body is used to make men's chuba (*pu-chuba*) 【3-26】, men's raincoats (*tshamzhi*) 【3-27】and blankets, while the slightly coarser, stiffer hair, which is cut from the lower abdomen, is called *tsid-pa* , and the *tsid-pa* of male yaks is used to make a variety of products such as tents, rain-proof cloth, *liu* 【3-28】and bags. However, the *tsid-pa* of female and male yaks is used exclusively for hats, of which the *tsid-pa* cut in the first year is called drab and is used to make thread (*kud-pa*) and rope for tying luggage to the back of a horse or yak (*nan-da*) 【3-33, 3-28】. The longest and coarsest part of the yak's hair is the *nga-ma*, which grows on the tail of the yak and is used to make bags called *pha-chung*.(8) 【3-29】and ropes called gida to tie the female yak's front legs while milking 【3-30】.

The method of making the *tsid-pa zhamo*, a Brokpa hat with five tassels, is described in the caption of the photographs in this chapter 【3-31】–【3-36】. In the photos taken in the 1980s(9), the Brokpa hat has a round top, and the five tassels were thicker, like those of the Monpa hat, but nowadays the top is flatter and the tassels are thinner. In Merak, at the end of shaping, the short, shaggy hairs on the surface are burned off with a piece of firelit wood.

Nyari instead of *kabne*, *lhemba* instead of *rachu*

In Bhutan, it is generally compulsory for men to wear a scarf called *kabne* over the go, and for women to wear a red ceremonial shoulder cloth called *rachu* over the left shoulder of the *kira*, when entering the Dzong, where the government offices and monasteries are located, and for official functions 【3-37】. The *kabne* and *rachu* are meant to show respect for the place.

The Merak and Sakteng people wear different traditional costumes and are not obliged to wear the *kabne* or *rachu*, but the *nyari* (for men) 【3-38】and *lhemba* (for women) 【3-10】take their place. The *nyari* is a rope-like cord made of black and white yak hair that can be *ngama* or *tsid-pa*. It is a kind of sash that hangs from the left shoulder to the right armpit. It is the same in use as the *nyare* worn by Bhutanese army and police officers in place of the *kabne* 【3-39】. However, until the early 1990s, the Brokpa men wore a cloak called a *tshamzhi* instead of a *nyari*【3-40】. The cloak worn by monks is of the same shape as the *tshamzhi*, but it is called a *dagam* 【3-41】. The *dagam* is still worn by monks, but the *tshamzhi* has almost disappeared. The *lhemba* of women is a thick, square woollen shoulder cover used for warmth or as a raincoat. Although it was part of the formal attire worn to show respect to others, it was not worn by all women. At Merak, the *lhemba* is embroidered with various one-point embroideries, just like the men's *chuba* 【3-10】.

Until 2019, in Sakteng, there was a building called *Nagtshang* which was used as the office and court of the Sakteng drungkhag, which had jurisdiction over the two gewgs of Sakteng and Merak (it has since been moved to another location in Sakteng), and it has been a rule for some time that the *nyari* and *lhemba* should be worn when visiting the *Nagtshang* and during public gatherings. Because some people did not comply with this rule, in the summer of 2017, a notice was issued by the government of Trashigang district to comply with the rule and it became stricter, applying also when going to the gewog office. There are no such rules in the case of the Monpa in India, which clearly shows the difference between the states to which they currently belong.

Costumes for the wedding

During my stay in Merak in September 2008, I had the opportunity to attend a wedding 【3-42, 3-43】. The ceremony consisted of picking up the bride in Sakteng, welcoming her in Merak with celebrations by the neighbours in various places, and taking her to the groom's home. In Brokpa society, 90% of the time a woman marries into a man's family, and 10% of the time a man becomes a son-in-law in a woman's family, usually if there are no boys in the family.

It should be noted that some Brokpa families have polyandrous marriages in which the wife marries two or three husbands. In this case, the husbands are often brothers. This form of marriage was used to prevent the fragmentation of inherited property such as livestock and land, and also because households in which one or more husbands were away from home for long periods of time for grazing the cattle needed other husbands to take care of the household and conduct trade. However, this custom is no longer practised by the younger generation.

Returning to the wedding ceremony, the bride, her head covered with a five-coloured cloth and her face turned down throughout, was rarely seen until she entered the house, dressed in a new *shingka* and *tothung*. The groom was dressed in a new chuba and nylon sports trousers. The villagers also wear new clothes, and what was unusual was that almost all the participants wore a *pangkheb*, a cotton ceremonial cloth, around their necks. This is a multipurpose cloth and is mainly used as a gift, but it can also be used as a cloth to carry children or luggage, or as a tablecloth, etc. The weavers of *pangkheb* are the village women of the Gamri river valley, such as Radhi and Phongme. Before the wedding ceremony, the bridegroom and bride's family order the dozens of these cloths and distribute them to their relatives and other wedding participants.

Cloths are an essential gift for many occasions in Bhutan, and it is the same in the Brokpa society. For example, a man gives a female relative a cloth for a *tothung* if she is a woman, and a cloth for a *kanggo* if he is a man. Cash gratuities for the attendants and helpers are also required, so only wealthy families can afford such grand weddings.

There is an interesting description of the marriage customs of the Brokpas in a booklet written by Dasho Tenzin Dorji(10). The original text was written in classical Tibetan (Chöke), published in 2002 and later translated into English, and the author writes that the tradition and customs of marriage among the Brokpas are undergoing changes.

The kind of wedding I saw may have already changed too.

Costumes and Clothes of the Three Major Events in Merak

There are three major annual religious events in Merak. All of them take place in the summer, when many people return to the village from their pastures and schools.

(1) *Choekor* **Festival's** *arpha* **costume is derived from** *the Epic of King Gesar of Ling*

The first festival is the *Choekor*, which involves the villages of Merak and Gengo. It represents the first turning of the wheel of Dharma (teachings of Buddha). This event is also held in Sakteng and the Monpa settlements on the Indian side. In the case of Merak, it is celebrated one day between the 12th and the 21st day of the 5th month in the Bhutanese calendar. It is a day-long walk around the perimeter of the two villages, with villagers carrying sacred texts from Samtenpheling Lhakhang, commonly known as Merak Lhakhang in Merak and Trashicholing Lhakhang, commonly known as Gengo Lhakhang, in Gengo 【3-44, 3-45】, while some sacred texts are from their own family altars. It is mainly women and children who carry the sacred texts. As the event is in July, during the school holidays, many young men and women return to their villages, and the usually quiet village comes alive with a large number of people. Because it is the rainy season, umbrellas are a necessity, but various cloths are placed over the sacred texts to keep them dry 【3-46, 3-47】.

By performing the *Choekor*, the people believe they will benefit from timely rainfall, bountiful harvests in the surrounding area, healthy growth of livestock, and the disappearance of diseases, conflicts and misunderstandings among the villagers.

A unique feature of the Merak's *Choekor* is the *arpha* (or *arpa*), or five men dressed as soldiers【3-48, 3-49】. They represent five groups in Merak and Gengo, called t*okhag*, who lead and protect the people carrying the sacred texts. The word *tokhag* means group. At the resting place of every tokhag, the women who belong to that particular *tokhag* entertain the guests, such as the monks, the *gomchen*(11) and officials with tea, alcoholic drinks and snacks, while the *arphas* have to recite poetry and dance 【3-50, 3-51】. It is interesting to note that the five *arphas* represent King Gesar and his four generals from the famous Tibetan heroic epic, *the Epic of King Gesar of Ling*. Their costumes and attributes / accessories, such as helmets, armour made of colourful cloth tied into mesh-like forms, and swords, are also derived from this story. The role of the *arphas* is to protect Buddhism from its enemies. Originally, there were two arphas, but this number was later increased to accommodate the five *tokhags*. The role of *arpha* is not hereditary but is chosen from among those who have memorised the verses from *the Epic of King Gesar of Ling* and learned the dance steps. The poems they recite are from this epic and are called *konglu* (songs of fulfilment) and are all in praise of the local gods[12]. The costume of the *arphas* reminds me of the costume of the soldier *arpo* (or *arpa*) who carries the "evil torma" at the *Torgya* and *Dungyur* festivals of Tawang monastery, but the Merak costume is more elaborate than the Tawang version 【7-12】. The Tibetan word *arpa* means 'thief, bandit, barkeeper, bricklayer' etc., but *arpo* can, depending on the circumstances, also mean 'labourer, assistant, bodyguard', and he is sometimes referred to as the assistant of a Bon priest[13]. In the case of the *arpo* of the *Torgya* and *Dungyur*, and the *arpha* of *Choekor*, 'bodyguard' seems to be the best explanation. The *arpha* also appears at the *Choekor* that is held in Sakteng twice a year[14] and at the *Mang Kurim* of Sakteng, a village-wide ritual of exorcism held every three years.

The most famous performance during the *Mang Kurim* festival is the naked masked dance called *tercham* (also called *terkong cham*). Besides the *arpha*, two *kengpa* wearing skull masks follow the procession of the *Choekor* of Merak 【3-46, 3-52】. They do not wear special costumes, but are dressed in western jackets, trousers and rubber boots, and their role is similar to the clown (*atsara*) seen at *Tshechu* festivals around Bhutan. The *tercham* dancers in Sakteng are also wearing skull masks, but they are fully naked except for a decorative collar with a hole to put the head through[15]. This collar is called *tser-nga*. *Tser* means on top, and *nga* means five. This is said to denote the four cardinal directions plus one upward to form the five directions[16]. In the Dzongkha language, it is called *dorji gong*, as the collar (*gong*) consists of four vajras (*dorji*) 【3-53】[17].

Although the *kengpa* seen in Merak is dressed, it is thought that originally, they used to be fully naked, with a wooden phallus hanging from their waist[18]. It is believed that the naked *kengpa* was found in various villages in Bhutan, especially in eastern Bhutan, such as along the Drangme river and Gamri river valleys in Trashi Yangtse and Trashigang districts. It has been observed in village rituals and festivals in the Monyul Corridor too[19]. In Chug village in the Dirang area, during the yearly *choskor* (same as *choekor* in Merak and Sakteng) procession, they were naked till recently, but now they wear shorts and some cloth around the shoulder, and they hang a wooden phallus from the belt[20].

(2) The Yak *Cham*, performed in *Nyungne*

The second festival occurs during the *Nyungne*, a Buddhist ritual of fasting and silence, held between the 11th day of the 6th month and the 1st day of the 7th month in the Bhutanese calendar. Lay women who participate in this ritual are confined in Samtenpheling Temple in Merak and the Trashicholing Temple in Gengo for the duration of the ritual. On the last day of the ritual, a holy fire is burned, and the yak mask dance is performed by the villagers between the two wang empowerment ceremonies that are conducted by the monks, one in the early morning and the other in the evening 【3-54, 3-55】. At this time, stalls are set up to sell children's toys, and people dress up and spend the day to receive wang twice and enjoy the yak cham with their families. For more information on yak cham, please refer to Chapter 6.

(3) *Jomo Kora*

The third festival is the propitiation ceremony to Ama Jomo, the 'mountain goddess' also worshipped by people in other parts of Bhutan and in the Monyul corridor. The people of Merak and Sakteng have their own legend and worship Ama Jomo with awe as their saviour and protector. Ama Jomo is believed to have led the Brokpa from the oppressive rule of the lord of Tshona in southern Tibet to their present land[21]. It is assumed that Ama Jomo is based on pre-Buddhist beliefs, but nowadays the people of Sakteng and Merak identify Ama Jomo with Jomo Remati, another form of the Buddhist protector deity Palden Lhamo. In the legend, she is described as a girl carrying an infant on her back, but in the wall paintings and statues in the temples, she often takes the form of a fierce goddess 【3-56】.

Jomo Kukhar or Jomo Phodrang, where Ama Jomo's palace is said to be located, can be seen from the village of Merak, and is a sacred mountain with an altitude of 4,383 m 【3-57】. The pilgrimage, called *Jomo Kora*, takes place on the 14th and the 15th day of the 8th month of the Bhutanese calendar, but some people make it in the 7th month.

A group of families who are called *jinda* 'sponsors' make the pilgrimage, which lasts three days and two nights. It is advisable for participants to wear new clothes, but because of the high altitude and cold weather, many women wear two layers of *shingka*.

Jomo Kora has strict taboos relating to 'death', 'blood', 'food' and 'smoke'. The household where death has occurred is not allowed to participate in the pilgrimage for one year, and that household must not provide any offerings such as cheese or butter for the pilgrimage, nor can they provide a horse. If there is a death or a birth in the village, no one is allowed to enter the mountain for three days. In other words, if there is a death in the village between three days before the day of departure, the mountain will be closed. The abomination of death is also present in the daily life of the people in Merak. In Sakteng, for example, it was customary to cut up the body into 108 pieces and throw into the river, although the corpse is now more commonly cremated in a crematorium near the disposal site. However, in the case of Merak, the home of Ama Jomo's palace, both of these practices are strictly forbidden, and it is customary to take the body to Rangjung in the Gamri river valley for cremation.

Menstruating women are not allowed to participate in the pilgrimage, and those women who are not menstruating are only allowed to go as far as the *Latsho* (spirit lake). The lake is at an altitude of 4,150 m, just below the summit 【3-58】. In other words, the summit is forbidden to women. When I attended in 2008, all the prayer flags and incense I had prepared were given to the men to offer at the top. While waiting for the men to return, the women would make offerings to Ama Jomo by the lake. They first repeat the prostration, then make animals out of butter and throw them into the lake to pray for successful breeding of their livestock 【3-59, 3-60】.

From the day before to the day of the descent, participants are not allowed to eat pork, chicken, eggs, garlic, or onions. It is also forbidden to bring in these foodstuffs. So, I had to carefully check the ingredients of the instant food I had brought with me. Smoking is also strictly forbidden. In the past, a female Indian journalist insisted on climbing to the top. The villagers refused and her climb to the top was abandoned, but the story goes that she smoked during the climb, which led to bad weather and a bad year for the Kora.

Costumes of the dancers of *Ache lhamo*

Ache Lhamo, which is found in the villages of the Monpa and Sherdukpen in Arunachal Pradesh, is also performed in Merak and Sakteng. However, like the yak cham, it is often a shortened version for presentation to the guests, government officials and tourists. The photograph 【3-61】 shows the costumes of the dancers when the play was performed at Merak.

For more information on Ache Lhamo, see Chapter 6.

(1) The name of the place comes from *mereg* in Brokpake, meaning "burn by fire". A legend has it that when the Brokpa people arrived here from Tibet, they burnt the area down with cooking fires.
(2) The name derives from *sateng* in Brokpake, meaning "on top of the land/ the top land."
(3) The reason was the loss of some antiques from the village (according to the head of Merak village, March 2004).
(4) [Pommaret 1999: 53]
(5) I interviewed the headmaster in September 2008.
(6) It is in Darranga Mela village of Baksa district in Assam.
(7) The method of dyeing *chuba* cloth will be explained in the chapter 4.
(8) The basic information on this yak hair is provided by [Karchung 2011: 33-34] but revised with my Brokpa friends.
(9) [Edmunds 1988: 150-155].
(10) [Dorji 2008].
(11) *Gomchen* is a lay person who performs religious duties but can also marry and do agricultural work. In Merak and Sakteng, where there are not enough monks, they play an important role in daily life.
(12) Lama Tashi Wangdi gave me the basic information of the *Choekor* at Merak on 23 July 2019.
(13) [Huber 2020a: 397].
(14) The first *Choekor* in Sakteng is on the 15th day of the 3rd month and the second *Choekor* is on the 15th day of the 7th month of the Bhutanese calendar.
(15) I have never seen the *tercham* of Sakteng but we can find the photo in [Choden 2014: 36].
(16) By personal instruction from Lama Tashi Wangdi in May 2021.
(17) The *dorji* or *vajra* in Sanskrit translated as the diamond thunderbolt is a name of the Buddhist ritual objects and the symbol of Vajrayana Buddhism.
(18) A 92-year-old man from Merak said that he had no memory of the Kengpa being naked, but Mr. Jamba, one of the *gomchens* of Merak, said that *kengpa* might have been naked a long time ago (31 May 2021).
(19) [Huber 2015: 220].
(20) By personal instruction from T. A. Bodt in May 2021 and [Bodt 2020: 97].
(21) The legend of Ama Jomo is presented in the oral tradition and in several biographies in Tibetan script, as well as in English works such as [Wangmo 1990], [Wangchuck 2006], [Chand 2004], [Bodt 2012] etc.

CHAPTER 4
Dyeing, Weaving and Trading

第4章 染める・織る・運ぶ

　本章では、モンパやブロクパ女性の貫頭衣シンカ、そして上着のトトゥンの製作と運搬について手短にまとめておこう。第2章、第3章でも述べたように、シンカやトトゥンは、エリ蚕から紡いだエリ・シルク糸をラック染料で染めたものを材料とする。だが、エリ蚕もラック染料も、着用する人々の居住地にはないものである。

　かつては、帯や紐などはカード織によって織られてきたが、ブータン同様にモンパの地でも稀にしか見られなくなっている。加えて、本章では、モンパ独特の工芸品として有名なダンガー（*dangnga*）と呼ばれるカラフルなバッグについても報告する。

ラック染め

　1906年にブータン東部のタシガンを訪れたイギリス人のシッキム行政官ホワイト（John Claude White）はその著書の中で、「タシガン周辺の谷で大量のスティック・ラックが飼養されているが、ブータン人はその養殖を体系的に行っていない。もし適切な監督のもとに置かれれば、この産業には大きな未来が待っているかもしれないのに、残念なことである」と述べている(1)。スティック・ラックとは、樹木の枝に無数に群がったラック・カイガラムシ（学名*Kerria Lacca*）の雌の粘着性の分泌物が固まったもので、外見は鉱物のように見える。

【4-1】小枝が付いたまま乾燥したスティック・ラック（左）と、小枝を除いたスティック・ラックの内側。Dry stick lac with twig still attached (left), and the inside of stick lac without twig. (Khaling, November 1999)

【4-2】木の種類はわからなかったが、ラック・カイガラムシの幼虫が白い粉のように枝を覆っている。
The type of tree was not identified, but lac insect larvae were covering the branches like white powder. (Gom Kora, March 2005)

【4-3】ブータンでは、ダショーの称号を持つ男性のスカーフ（カブネ）は臙脂色と決められている。この写真のダショーのカブネはラック染料で染められている。
In Bhutan, the scarf (*kabne*) of men with the title of *dasho* is specified to be a dark red colour. The *kabne* of the *dasho* in this photograph is dyed with lac. (Thimphu, January 2024, photograph by Siok Sian Pek-Dorji)

英語のラック（*lac*）は、サンスクリット語のラクシャ（*laksha*）からヒンディー語のラック（*lakh* 10万）を経て、ポルトガル語のラッカー（*laca*）、中世ラテン語のラッカー（*lacca*）に最終的に派生したものである。小枝の周りに無数のラック・カイガラムシがたかってラックを生産していることからきているという(2)。固まった分泌物が小枝を棒状に囲む様子は、まるでひき肉で作った串刺しのシシカバブのようである【4-1】。

　ブータンでは、近年まで、モンガル県のヤディ（*Yadi*）村周辺で、伝統的なラックの飼養が続いていた。しかし、生産した染料を運ぶための運搬に費用がかかるため、生活をやっと支えるくらいの利益しかなかったという。それでも飼養を続ける家庭はあったが、2018年頃に一度衰退した。衰退の理由は、経済的な理由だけではない。【4-2】は、私が、2005年にタシガン県とタシ・ヤンツェ県の境にあるゴム・コラ（Gom Kora）付近の河原で、木の枝に白い粉を吹いたように固まっているラック・カイガラムシを見かけた時に撮影したものである。地元の人の話では、以前は、この周囲でもラック・カイガラムシの飼養が盛んに行われていたという。しかし、仏教僧が、殺生に結び付く行為をやめるようにと戒めたこともあり、タシガン県やモンガル県の多くの人が飼養を

［ラック染色の工程］

【4-4a】このミョウバンは、ラック染めの媒染剤として使われている。This alum is used as a mordant in lac dyeing. (Dirang, December 2004)

【4-4b】砕いて粉にする前のスティック・ラック。Stick lac before crushing it into powder. (【4-4b】-【4-4f】: Dirang, March 2004)

【4-4c】スティック・ラックを臼で挽いて粉にする。
Stick lac is ground to powder in a mortar.

【4-4e】薄手の布を使ってラック染料を漉す。
Straining the lac dye using a thin cloth.

【4-4d】アルミニウムの鍋や洗面器に入れた粉状のラック染料に熱湯をかけ、手で揉みほぐす。
Pouring boiling water over powdered lac dye in an aluminium pot and washing basin and kneading it well by hand.

【4-4f】漉した染料を絞り出す。絞ったラック染料を再び鍋に戻して【4-4d】-【4-4f】の作業を20回以上繰り返す。
Squeezing the liquid out of the strained dye. Returning the strained dye back into the cooking pot and repeating steps 【4-4d】-【4-4f】 at least 20 times.

あきらめたという。ヤディ村及び周辺の村では、新型コロナウイルスの流行がほぼ収まった2023年秋頃から、数家族が飼養を再開したと聞く。彼らには、織り手からの需要があるため再開したとはいえ、仏教の教えとの葛藤があるようである。

ブータンの伝統的な手織布に、ラック染料は、欠かせないものの一つである。かつては僧侶の衣もラック染料で染められていた。現在では、国家に功績を残し、国王からダショーの爵位を賜った人々だけが身に着けることを許される臙脂色のカブネ（*kabne*）と呼ばれる野生絹ブラ（*bura*）のスカーフは、現在でも多くがこのラック染料で染められている【4-3】。化学染料が増えた現在でも、天然染料であるラック染料の深い色合を好む顧客の需要に応えるため、ラック染料を購入してシルク糸を染める織り手は絶えない。

　東ブータンのラック・カイガラムシの飼養方法はアッサムで行われているものと同様で、ラック染料は多くはアッサムから輸入されてきた。そのことは、ブータンでラック染料がギャツォ（*gyatsho*）と呼ばれ、その意味が「インドの色あるいは染料」という意味であったことからもわかる(3)。

　私が2002年にディランで会ったアッサムからの行商人RBは、彼が運ぶラック染料は、アッサム西部のゴアルパラ（Goalpara）で仕入れたものだが、産地はその南に位置するメガラヤ州のガロ丘陵にあるバジェンドバ（Bajengdoba）周辺であるという。過去30年間で仕入れ値は13倍に上昇していると語っていたが、現在は、さらに高くなっているようだ。

　ディランでのラック染色の工程は、2004年3月当時、以下の通りであった。

　　エリ・シルクの糸は、氷砂糖のような岩石を砕いて煮た液体に漬けておく。この岩石は、地元ではツール（*tsur*）と呼ばれていたが、ヒンディー語のフィトゥキリー（*phitkiri*）、つまりミョウバンのことである【4-4a】。ミョウバンは、ブータンとの国境近くのマンダラフォドンの崖や山で採れるという。ルパやジーガオン、シェルガオンの間の川沿いや道路沿いの急な断崖でも見つけることができる。染色は、まず、ラックを臼で粉にする【4-4b, 4-4c】。次に、アルミニウム製のたらいや鍋の中に入れた粉状の染料に熱湯をかけ、よく揉みほぐして色を抽出する【4-4d】。しばらく揉んだ後、薄い布を使って漉し、さらに絞り出す【4-4e, 4-4f】。再び同じ粉をたらいに戻して熱湯を入れて揉み、漉して絞り出すという工程を色が出なくなるまで20回以上繰り返す。こうして絞り出された赤い液体を火にかけ、その中に媒染剤に漬けておいた糸を入れて約1時間煮出す。煮出した糸を天日で干す。

【4-5】コマンと呼ばれるボケの実を輪切りにしたもの。冬にタシガン県のチャリンで収穫され、メラに運ばれた。
Japanese quince called *khomang* harvested in winter in Chaling, Trashigang district and brought to Merak. (Merak, August 2007)

【4-6】メラでもラック染めの媒染剤としてコマンが使われるが、ウールを赤い化学染料で染める場合には、このショマという植物が媒染剤として使われる。
In Merak, *khomang* is also used as a mordant for lac dye, but when wool is dyed with red chemical dye, this plant, called *shoma*, is used as a mordant. (Merak, August 2007)

【4-7】タマリンドは、マメ科の植物で、その実は食用にもなる。これはペースト状にしたもので、媒染剤として使う。
Tamarind is a leguminous plant, the fruit of which is also used for food. It is made into a paste and used as a mordant. (Tangla, Assam, August 2005)

ラックの媒染剤には、ミョウバン以外にも、場所によってさまざまな物が使われるが、ブータンのラディ村の場合には、ツァンラ語でコマン (*khomang*) と呼ばれるボケ (学名 *Chaenomeles speciosa*) の実を輪切りにして干したもの【4-5】を使っていたが、ディランでもボケの実を使うことがあり、トゥン (*thung*) と呼ぶという。メラの人々もラック染めにはコマンを使うが、ウールを化学染料で染める時には、現地語でショマ (*shoma*) と呼ばれる雑草を媒染剤として使う。この植物は英語のネパール・ドック (Nepal dock 学名*Rumex nepalensis*) のことで、ゾンカ語でショムダ (*shomda*) と呼ばれるものである【4-6】。日本では、貴船大黄 (キブネダイオウ) が学名 (*Rumex nepalensis*) が同じである。アッサムの、タンラでは、タマリンド (学名*Tamarindus indica*) の実がラック染めに使われている【4-7】。

モンパ女性がシンカやトトゥンを買い求める時、唾を付けた指先で布を挟んで色が付くかどうか調べているのを見たことがある。ラック染めでは色は付かないが、化学染料のものだと指先が真っ赤になるという。そして色がより長く保たれるのもラック染料によるものだという。

シンカ、トトゥンを織る人、運ぶ人

タワン地方では、織物は盛んではなく、シンカやトトゥンを織る人を見かけ

【4-8】ラディのこの女性の家では、祖母の時代から女性たちがメラの女性用のシンカやトゥンを織ってきた。
In this Radhi woman's home, women have been weaving *shingkha* and *tothung* for Merak women for three generations, since the time of her grandmother. (Radhi, March 2005)

【4-9】メラで、トゥンを織る若い女性。
Young woman weaving a *tothung* in Merak. (March 2006)

【4-10】ディランのシルク織りセンター。織り機はすべてマニプル製で、織っているのもマニプル女性たち。
Silk weaving centre in Dirang. The looms are all made in Manipur, and the weavers are also Manipuri women. (November 2012)

たことはない。

　東ブータンでは、タシガン県のラディ、ポンメ、バルツァムなど織物の盛んな村で、メラやサクテン、そしてタワンやディラン地方のブロクパやモンパのために、シンカやトトゥンが織られていた。

　メラやサクテンの高地に住む牧畜民は、バターやチーズ、肉などを麓の村に運んで、コメや野菜、布などと物々交換していたが、現在は、現金での取引に変わっている【4-8】。

　2006年に私が初めてメラを訪れた時、数人の若い女性がシンカやトトゥンを織っていたが、彼女たちはラディなどの麓の村で織りを習ったとのことだった。多くの中高年の人々は、模様のないウール布は織れても縞柄や細かな模様のあるエリ・シルク布は織れないと言っていた【4-9】。

　2005年当時、西カメン県のディランには、3軒の織物工房があった。第2章にも書いたが、2002年頃に政府が主催した「女性による地域の手工芸品製作を促進する織物研修プロジェクト」に、約40人から50人のモンパ女性が参加して、最後まで残った人々のうち3人がそれぞれ開いた工房である。3軒の工房ともオーナーはディランのモンパ女性だが、そのうちの2軒の工房の織り手は、モンパではなかった。1軒はアッサムから、もう1軒はマニプル州から来て、いずれも住み込みで働いている若い女性たちのグループであった。彼女たちの出身地は、いずれもシルク織りが盛んな村である【4-10】。同時期に開設された工

【4-11】ディランのニュー・マーケットの端にあった織物工房の一つでトトゥンを織っていた女性は、若い頃からシンカやトトゥンを織ることができた。その後、この工房のあったマーケットの一角は、火災でなくなってしまった。
The woman in the photograph, who was weaving a *tothung* in one of the weaving workshops at the edge of the market in Dirang, had been weaving *shingka* and *tothung* since she was young. The corner of the market where this workshop was located was later destroyed by fire. (November 2003)

【4-12】若い頃からシンカやトトゥンを織ってきたもう一人の女性。
Another woman who has been weaving *shingka* and *tothung* since she was young. (Old Dirang, December 2004)

【4-13】アッサムのタンラの村外れで、簡素な織り機を使って、モンパのシンカを織るラブハ族の女性。
On the outskirts of Tangla village, Assam, a Rabha woman weaves *shingka* for the Monpa people on a simple loom. (August 2005)

房が、ボムディラやカラクタンにもあった。

ディランでは、モンパの所有する工房でシンカやトトゥンが織られるようになる以前から、自宅でそれらを織る女性が2人いた。私が訪問した2005年頃は、元気で仕事を続けていたが、数年後に訪問した時には、2人ともう機織りはしていなかった。彼女たちは、アッサム商人からラックで染められたエリ・シルクの糸を購入して、自宅の庭先やベランダで、腰機を使ってシンカなどを織っていた【4-11, 4-12】。だが、彼女たちは数少ない例外で、基本的にモンパの女性たちは、ウールの布やバッグなどは織るが、シンカやトトゥンは織っていなかった。

モンパ女性たちは、ブータン東部やアッサムで織られた布を手縫いするか、インドの平原から来た人たちが経営する仕立て屋に布を渡して縫ってもらっていた。最近では、既製品に仕立てられたシンカやトトゥンもいくつかの店で売られている。

アッサム州では、アルナーチャル・プラデーシュ州との州境に近いウダルグリ（Udalguri）やタンラ（Tangla）、そしてブータンとの国境近くの通称メラ・バザールと呼ばれているダランガ・メラ（Darranga Mela）[4]近くの村で織られてきた。織っているのは、アッサムのボド（Bodo）やラブハ（Rabha）などの

【4-14】メラ・バザールで、ブータンの国民服、モンパやブロクパの人々の衣装、織物や染織の原材料などを商うマールワーリー商人の店。
A Marwari merchant's shop in Mela Bazar selling textiles and dyed raw materials for the Bhutanese national dress and the costumes of the Monpa and Brokpa people. (November 2015)

【4-15】メラ・バザールの近くの村には、ブータンの男性のゴの生地を織るボド女性の家が数十軒ある。彼女たちに材料を渡し、織り賃を支払うのは、マールワーリー商人である。
In the villages near Mela Bazar, there are dozens of Bodo women who weave the fabric for Bhutanese men's *go*. It is the Marwari merchant who hands over the materials and pays the weaving wages to these women. (November 2015)

部族の女性である【4-13】。アッサムの場合には、店のオーナーが近隣の村の織り手の女性たちに材料の糸を渡して、織り賃を支払う形式である。人件費の安いアッサム製の製品は、ブータン製よりも安価である。メラ・バザールの布を扱う店のオーナーの多くはマールワーリー商人(5)で、インド独立後70年以上商いを続けている家族もいる【4-14】。シンカやトゥンだけでなく、ブータンの国民服であるゴやキラ用の布も多く織られている【4-15】。

　タシガン県のラディ村で出会った2人の男性は、祖父や父と同じように、村の女性たちが織ったシンカやトゥンの布を徒歩でタワンまで運んで売っていた【4-16】。私も何度かタワンの村でラディ村から風呂敷包を担いで売りに来ていた行商人に出会ったことがある。同じくタシガン県のバルツァムでは、1980年代から90年代にかけて、アッサムのウダルグリの市が立つ日に、シンカなどを安く仕入れ、それを馬に乗せてタワンまで運んで売ったことがあるという男性にも会った。

　ウダルグリは、アルナーチャル・プラデーシュ州とアッサム州の州境、そしてブータン国境にも近く、アホム王国(1228-1838)時代からの定期市があった

町である。第1次イギリス・ビルマ戦争（1824-1826）当時、市は閉鎖されていたが、1833年にイギリス植民地政府によって再開された。アッサムと、チベット、そして丘陵部の諸部族との交易を促すためである。チベットからアッサムへは岩塩、アッサムからは、コメ、シルクの布、鉄、ラック染料が交易品であった。チベット各地やブータンからも商人が集まり、19世紀の後半まで、ウダルグリは、大変繁栄していたという(6)。

ディランで織られたシンカは、ラック染料で何度も染められた臙脂色のもので、織りも精巧にできていたこともあり、アッサムからの安物と区別するために、「ディラン・シンカ」と呼ばれている。2018年頃には、シンカは6,000〜6,500ルピー、トトゥンは6,500〜7,000ルピーと高額になっていた。その後のラック染料の高騰と、高級品としての需要が一巡したことのためか、2019年にディランを訪れると、ほとんどの工房が閉鎖されていた。

【4-16】この男性2人は、祖父や父と同じように、ラディ村の女性たちが織ったシンカやトトゥンをタワンまで徒歩で売りに行っていた。
Like their grandfathers and fathers before them, these two men used to walk to Tawang to sell the *shingka* and *tothung* woven by the women from Radhi. (Radhi, September 2008)

【4-17】後帯機でカード織をするドゥフンビ女性。
Duhumbi woman doing card weaving on a backstrap loom. (Photograph by T. A. Bodt, Chug, October 2018)

モンパのカード織

　カード織は、ヨーロッパではタブレット織（Tablet weaving）、アメリカではカード織（Card weaving）と呼ばれている【4-17】。タブレットとは木片の

ことだが、19世紀末のドイツの研究者が初めて見たカード織がアイスランドのもので、小さな木の板が使われていたことから命名されたという(7)。

カード織の基本は、木・紙・動物の皮・プラスチックなどの四角形の薄い板の四隅に穴を開け、その穴に縦糸を通して回転させ、上下に分かれた縦糸の間に横糸を入れて、再びカードを回転させて織ってゆく作業を繰り返すというものである。回転の方向や糸の色によって異なる模様が生まれる。カードを使った織物は、紀元前に始まり、ヨーロッパから北アフリカ、中近東、ロシア、中国、東南アジアに至るユーラシア大陸全体に分布しているが、20世紀に入り多くの国で姿を消し、忘れられた織物になってしまったという(8)。チベットやブータン、そしてアルナーチャル・プラデーシュ州のモンパの間でもカード織が行われてきたが、次第に織っている人の数は減ってきている。

ディランのチュグ谷とリシュ村に住むモンパは、それぞれドゥフンビ (Duhumbi)、キスピ (Khispi) が自称で、多数派のツァンラ語とは異なる独自の言語を持っている。アルナーチャル・プラデーシュ州の中では、このドゥフンビとキスピの人々の中にカード織が残されている。ただし織れる人の数はごく少数になっている。彼らのカード織は、どちらもシャコック（*shakhok*）と呼ばれるが、これは「獣皮」のことである。メラやサクテンのブロクパはパーパ（*papha*）と呼ぶが、こ

【4-18a】自分の足を使って織る、キスピ女性のユニークなカード織。
Unique card weaving by Khispi woman using her feet. (【4-18a】-【4-18c】: Lish, July 2012)

【4-18b】カード織の織り具は、畳むとこのようにコンパクトになる。
Card looms are very compact when folded.

郵便はがき

6008790

110

料金受取人払郵便

京都中央局
承　認

7416

差出有効期間
2026年10月
30日まで

（切手をはらずに
お出し下さい）

京都市下京区
　正面通烏丸東入

法藏館 営業部 行

愛読者カード

本書をお買い上げいただきまして、まことにありがとうございました。
このハガキを、小社へのご意見またはご注文にご利用下さい。

|ııı||ı|·ı·||ı|l|ıı·||·|||ı|ı·ı·ı·|·|ı·|·|·|·|·|ı·|·|·|||||

お買上 **書名**

＊本書に関するご感想、ご意見をお聞かせ下さい。

＊出版してほしいテーマ・執筆者名をお聞かせ下さい。

| お買上 書店名 | 区市町 | 書店 |

◆ 新刊情報はホームページで　http://www.hozokan.co.jp
◆ ご注文、ご意見については　info@hozokan.co.jp　　24.11.50000

ふりがな ご氏名		年齢　　歳　男・女	
☎ □□□-□□□□		電話	
ご住所			
ご職業 （ご宗派）		所属学会等	
ご購読の新聞・雑誌名 （PR誌を含む）			

ご希望の方に「法藏館・図書目録」をお送りいたします。
送付をご希望の方は右の□の中に✓をご記入下さい。　□

注　文　書

月　　日

書　　名	定　価	部　数
	円	部
	円	部
	円	部
	円	部
	円	部

配本は、○印を付けた方法にして下さい。

イ．下記書店へ配本して下さい。
（直接書店にお渡し下さい）

─ （書店・取次帖合印） ─

ロ．直接送本して下さい。
代金（書籍代＋送料・手数料）は、お届けの際に現金と引換えにお支払下さい。送料・手数料は、書籍代計16,500円未満880円、16,500円以上無料です（いずれも税込）。

＊お急ぎのご注文には電話、
FAXもご利用ください。
電話 075-343-0458
FAX 075-371-0458

書店様へ＝書店帖合印を捺印の上ご投函下さい。

（個人情報は『個人情報保護法』に基づいてお取扱い致します。）

【4-18c】使われている30枚のカードは、破れた太鼓の皮を利用したものである。
The 30 cards are made from torn drum skins.

れは、チベット語のパーパ (*pags-pa*) と同じで、「獣皮」を意味している。それは、この織りに使用するカードにしばしば破れた太鼓の皮が用いられているからである。ブータンのゾンカ語では、カード織機は、「紙の織機」を意味するショグ・タンシン (*shogu thangshing*) と呼ぶ。ショグとは紙のことである。これはかつてカードが地元の厚手の手漉き紙で作られていたことに由来している。最近は、代用品として、使用済みのレントゲン撮影用のフィルムが使われるようになってきている。現在、日本では、手芸用のカード織セットが販売されているが、そのカードは、厚紙で作られている。

　ドゥフンビ女性のカード織は、皮製のカードを使って、後帯機で織る。ブーツの紐などのような3cm程度の幅のものは30枚、男性用の厚手の上着をしっかり締めるためのベルトの場合は、40枚以上のカードが必要となる。一方、キスピ女性のカード織は、ブータンでも見られない独特なものである。固定された織機は使わず、縦糸を保持するのは、腰の帯と自身の両足と手元の横棒で、その張力を調整するための棒が先端にあり、足で支えられている【4-18a】。すべての道具を折り畳むと両腕で楽に抱えられるくらいの大きさである【4-18b】。この写真で織られている紐は幅2.7 cmで、30枚のカード

【4-19】アチェ・ラモあるいはアジ・ラム仮面舞踏の衣装に使われているカラフルなベルトもカード織による。
The colourful straps adorning the *Ache Lhamo* or *Azhi Lamu* masked dance (see Chapter 6) costume are also woven by card loom. (Rama Camp, November 2012)

第4章　染める・織る・運ぶ

【4-20】キスピ女性たちのカード織を保護・促進するためのワークショップ。
Workshop to protect and promote card weaving among the Khispi women. (Dirang, November 2012)

が使われていた。この皮は破れた太鼓の皮を使用したものだが、大きさは、多少ばらつきがあるが、およそ5 cm四方である【4-18c】。このような細い紐は、背負い籠のベルトや布製ブーツを膝下で締めるのに使われてきた。第6章で取り上げるアチェ・ラモあるいはアジ・ラムという仮面舞踏の衣装にも使われている【4-19】【6-9a, 6-13b】。

キスピの人々のカード織を保護・促進しようとする「モン・社会経済開発協会」という団体が主催するワークショップが2012年11月に開催された。3人のキスピ女性がデモンストレーションを行っていたが、女性たちも日中は農作業に忙しく、現在も続いているのかどうかはわからない【4-20】。チュグ谷でカード織ができた最後の女性は、今はカード織をやめてしまっている。

カラフルなモンパのバッグ

モンパ女性がよく持ち歩いているのが、ディラン地方ではカルツァ・ダンンガーあるいはダンンガーと呼ばれるカラフルなバッグで、タワンではカルツァ・コプと呼ばれている【4-21】。ブータン東部でも織られているが、元々は、アルナーチャル・プラデーシュ州のモンパの伝統的な工芸品である。ブータンのタシ・ヤンツェからバッグを売りに来た男性に、いつからこれらのバッグを作り始めたかを尋ねたことがある。彼の返答によると、1962年の中印国境紛争の際にブータン側に逃れてきたモンパ女

【4-21】多くのものを運べるダンンガーは、モンパの外出には欠かせない。
The *dangnga*, which can carry many things, is indispensable for the Monpa people's excursions. (Tawang, August 2010)

【4-22】タワン僧院の祭りにブータンのタシ・ヤンツェからバッグを売りにやってきた男性。
A man from Trashi Yangtse, Bhutan, came to sell bags at the festival of Tawang monastery. (Tawang, August 2010)

【4-23】伝統的なダンンガー布から作られたモダンなハンドバッグを持つタワンのモンパ女性。
Tawang Monpa lady with modern handbag from traditional *dangnga* cloth. (Tawang, April 2017)

性から、村の女性たちが織り方を習ったのが契機だという。タワン僧院の祭りの際に、国境を越えて売りに来ているブータン人の姿を必ず見かけるが、バッグのデザイン・色彩・織りの技術は、モンパのものの方がはるかに優れている【4-22】。本来は、男女共に穀物その他の荷物を運ぶ際に用いていたが、最近では、小型のハンドバッグを含むさまざまなお土産品が生まれている【4-23】。

バッグに関しては、T. A. ボットが本章のコラムに詳しく書いているので、そちらをお読みいただきたい。

(1) [White 1971(1909): 190]。
(2) [クラウセン 1972: 79-80]。
(3) [Pommaret 2000: 42]。
(4) ウダルグリとタンラはアッサム州ボドランド領域地域内のウダルグリ県にある。ダランガ・メラもボドランド領域地域内のバクサ県にあり、旧名をグダマ (Gudama) という。ブータンのサムドップ・ジョンカルからアッサムへの国境の門をくぐって車で5分ほどのところにある。
(5) これらの商人たちは、現在のラージャスターン州中部のマールワール地方の出身者で、16世紀半ばにはベンガル地方で商業活動の基盤を確立し、19世紀にはインド全体に商圏を拡大した。アルナーチャル・プラデーシュ州では、1962年の中印国境紛争後にタワンなどの国境の町にも多くのマールワーリー商人が店を構えている。
(6) [Mackenzie 2001 (1884): 15-16]。
(7) [日下部 2019: 3]。
(8) [日下部 2019: 3]。

第4章 染める・織る・運ぶ 143

CHAPTER 4
Dyeing, Weaving and Trading

In this chapter, I will briefly summarise the production and trading of the *shingka* 'tunic' dress, and the *tothung* 'upper garment' of the Monpa and Brokpa women. As mentioned in chapters 2 and 3, the materials for the *shingka* and *tothung* are *eri* silk yarns spun from *eri* silkworms and dyed with lac dyes. However, neither *eri* silkworms nor lac dyes are available in the area inhabited by the Monpa and Brokpa people who wear them. In the past, belts and straps were woven by card loom, but these are now rare in both the Monpa areas and in Bhutan. This chapter also describes the colourful bags known as *dangnga*, a well-known craft unique to the Monpa.

Lac Dyeing

The British administrator of Sikkim, John Claude White, who visited Trashigang in eastern Bhutan in 1906, wrote in his book, 'There is a great deal of stick lac grown in the valley of Trashigang, but the Bhutanese do not carry on its cultivation in any systematic manner, which seems a pity, as if placed under proper supervision the industry might have a great future before it'(1). Stick lac is a hardened mass of sticky secretions produced by the female lac insect (*Kerria lacca*), which swarms in countless numbers on tree branches. The stick lac looks like a mineral. The English word lac is ultimately derived from the Sanskrit *laksha* via Hindi lakh 'one hundred thousand'(2), via Portuguese *laca* and Medieval Latin *lacca*. This name is said to refer to the numerous lac insects that colonise the twigs and produce the lac. The hardened secretions that surround the twigs resemble minced meat kebabs on skewers 【4-1】.

In Bhutan, traditional lac cultivation continued until recently in and around Yadi village in Mongar district. However, due to the cost of transporting the dyes produced, the profits were barely enough to support their livelihoods. Despite this, some households continued to cultivate lac insects, but the practice declined around 2018. The reasons for the decline were not only economic. Photo 【4-2】 was taken in 2005, when I saw lac insects clinging to tree branches like a white powder on the riverbank near Gom Kora, on the border between Trashigang and Trashi Yangtse districts. According to local people, cultivating and harvesting lac insects used to be popular in the Gom Kora area also. But many people in Trashigang and Mongar districts gave up cultivating the insects, partly because Buddhist monks warned them to stop the practice, because it involves killing. In Yadi village, I heard that several families have resumed the practice since the autumn of 2023, when the Covid-19 epidemic was almost over. Although they have resumed because of demand from the weavers, there seems to be a conflict with Buddhist teachings.

Lac dye is one of the essential components of traditional Bhutanese handwoven cloth. Monks' robes were once dyed with lac dyes. Most of the dark red wild silk (*bura*) shawls called *kabne*, now only worn by those who have made meritorious contributions to the nation and have received the title of *dasho* from the king, are still dyed with lac dyes 【4-3】. Even with the increased availability of chemical dyes, weavers continue to buy lac dyes to dye silk yarns to satisfy customer demand for the deep colour tones of the natural lac dye.

The method of cultivation of lac insects in eastern Bhutan is the same as that practised in Assam, and a lot of lac dye used to be imported from Assam. This is evidenced by the fact that lac dye was called *gyatsho* in Bhutan, meaning 'Indian colour / dye'(3).

RB, an Assamese trader I met in Dirang in 2002, told me that he brings the lac dye from Goalpara in western Assam, but that it originates from the area around Bajengdoba in the Garo Hills of the state of Meghalaya to the south. He said the buying price had increased thirteen times in the last 30 years, but now it seemed to be even higher.

In March 2004, the process of lac dyeing in Dirang was as follows:

> The *eri* silk threads are placed in a liquid made from a crushed and boiled rock that resembles crystal sugar. This rock is alum, locally known as *tsur*, which in Hindi is called *phitkiri* 【4-4a】. It is said to be found in a cliff near Mandalaphudung, near the border with Bhutan. It can also be found in the steep cliffs along the river and the road between Rupa, Jigaon and Shergaon. To dye, the lac is first ground into a powder in a mortar 【4-4b, 4-4c】. The powdered dye is then placed in an aluminium wash basin and cooking pot, poured over with boiled water and rubbed well to extract the colour 【4-4d】. After a while, it is strained through a thin cloth and squeezed out again 【4-4e, 4-4f】. The same powder is then put back into the tub and rubbed with boiling water, strained, and squeezed out again, repeating the process more than 20 times until no more colour is produced. The red liquid thus squeezed out is placed in a pot over a fire, into which yarn soaked in mordant is placed and then boiled for an hour. The boiled yarn is dried in the sun.

In addition to alum, various other substances are used as mordants for lac depending on the location, but in the case of Radhi village in Bhutan, the locals use the fruits of Chinese or Japanese quince (*Chaenomeles speciosa*), known locally as *khomang*, which are sliced and dried 【4-5】. These are also sometimes used in Dirang, where they are called *thung*. In Merak, *khomang* is also used as a mordant for lac dye, but when wool is dyed with red chemical dye, a weed called *shoma*, in the local language, is used as a mordant. This plant is Nepal dock (*Rumex nepalensis*) in English and *shomda* in Dzongkha 【4-6】. In Japan, *Kibunedaiou* has a close scientific name. In Tangla, Assam, the fruits of the tamarind (*Tamarindus indica*) are used for lac dye 【4-7】.

I have seen Monpa women, when buying *shingka* or *tothung*, pinch the cloth between their spit-dipped fingertips to see if they can get some colour. They said that with lac dye there was no colour, but with chemical dye the fingertips turned bright red. They also indicated that colour of the lac dye would last longer.

Weavers and Traders of *Shingka* and *Tothung*

Weaving is not popular in the Tawang region, and I have not seen any weavers of *shingka* or *tothung* there. In Radhi, Phongme, Bartsham, and other textile-producing villages in Trashigang district of Eastern Bhutan, *shingka* and *tothung* are woven for both the Brokpa people of Merak and Sakteng, and for the Monpa people of the Tawang and Dirang regions.

The Highland pastoralists, the Merak and Sakteng people, used to transport butter, cheese and meat to the villages in the lower areas where they barter and exchange for rice, vegetables, and textiles, but this has now changed to cash transactions 【4-8】.

When I first visited Merak in 2006, a few young women were weaving *shingka* and *tothung*, and they told me that they had learnt weaving in the lower-lying villages such as Radhi. Most of the middle-aged and older people said that when they were young, they could weave woollen cloth without patterns, but not eri silk cloth with stripes and fine pattern 【4-9】.

In 2005, there were three weaving workshops in Dirang, West Kameng District. As mentioned in Chapter 2, around 2002, about 40-50 Monpa women participated in a government-sponsored weaving training project to promote local handicraft production by women, and three of those who remained until the end of the project opened their own workshops. While these three workshops were owned by Monpa women from Dirang, the weavers in two of them were not Monpa. In one of the workshops, the weavers were young women from Assam, and in the other one the weavers were young women from Manipur. In both cases, there were live-in workers who came from villages where silk weaving is popular 【4-10】. At the same time, there were also workshops established in Bomdila and Kalaktang.

In Dirang, there were two women weaving *shingka* and *tothung* at home, even before the weaving in the workshop owned by the Monpa started. When I visited in 2005, they were in good health and continuing their work, but when I visited a few years later, neither of them were weaving anymore. They used to buy lac-dyed eri silk yarn from an Assamese trader, and they would weave *shingkas* and *tothungs* in their gardens or on their verandas using a back strap loom 【4-11, 4-12】. However, they were the only exceptions; basically, Monpa women would weave woollen cloth and bags, but not the *shingka* and *tothung*.

The Monpa women would either hand-sew cloth that was woven in eastern

Bhutan and Assam, or they would give the cloth to tailoring shops run by people from the plains of India to have it sewn. More recently, ready-made, tailored *shingkas* and *tothungs* are also being sold in a few shops.

In Assam, weaving was done in villages near Udalguri and Tangla, near the border with Arunachal Pradesh, and near Darranga Mela(4), commonly known as Mela Bazar, near the Bhutanese town of Samdrup Jongkhar. The weavers are women from tribes such as the Bodo and Rabha of Assam 【4-13】. In the case of Assam, shop owners give yarn to weaver women from neighbouring villages and pay them for weaving the cloth. Products made in Assam, where labour costs are lower, are cheaper than those made in Bhutan. Many of the owners of cloth shops in Mela Bazar are Marwari traders (5), and some families have been trading since India's independence, so for more than 70 years 【4-14】. These weavers make cloth for *shingka* and *tothung*, but also for go and kira, the national dress of Bhutan 【4-15】.

Two men I met in Radhi village, Trashigang district, told me that like their grandfathers and fathers before them, they used to walk to Tawang to sell the *shingka* and *tothung* cloth woven by the village women 【4-16】. On several occasions, I have met traders who were walking from Radhi to Tawang to sell clothes. In Bartsham, in Trashigang district, I also met a man who said that in the 1980s and 1990s, he used to buy *shingka* and other items at low prices at the Udalguri market in Assam and carried them on his horse to Tawang to sell them.

Udalguri, on the border between Arunachal Pradesh and Assam and close to the Bhutan border, had a regular market during the Ahom Kingdom (1228-1838). The market was closed at the time of the first Anglo-Burmese War (1824-1826) but was reopened by the British colonial government in 1833. The purpose of the reopening was to facilitate trade between Assam, Tibet, and the hill tribes. The trade goods were rock salt from Tibet to Assam, and rice, silk cloth, iron, and lac dyes from Assam. Merchants came from all over Tibet and Bhutan, and until the second half of the 19th century, Udalguri was very prosperous (6).

Shingkas woven in Dirang are dark rouge, dyed many times with lac dyes, and are called "Dirang *Shingka*", distinguishing them from the cheap ones from Assam, as both the dying and the weaving was done elaborately. Around 2018, a Dirang *shingka* cost 6,000-6,500 rupees and a *tothung* 6,500-7,000 rupees, which was already expensive at that time. Due to the subsequent rise in the price of lac dyes and the reduced demand for this luxury product, most of the workshops had closed when I visited Dirang in 2019.

Card Weaving of the Monpa.

Card weaving is called tablet weaving in Europe and card weaving in the USA 【4-17】. The word 'tablet' refers to a piece of wood. Card weaving was first described by German researchers at the end of the 19th century from Iceland and the weaving practice was named after the small wooden planks that the people there used(7). The basic principle of card weaving is to make holes in the four corners of thin rectangular boards of wood, paper, animal skin or plastic, pass the warp thread through the holes and rotate the board, insert a weft thread between the upper and lower warp threads, rotate the card again and repeat the weaving process. Different patterns are produced depending on the direction of rotation and the colour of the thread. Card weaving originated before the Common Era and was distributed throughout Eurasia, from Europe to North Africa, the Middle East, Russia, China, and in South-East Asia. Since the turn of the 20th century, card weaving has disappeared from most countries, and it has become a forgotten weaving practice(8). While card weaving was also practiced in Tibet, Bhutan and among the Monpa of Arunachal Pradesh, the number of weavers is rapidly declining.

The Monpa living in the Chug valley and in Lish village in Dirang have their own language, which differs from the majority Tshangla language. They call themselves Duhumbi (in Chug) and Khispi (in Lish), respectively. Within Arunachal Pradesh, card weaving continues to be practiced among these Duhumbi and Khispi people. However, the number of weavers is very small. Both their card weaves are called shakhok, which means 'animal skin'. The Brokpa of Merak and Sakteng also called it *papha*, from the Tibetan word *pags-pa*, which also means 'animal skin'. This is because the cards used for this weaving are often made from the skins of torn drums. In the Bhutanese Dzongkha language, card looms are called *shogu thagshing*, meaning 'paper loom', because shog means paper. This derives from the fact that the cards used to be made from thick local handmade paper. Nowadays, recycled x-ray film is increasingly used as a substitute. Card weaving sets for handicrafts are now available in Japan, but these cards are made of cardboard.

The Duhumbi women use a backstrap loom with leather cards for card weaving. For a belt that is about 3 cm wide, such as bootstraps, 30 cards are needed, while for a man's belt for securely fastening a thick jacket, 40 or more cards are needed 【4-17】. The Khispi women's card weaving, on the other hand, is unique and not even found in Bhutan. No fixed loom is used, and the warp thread is held in place by the belt at the waist, and the weaver's own feet, while holding the weft in her hand, with a rod at the end to adjust the tension, which is supported by her feet 【4-18a】. When all the tools are folded, they are large enough to be held comfortably in both arms 【4-18b】. The strap woven in this picture is 2.7 cm wide and was made from 30 pieces of card. The cards that are used were torn drum skins and are approximately 5 cm square, although the size varies slightly 【4-18c】. Such narrow cords have been used to weave the strap of a small carrying basket or the straps of cloth-and-leather boots. These straps are also used in the Ache Lhamo or Azhi Lamu masked dance costume discussed in Chapter 6 【4-19】【6-9a, 6-13b】.

A workshop organised by the organisation 'Mon Socio-Economic Development Association', which aimed to protect and promote card weaving among the Khispi people, was held in November 2012; three Khispi women gave demonstrations, but the women were also busy farming during the day, and it is not known whether the card weaving practice is still going on today 【4-20】. The last woman that was able to weave using cards in the Chug valley has given up the practice now.

Colourful Monpa Bags

Monpa women often carry colourful bags, which in the Dirang region are called *kartsa dangnga* or *dangnga*, and in Tawang they are called *kartsa kop* 【4-21】. While these bags are nowadays also woven in eastern Bhutan, they were originally a traditional craft of the Monpa of Arunachal Pradesh. I once asked a man from Trashi Yangtse who came to sell bags in Tawang, whether he knew when Trashi Yangtse people started weaving these bags. According to him, the women in his area learned how to weave the bags from Monpa women who had fled to Bhutan during the Sino-Indian border conflict in 1962. During the festival at Tawang Monastery, Bhutanese are always seen crossing the border to sell their products, but in terms of design, colour, and weaving techniques, the Monpa bags are far superior to those from Bhutan 【4-22】. Originally, both men and women used them to carry grain and other goods, but recently a variety of souvenirs have been created, including small handbags 【4-23】.

For more information on the bags, please read the column written by T. A. Bodt in this chapter.

(1) [White 1971 (1909): 190].
(2) [Clausen 1962: 157].
(3) [Pommaret 2000: 42].
(4) Udalguri and Tangla are in Udalguri district within the Bodoland Territorial Region in Assam. Darranga Mela is in Baksa district, also within the Bodoland Territorial Region and formerly known as Gudama. It is a five-minute drive from Samdrup Jongkhar in Bhutan through the border gate to Assam.
(5) These merchants from the Marwar region of what is now central Rajasthan, they established a commercial base in Bengal in the mid-16th century and expanded across India in the 19th century. In Arunachal Pradesh, many Marwari traders set up shop in border towns such as Tawang after the Sino-Indian border dispute of 1962.
(6) [Mackenzie 2001(1884): 15-16].
(7) [Kusakabe 2019: 3].
(8) [Kusakabe 2019: 3].

COLUMN　The Monpa's Multi-Purpose Bag: the *Dangnga*

コラム
モンパの多目的バッグ、ダンンガー

（本コラムの原文は英語で、筆者及び写真はティモテユス・A・ボット）

　モンパのカラフルな衣装のほかに、モンパ女性はもう一つの工芸品であるダンンガーと呼ばれる、とても目を引き、とても有名な伝統的な織物の布製バッグで知られている【4-21, 4-22】。ダンンガーはブータン東部、西カメン県、タワン県のいくつかの村で織られているが、最も精巧なものは西カメン県のディラン地域で織られたものである。ディランとその周辺の村々に住むツァンラ語話者の人々も、リシュ村やチュグ村の人々もこのバッグを織る。ディラン地域のダンンガー・バッグは、織りがしっかりしているため非常に丈夫で長持ちすること、色彩の設定、さまざまなデザインが丁寧に施されていることなどが評価されている。ディラン地方のよく織られたダンンガー・バッグは、今では簡単に3,000ルピー（日本円で約5,400円）以上の値がつく。

　ここ10年ほどの間に、ジャンフー、ヤラン、メロンカールといったブータンのタシ・ヤンツェ県南部のダクパやツァンラ語話者の人々も、ダンンガー・バッグを織り始めた。しかし、その織りは非常に粗く、使用される糸の質も低いため、バッグはあまり丈夫ではなく、長持ちせず、デザインも大まかで、紐の幅も狭いことが多いため、持ち運びには不便である。それにもかかわら

【4C-1】ンゲイツォクと呼ばれるショクメ（縁）。
Shokme called ngeytshok.

【4C-2】シュルマ（境界）。
Shurma 'border'.

ず、タワンやディランでもあまりしゃれていない用途で需要があるのは、アルナーチャルで織られるバッグよりも価格がはるかに安く、通常数百ルピーしかしないからである。

モンパの
ダンンガー・バッグのデザイン

　伝統的に、モンパのバッグの縦糸と横糸は、オレンジまたは赤・黄・緑・黒・白の5色で織られている。現在では、糸の入手状況に応じて、織り手個人がこれらの色を他の色、例えば黒を青に置き換えることもある。

　ダンンガー・バッグのデザインは、一括してメント（花）と呼ばれる。ダンンガー・バッグには十数種類のデザインがある。しかし、この十数種類のデザインでさえ、織り手によって表面の形状が異なる。異なるサイズと色の組み合わせは、独特のデザインを作り出し、個人的な技法を加え、地元の織り手たちは、特定のバッグを誰が作ったのかを識別することさえできる。個々のメントのデザインに加え、伝統的なスタイルで織られたダンガーのパネルに沿ったショクメ「縁（フチ）」（*shokme*）【4C-1】のデザインと色は、どの村にも独自の伝統があり、その地理的な産地を示している。例えば、チュグ村の織り手はンゲイツォク（*ngeytshok*）と呼ばれる小さな菱形の列を織り、ディラン村の織り手はカン

【4C-3】ゴウ「お守り箱」。
Gow 'Amulet box'.

【4C-4】ゴウ「お守り箱」。
Gow 'Amulet box'.

【4C-5】ゴウ「お守り箱」。
Gow 'Amulet box'.

【4C-6】ゴウ「お守り箱」。
Gow 'Amulet box'.

【4C-7】黄色い時計周りのエムリン「卍字」。
Yellow clockwise emring 'swastika'.

【4C-8】赤い反時計回りのエムリン「卍字」。
Red counter-clockwise emring 'swastika'.

COLUMN

ジラ・ワロン（*khangjila warong*）「蟻の角」、リシュ村の織り手はミクシュ（*mikshu*）「矢尻」と呼ばれるデザインを用いる。個々のメントのデザインを区切るシュルマ（*shurma*）「境界」【4C-2】は、通常比較的平易で織りやすい。そのため、個々の文様の列の間のボーダーが広いのは、経験の浅い織り手や、より営利的な織り手の特徴である。例えば、チュグの熟練した織り手は、赤・黒・緑の正方形を交互に並べた列を2セット（4列）だけ使い、メントの間に黄色と白の正方形を並べる。

　絵柄の名称は言語によって、また村によっても異なる。以下のいくつかの最も人気のあるモンパのダンガーの名前は、ドゥフンビ語を話すチュグ村のものである。

(1) ゴウ「お守り箱」。このデザイン（チベット語の*ga'u*ガウ）は、邪悪なもの・嫉妬・噂話・陰口・災難から身を守ることを表している。ゴウのデザインは、大きな単一のデザインから、小さな繰り返しのデザインまで、さまざまな形や大きさがある【4C-3】−【4C-6】。
(2) エムリン（*Emring*）「万字・卍」。このシンボル（チベット語の*g.yung-drung*ユンドゥン）は、不変・恒常・永遠を象徴する。仏教を表す時計回りの万字【4C-7】と、ボン教を表す反時計回りの万字【4C-8】の両方がダンガー・バッグに見られる。万字の地色は通常、赤か黄である。
(3) ジャチュール（*Jachur*）「屋根葺きマット」。このデザインは、家の屋根裏で屋根葺きや風除けに使われる竹製のマットにちなんで名付けられた。このデザインは、悪天候や外敵からの保護などを象徴している【4C-9】。
(4) ポクポクマ（*Pokpokma*）「菱形」。このデザインは、ロサル「新年」の頃に供えられ、食べられる黒粟粉で作られた菱形のビスケット（ポクポクマ）にちなんでいる。このデザインは「一新」を表している【4C-10】。
(5) ポルツィ「香炉」。チベット語で「香炉」（*spos-phor* ポポル）を意味するこの文様は、土製の香炉の形をしたもので、ポルツィ・ゲイタン（*phortsi geytang*）とも呼ばれ、清浄を表している【4C-11】。
(6) ミクシュ（*mikshu*）、「矢尻」（ツァンラ語でシャクチュンマ*shakcungma*）。このデザインは鉄の矢尻にちなんで名付けられ、強さと保護を象徴している【4C-12】。
(7) ズィウ（*ziw*）「鍵」。鍵のデザイン（ツァンラ語でズィウ またはズは「とげ」のこと）は、繁栄・富・財宝を表す【4C-13】。

　これらのデザインとその名前が示すように、モンパのダンガー・バッグには象徴的な機能もある。バッグを持つ人の富と繁栄を表し、それを与え、

【4C-9】ジャチュール「屋根葺きマット」。
Jachur 'roofing mat'.

【4C-10】ポクポクマ「菱形」。
Pokpokma 'diamond'.

彼らを害悪や不幸から守ってくれるのである。

　かつては1つのバッグに3、4種類のデザインが繰り返されるだけだったが、現在では、より多くの異なるデザインを加えることで、織り手の技術を誇示している。モンパ独自のダンンガー・バッグのスタイルとそのデザインの起源は不明だが、おそらく土着のものが発展したものであろう。

モンパの
ダンンガー・バッグの織り方

　ダンンガーは後帯機で織られる。典型的なバッグは、現地ではカルツァ・ダンンガー（*kartsa dangnga*）と呼ばれ、ペクパ（*pekpa*）と呼ばれる2枚の細長い布が縦に縫い合わされ、タクパ（*thakpa*）と呼ばれる幅の広い紐が、バッグの前面と背面を側面でつないでいる。2枚の細長い布の縦糸は丸みを帯びており、パネルは通常1メートルほどの長さで、真ん中で区切られながら一続きに織られている。伝統的には、布の両面の少なくとも一部のデザインを同じ水平レベルで繰り返すように注意し、これがバッグの「前面」を作る。伝統的なスタイルのバッグでは、この前面にもメント「花」の形をした小さな糸の房があしらわれるパネルのデザイン（カバー裏の写真参照）は、ストラップにも小さく繰り返される。ペクパの幅は15〜20cmで、織り手やバッグの用途によって異なる。

　ダンンガー・バッグを織るとき、メント・ニー（*mentok nyi*）「綜絖棒」を使わず、マパ・ニー（*mapa nyi*）「巻き棒」またはリース・スティック「綾竹」1本とタクチュン（*thakcung*）「筬（おさ）」1本だけで織る織り手もいる。その場合、経糸のすべての糸を別々に持ち上げて横糸を作らなければならず、織物には大変な労力と時間がかかる。それでも、熟練した織り手であれば、

COLUMN

1つのバッグを丸2日で作ることができる。

後帯機とその道具は母から娘へと受け継がれ、ダンンガー・バッグを織る技術も受け継がれる。しかし近年、学校に通う女子が増えており、バッグを織ることで現金収入が得られるにもかかわらず、バッグを織ることを学ぶ時間も興味もない。結婚して学校に通う子供ができて初めて、再び織物を始める女性もいる。

モンパの ダンンガー・バッグの用途

布を2枚使ったダンンガー・バッグは、買い物袋としてや、お弁当、宗教的なお供え物、畑で採れた野菜など、軽いものから中程度の重さの、価値の低いものを徒歩で運ぶために使われる。バッグは上から閉じないため、横に広がることができ、かなりの量を持ち運ぶことができる。また、近年は一枚布のバッグも人気があり、特に小物を入れる「女性のハンドバッグ」として、また観光客へのモンパの代表的な土産物として人気がある。

ダンンガー・バッグの幅広のストラップは、肩にかけても額にかけても快適で、結び目を作ってバッグを上から「ロック」することもできる。伝統的にダンンガー・バッグには、垂れ蓋やジッパーなどの上部を閉じる手段はない。ダンンガー・バッグを額から吊り

【4C-11】ポルツィ・ゲイタン「香炉」。
Phortsi geytang ' incense burner'.

【4C-12】ミクシュ「矢尻」。
Mikshu 'arrowhead'.

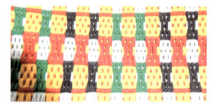

【4C-13】ズィウ「鍵」。
Ziw 'key'.

下げて運ぶのは、空いた両手で紡錘車や羊毛など他のものを運べるため、好んで使われる運搬方法の一つである。アルナーチャル・プラデーシュ州の農村部では安全だが、他の地域ではそうではないかもしれない。時には、巡礼や買い物、治療のためにインドの平原を訪れるモンパの村人たちが、スリに遭うことも想定せず、荷物を入れて開けたままのダンンガー・バッグを、のんきに背中に背負っているのを見かけることがある！

The Monpa's Multi-Purpose Bag: the *Dangnga*

Written and photographed by Timotheus A. Bodt

Besides the colourful dress of the Monpa people, the Monpa women are renowned for another artifact that is both very visible and very famous: the traditional woven cloth bag, called *dangnga* 【4-21, 4-22】. While the *dangnga* is woven in several villages in eastern Bhutan and West Kameng and Tawang districts, its most exquisite examples originate from the Dirang area of West Kameng. Both the Tshangla speakers of Dirang and its surrounding villages and the people of Lish and Chug villages weave this bag. *Dangnga* bags from the Dirang area are appreciated for the tightness of the weaving, making the bags very sturdy and long-lasting; the colour settings; and the careful execution of a wide variety of designs. A well-woven *dangnga* bag from the Dirang area now easily fetches over 3,000 rupees.

In the last decade or so, the Dakpa and Tshangla people from villages in southern Trashi Yangtse district of Bhutan, such as Jangphu, Yalang and Melongkhar, have also started to weave the *dangnga* bags. However, their weaving is very coarse, the thread used is of lower quality making the bags not very sturdy and lasting, the designs are more crude, and the straps are often narrow, making it uncomfortable to carry them. They are nonetheless in demand even in Tawang and Dirang for less sophisticated uses as their price is much lower than the bags woven in Arunachal itself, typically a few hundred rupees only.

Designs of the Monpa *dangnga* bags

Traditionally, the warp and weft of Monpa bags are executed in five colours: orange or red, yellow, green, black, and white. Nowadays, and depending on availability of thread, individual weavers may also replace these colours by other colours, for example, replacing black with blue.

The designs of the *dangnga* bags are collectively known as *mentok* 'flowers'. There are a dozen different designs for the *dangnga* bags. But even these dozen underlying designs can have distinct surface forms depending on the individual weaver. Different sizes and colour combinations make distinct designs and add a personal touch, even enabling the local weavers to identify who created a particular bag. In addition to individual *mentok* designs, the design and the colours of the *shokme* or rim along the panels of a *dangnga* woven in traditional style will indicate its geographical provenance, with every village having its own tradition. For example, the weavers in Chug will weave a row of small diamonds called *ngeytshok*, while the weavers in Dirang village use a design called *khangjila warong* 'ant's horn' and the weavers of Lish use the *mikshu* 'arrowhead' 【4C-1】. The *shurma* or border separates the individual *mentok* designs and is usually relatively plain and comparatively easy to weave. Therefore, broader borders between the individual rows of designs are usually a hallmark of less experienced or more commercial weavers. A seasoned weaver in Chug, for example, will only use two sets (four rows) of a row of alternating red, black and green squares, and a row of yellow and white squares between the *mentok* 【4C-2】.

The names of the designs differ from language to language and even from village to village. The following names for some of the most popular Monpa *dangnga* designs are from Chug village where the people speak Duhumbi.

1) *Gow* 'amulet box'. This design (Tibetan *ga'u*) represents protection from evil, jealousy, gossip, backbiting and misfortune. The *gow* design occurs in various shapes and sizes, from large single designs to smaller, repetitive designs 【4C-3】–【4C-6】.
2) *Emring* 'swastika'. This symbol (Tibetan *g.yung-drung*) symbolises changelessness, constancy, and eternity. Both the clockwise-turning *emring* representing Buddhism 【4C-7】 and the anti-clockwise-turning *emring* representing Bon are found on *dangnga* bags 【4C-8】. The emring usually has a red or yellow base colour.
3) *Jachur* 'roofing mat'. This design is named after the bamboo mats that is used for roofing and as windscreen for the attic of the house. The design symbolises protection, for example against the elements and external forces 【4C-9】.
4) *Pokpokma* 'diamond'. This design is named after the *pokpokma*, diamond-shaped puffed biscuits made of black millet flour offered and eaten around *losar* 'new year'. The design represents renewal 【4C-10】.
5) Phortsi 'incense burner'. This design (Tibetan *spos-phor* 'incense pot'), also called *phortsi geytang*, is in the shape of an earthenware incense burner and represents purity 【4C-11】.
6) *Mikshu* 'arrowhead' (Tshangla *Shakcungma*). This design is named after the iron arrowhead and symbolises strength and protection 【4C-12】.
7) *Ziw* 'key'. The key design (Tshangla *ziw ~ zu* 'thorn') represents prosperity, wealth, and treasures 【4C-13】.

As these designs and their names indicate, the Monpa dangnga bags have a symbolic function as well: they represent and confer the bag carrier's wealth and prosperity and protect him or her from evil and misfortune.

While in the past only three or four different designs could be found repeated on a single bag, nowadays, weavers show off their skills by adding a larger number of distinct designs. The origin of the uniquely Monpa *dangnga* style of bags and their designs is unknown, but most likely represents an indigenous development.

Weaving the Monpa *dangnga* bags

The *dangnga* is woven on a backstrap loom. A typical bag, locally called *kartsa dangnga* in full, consists of two panels called *pekpa* stitched together vertically, with a broad strap called *thakpa* connecting the front and the back of the bag at the sides. The warp of the two panels is set up and the panels are woven in a single stretch, usually around one meter long, with a separation in the middle. Traditionally, care is taken to repeat at least some of the designs on both panels on the same horizontal level, which will create the 'front' of the bag. In traditional-style bags, this front is also marked by small tufts of thread shaped into *mentok* 'flowers' (see photo on the back cover). The designs on the panel are also repeated in smaller size on the strap. The width of the *pekpa* varies between 15 and 20 centimetres and also depends on the weaver and the purpose of the bag.

When weaving the *dangnga* bags, some weavers do not use *mentok nyi* 'heddle rods' but only a single *mapa nyi* 'coil rod' or 'lease stick' and a single *thakcung* 'batten'. In that case, every thread of the warp has to be lifted separately to create the weft, making the weaving very labour-intensive and time-consuming. Still, an experienced weaver can make a single bag in two full working days.

The backstrap loom and its implements is passed on from mother to daughter, and so is the skill of weaving the *dangnga* bags. But in recent years, more and more girls are attending school and lack the time and interest to learn how to weave, even though weaving can provide them a good supplementary cash income. Only after marrying and having school-going kids themselves do some women pick up the craft again.

Uses of the Monpa *dangnga* bags

Double-panel *dangnga* bags are mostly used for light-to-medium-heavy, low-value items that need to be transported on foot for some distance, such as shopping items, pack lunches, religious offerings, vegetables from the fields, etc. Because the bags do not close from the top, they can expand sideways, and thus carry considerable quantities, making them look distinctively 'bulky'. Single-panel bags have also become more popular in recent years, especially as 'ladies' handbags' for carrying small personal items and as typical Monpa souvenir item for tourists.

The broad strap of the *dangnga* bag makes it comfortable to carry the bag both over the shoulder and on the forehead, and also makes it possible tie a knot to 'lock' the bag from the top. Traditionally, the *dangnga* bag does not have a flap, zip, or other means of closing the top. Carrying the *dangnga* bag suspended from the forehead is one of the favourite ways of transporting things, as it keeps the hands free for carrying other things, such as a spindle and wool. While this is safe in the rural areas of Arunachal, it may be less so elsewhere. Sometimes, Monpa villagers visiting the plains of India for pilgrimage, shopping or treatment can be observed to carry their belongings suspended on their back in their open *dangnga* bags in a carefree manner, not expecting anyone to pickpocket them!

CHAPTER 5
The Back Apron is Essential for *Shingka*
第5章 シンカに必須の腰当て布

　貫頭衣シンカを着用する際には、帯の下に腰を覆う長方形の腰当て布を挟み込む。これは、既婚・未婚を問わず、たとえ幼い少女でもシンカには必須のものとなっている【5-1, 5-2】。タワンのモンパ語では、「テンキマ」（*tengkima*）あるいは「テンガ・キマ」（*tenga kima*）(1)、ディランのツァンラ語では「マクロム」（*maklom*）、ディランのチュグ村のドゥフンビ語では「ゲステン」（*gesten*）、サクテンやメラのブロクパ語では「メーキム」（*me-kim*）(2)など、それぞれの言語によって呼称が異なる。

【5-1】子供には、一人で腰当て布をベルトでしっかり締めるのは少し難しい。
It is a bit difficult for small children to fasten the back apron tightly with the belt. (Merak, September 2008)

　腰当て布には、さまざまな機能的側面がある。まずは、寒さ対策として機能する。家の木床に座る際、寺院で地面や床に座る際などに座布団の代わりにもなる。そして、野蚕シルク素材のシンカの汚れを防ぐ機能もある。しかし、地面や床に座る必要のない会議やパーティーでも必ず着用し、完全にシンカの一部となっている。おそらくそれは、慎み深さを保つ方法として機能しているのだろう。なぜならば、シンカはギャザーを前面に寄せるが、後面に

【5-2】幼女でもシンカには腰当て布は必須アイテムである。
Even for a little girl, the back apron is an essential item when wearing *shingka*.
(Zemithang, March 2009)

【5-3】シンカを着て、左の女性のように腰当て布をしていない女性は大変珍しい。
It is very rare to find a woman who does not wear a back apron on her *shingka*. (Zemithang, March 2009)

はそれがないので、腰当て布がないと、身体の線が露骨に出てしまうからである。

腰当て布の義務性の例外は、パンチェンパと呼ばれるゼミタンのモンパに見られる。2009年3月にゴルサム・チョルテンでの法要に参加した時に、集まったパンチェンパの中に、腰当て布を着けていない女性を数人見かけた【5-3】。それを見たタワンの町から来たモンパ女性たちは、眉をひそめていた。

実は、第2章にもあるように、ゼミタンの人々が現在のシンカを着るようになったのは、1962年の中印国境紛争の後に道路ができ、タワン僧院の祭りなどに出かけることが容易になってからのことだという。ゼミタンの人々の伝統

【5-4】タワン地方ではテンキマまたはテンガ・キマと呼ばれる赤と黒、両方のウールの腰当て布が着用されるが、写真中央の2人の女性のように、多くは赤いものである。
In the Tawang area, both red and black woollen back aprons called *tengkima* or *tenga kima* are worn, but they are mostly red. (Tawang, October 2003)

【5-5】ディラン地方の若い女性は、パンデンと呼ばれる縞柄の腰当て布を好む。
Young women in the Dirang area prefer striped back aprons called *pangden*. (Dirang, March 2004)

的な衣装では、子牛の皮を背中から腰のあたりまで背負っていて、今でも何人かの年配の女性たちにそれが見られる。最近になってシンカを着るようになった女性たちは、他のモンパ女性にとって腰当て布が必須のものだということに気づかなかったのかもしれない。

腰当て布は、タワン一帯では赤または黒のウール製だが、赤が多い【5-4】。ディラン周辺では、多くの年配や中年の女性は赤や黒のウール製を着けているが、若い女性たちは横縞のカラフルなものを好む【5-5】。これは、チベット人既婚女性が前掛けとして着けるパンデン（*pangden*）という布に似ている。しかし、サクテン、メラの女性たちは、黒いウール製のもの以外は着けない【5-6】。長さもモンパのものよりやや長い。このように、腰当

【5-6】サクテン、メラの女性の腰当て布メーキムは、黒いウールのもののみで、他の色は着けない。
Women of Sakteng and Merak wear only black woollen back aprons called *me-kim* and no other colours. (Merak, August 2007)

第5章　シンカに必須の腰当て布　161

【5-7】自宅の軒先でウールの布を織る西カメン県テンバンの女性。
A woman weaving woollen cloth under the eaves of the house. (Thembang, West Kameng district, November 2004)

CHAPTER 5

The Back Apron is Essential for *Shingka*

When wearing the tunic style *shingka*, a rectangular piece of cloth covering the waist is inserted under the belt at the back. This is compulsory for both married and unmarried women, even for little girls [5-1, 5-2]. In the Monpa language of Tawang, it is called *tengkima* or *tenga kima*(1) in the Tshangla language of Dirang, it is called *maklom*; in the Duhumbi language of Chug village in Dirang, it is called *gesten*; and in the Brokpa language of Sakteng and Merak, it is called *me-kim*(2).

The back apron has several functional aspects. First of all, it acts as a protection against the cold. It also serves as a substitute for a cushion when sitting on the wooden floor of the house or on the ground and floor of a temple. It also has the function of preventing staining of the raw silk *shingka*. However, it is also a prerequisite for meetings and parties where seating on the floor or ground is not required. Rather the back apron is an integral part of the *shingka* dress. Perhaps, it functions as a way to preserve modesty. Because the *shingka* is gathered at the front but not at the back without wearing the back apron, the contours of the buttocks of the wearer would be exposed.

An exception to the compulsory nature of the back apron can be found among the Monpa of Zemithang, who are called Pangchenpa. In March 2009, when I attended a Buddhist ceremony at Gorsam Chorten, I saw some Pangchenpa women wearing *shingka* without their back aprons [5-3]. The Monpa women from the town of Tawang saw them and frowned.

In fact, as mentioned in Chapter 2, the traditional dress of the Pangchenpa is

て布の色である程度、着る人の出身地を推し量ることができる。

　ウール織りは、インド側でもブータン側でも自宅の軒先で女性たちが後帯機で織っているのを見かける【5-7】。一方、縞柄のものは、西ベンガル州のカリンポンあたりで機械織りされたものがマーケットで売られている。

　第9章で取り上げるように、西カメン県のモンパではない集団の女性の衣装も、貫頭衣という形状は共通しているが、腰当て布を着けているのはモンパだけである。

(1) チベット語で「外面のカバー」を意味するテン・ケプ (*steng khebs*) と関係があるかもしれない。
(2) メーキムはチベット語の「下部のカバー」メーケプ (*smad-khebs*) と関係があるのではないか。

---

different from the other Monpa. It was only after the Sino-Indian border dispute in 1962, when roads were built and it became easier to go to festivals at Tawang monastery, that the people of Zemithang began to wear the *shingka* as they do today. The traditional costume, in which the skin of a calf is worn at the back, from the shoulders to the waist, is still worn by some of the older women. The Pangchenpa women, who have only recently started wearing the *shingka*, may not have realized that the back apron is an essential part of the dress among the other Monpa people.

　The back apron is made of red or black wool in the Tawang area, but it is mostly red [5-4]. Around Dirang, many older and middle-aged women still wear these traditional red or black woollen ones, but young girls prefer to wear a colourful back apron with stripes [5-5]. This apron resembles the *pangden* worn as a front cover by married Tibetan women. The women of Sakteng and Merak, however, wear only black woollen ones [5-6]. They are also slightly longer than those of the Monpa. Thus, the colour of the back apron can to some extent indicate the place of residence of the wearer.

　In both India and Bhutan, we can observe women weaving woollen cloth on backstrap looms in the eaves of their home [5-7]. The striped ones, on the other hand, are machine-woven in Kalimpong in West Bengal and elsewhere and sold in the local markets.

　The women's dresses of the non-Monpa groups in West Kameng are the similar shaped sleeveless tunics as *shingka*, as will be discussed in Chapter 9, but only the Monpa women wear the back aprons.

(1) The It may be related to the Tibetan word *steng khebs*, meaning "surface cover".
(2) The word *me-kim* may be related to the Tibetan word *smad-khebs* meaning "lower part cover".

CHAPTER 6
Costumes in Folk Performing Arts

第6章　民俗芸能に残る衣装

　一般的にはチャムは、仏教の教義に基づいた宗教的な舞い、あるいは仮面舞踏を指す用語である。モンユルの回廊地帯やブータン東部を含むモンユルには、寺院の祭礼などで僧侶によって舞われる仮面舞踏とは別に、村々で演じられるヤク・チャムやアチェ・ラモ（アジ・ラム）などの、より土俗的な仮面舞踏が残されている。

　それらの衣装は演じられる場所によって異なっているが、民族衣装と同様に、固定化したものではなく、変化してゆく可能性はあるだろう。本章では、私がこれまでモンゴル地方で見学したものについて、報告しておきたい。

ヤク飼育の起源を伝える仮面舞踏ヤク・チャム

　1999年2月に友人と初めてタワンを訪れた。ちょうどチベット暦の新年（ロサル）に当たる時期で、車でタワンを去る途中で、偶然ヤク・チャム(1)の一団に出会った。ヤクの胴体は、竹で編まれ、その上にヤクの毛皮やヤクの毛で織った敷物を被せてある。木製の頭部を付け、胴体の中に2人の人間が入っていた。その周りで濃紺の木製の面や牧畜民の衣装を着けた男たちが踊っていた。彼らは通りかかる車を停めさせては、傍らのテーブルの上に用意された酒を乗客に勧め、踊りを見せるというもので、私たちもその踊りを楽しんだ後、心付けを渡してその場を離れた【6-1】。

【6-1】新年に、道端で通りかかる車を停めて踊りを見せるヤク・チャムの一団
A group performing the Yak *Cham* stopped our car at the roadside to show their dance during New Year. (Tawang, February 1999)

【6-2a】ギャンカル村のヤク・チャムの主要キャラクター。左から父親、長男、三男、次男（主人公のトゥーパ・ガリ）、従者ナロ。
The main characters of the Yak *Cham* in Gyangkhar village. From left to right: father, eldest son, third son, second son (the main character Thupa Gali) and his servant Naro. (【6-2a】-【6-2d】 Gyangkhar, November 2012)

【6-2b】ギャンカル村では、最初に白い布を翼のように広げたガルーダが登場する。
First of all, a Garuda appears with a white cloth spread like wings in Gyangkhar village.

このヤク・チャムが、タワンのギャンカル村の場合には、本来、正月の時期に限った特別なもので、伝説をベースにしたモンユル地方の伝統的な仮面劇であることを知ったのは、それから4〜5年後のことであった。ギャンカル村では、ロサルの3日目に終日、村の広場で演じられる。ロサルの時期に家々を回っては舞い、酒を振る舞われたが、今はその習慣は失われつつあるという(2)。

西カメン県のディラン地方のいくつかの村々にもヤク・チャムはあると聞いたが、残念ながらまだ見学の機会はない。1939年にイギリスの登山家ティルマン（Harold William Tilman　1898-1977）

【6-2c】ガルーダは、最初に白、次にまだら模様、最後に黒い卵を巣の上に産みつけてゆく。
The Garuda lays a white, a spotted, and a black egg on its nest.

【6-2d】黒い卵から生まれたヤクの周りで主人公と兄が舞っている。ヤクの背中には土地神スンマ・ゴンプー・マリンが乗っている。
The hero and his brother are dancing around a yak born from the black egg. The yak is carrying the local deity Sungma Gonpu Maling on the back.

とそのチームが、ゴリ・チェン山（Mt. Gori Chen）からの帰りに、シェルドゥクペンの人々が住む西カメン県のルパを訪れて、ヤク・チャムの写真を撮っている(3)。1950年代には、エルウィン（Verrier Elwin 1902-1964）(4)もルパ、あるいはシェルガオンで、ヤク・チャムの写真を撮影している(5)。これら二つの写真の中のヤクは、背中に穏やかな顔の女神を乗せている。

　第3章にも書いたように、ヤク・チャムは、国境のブータン側のメラやサクテンでも今でも演じられている。メラの場合には、毎年ブータン暦6月から7月にかけて行われるニュンネと呼ばれる断食と無言の行を行う仏教行事の最終日に披露される。ストーリーに沿ったものではない短縮版である。

　ヤク（学名*Bos grunniens*）は、モンパやブロクパにとって重要な動物である。ヤクは、乳製品や肉としての食用だけでなく、その毛は帽子・上着・雨具などの衣服や、袋・敷物・テント地・ロープなどの生活用品の材料となり、糞は、畑の肥料や乾燥させて燃料などに使われている。

　そのヤクがどのようにしてモンパやブロクパの地にもたらされたかという異なる場面を、楽器と踊りによってドラマ仕立てに表現したものがヤク・チャムである。2013年11月当時、タワン周辺の村には伝統的なヤク・チャムを演じるグループが合計5つあった。その中でも最も古いのがギャンカル村のグループである。すべての物語を演じるには9時間から10時間かかるというが、私が見学したものはそれを2時間から3時間に短縮したものである。

ギャンカル村のこの短縮版の場合は、登場人物は主人公のトゥーパ・ガリを含む3人の息子と父親、トゥーパ・ガリの従者のナロの5人である【6-2a】(6)。それに2人の人間が中に入ったヤクと、3個の異なる色のヤクの卵を産み付けるガルーダが加わる【6-2b, 6-2c】。ヤクの上には、両手を上げたこの地方の土地の女神の一人、スンマ・ゴンプー・マリンが乗っている【6-2d】。メラの場合には、

【6-3】メラのニュンネで使われたヤクには、護法尊のパルデン・ラモが乗っている。パルデン・ラモはチベット仏教では女性の忿怒尊だが、このヤクの背に乗った女神は普通の表情である。
The yak which was used for the Yak *Cham* during *Nyungne* in Merak had the dharma-protecting deity Palden Lhamo riding on it. Palden Lhamo is a wrathful female deity in Tibetan Buddhism, but this female deity on the yak has an ordinary face. (Merak, August 2007)

ヤクに乗っているのは仏教の護法尊パルデン・ラモである。チベット仏教では、彼女は、女性の忿怒尊であるが、このヤクの上の女神は、忿怒形ではなく、普通の女性の顔である【3-55, 6-3】。

　伝統的なヤク・チャムとして認められるのは、女神が乗っているものだとギャンカル村で聞いたが、観光促進のためのタワン・フェスティバルなどのイベントの際に舞台で演じられるショーとしてのヤク・チャムのヤクは着ぐるみで、女神は乗っていない。演じているのもチベット人の若者のグループである。ヤク・チャムと呼ばれてはいるが、これはチベット・オペラの演目の一つ、「ドワ・サンモ」(7)の中のヤク飼いの遊牧民の家族が演じる有名なシーンからのものではないかと推測している。チベット語で「ヤクの劇」や「ヤクの踊り」を意味するヤク・ツェと呼ばれている(8)。踊りが激しく、舞台上で短時間に短縮して演じられるため、モンパのヤク・チャムよりもイベントで採用されることが多い。しかしながら、いくら短縮版であったとしても、モンユルのヤク・チャムとはどう見ても別物であると思う。モンユルのヤク・チャムは、主人公が苦難の旅の果てにようやくヤクを手に入れるなどのさまざまな長いストーリーから

【6-4】タワンの国際観光市で演じられたヤク・チャム。服装はチベット風である。2頭のヤクの背中には神は乗っていない。
A Yak *Cham* performed at the International Tourism Mart in Tawang. The costumes of the dancers are in Tibetan style. There is no deity on the back of the two yaks. (Tawang, October 2013)

【6-5】メラで来賓を歓迎するために演じられたヤク・チャムには神は乗っていなかった。しかし、ダンサーは伝統的な皮のレギンスのピシュを着けていた。
The Yak *Cham* performed to welcome the guests at Merak didn't carry the deity on its back. But the dancer was wearing the traditional leather leg guard *pishub*. (Merak, July 2012)

なり、ヤクが卵から出現するシーンや他の随所に、神話的な要素がちりばめられている。かつては、さまざまなイベントに招かれたギャンカルの人々は、このチベット人のヤク・チャムグループのもの【6-4】が採用されるようになって、自分たちの伝統的なヤク・チャムを公衆に見せる機会が減っていると嘆いていた。

　メラでも2012年ごろから外部からの賓客や観光客に見せるヤク・チャムに同じような着ぐるみが使われるようになった。演じているのは地元の人々で、ヤク・チャムのさわりを少しだけ見せている。だが、このヤクの背にパルデン・ラモは乗っていない【6-5】。しかし、2019年にパルデン・ラモが乗ったオリジナルの新しいヤクを購入し、現在は、着ぐるみとオリジナルのものの2つを使い分けているという。

　いずれのヤク・チャムも、登場人物は、典型的な牧畜民の衣装を身に着けている。モンパの村では、白いキュロット・スカートと丸い携帯型クッション（テンタン）は、ヤク・チャムの衣装として残っているだけになっている【6-6】。

チベットとは異なるアチェ・ラモ

　チベット・オペラ(歌舞劇)の「アチェ・ラモ」は、「姉女神」と訳され、複数のオペラ全般を意味する名称となっている(9)。一般的には「ラモ」と略されることが多い。しかし、モンユルの場合は、歌もところどころで歌われるが、歌舞劇というより仮面舞踊のチャムに近く、登場人物も5人ないし6人で、演者はすべて男性である。楽器は太鼓とシンバルだけで、それを演奏するのも男性である。ストーリーの多くはチベットの「ノルサン法王の伝記」とよく似た物語がベースとなっている(10)。

【6-6】タワンでは、白いキュロット・スカート(カンダムまたはカンノム)と携帯用座布団のテンタンは、ヤク・チャムの衣装としてしか着用されなくなってきている。このカンダムも本来のウールではなく、薄い木綿布で作られている。
In Tawang, the white culotte skirt (*kangdham* or *kangnom*) and a portable felt cushion (*tengtan*), are only worn as a costume for the Yak *Cham*. The *kangdham* they use is made of thin cotton cloth instead of the original ones, which are made of wool. (Gyangkhar, March 2004)

　現在でもモンユルのいくつかの村々で演じられているが、私が実際に見学したのは、ブータン東部のタシガン県のジ

【6-7】ルブランの小学生が校庭でアチェ・ラモの練習をしていた。
Primary school children in Lubrang practicing *Ache Lhamo* in the school yard. (Lubrang, August 2005)

ョンカルとメラ、アルナーチャル・プラデーシュ州では、タワン県のゼミタン、そして西カメン県のディラン・サークルのラマ・キャンプである。また、ディラン・サークルの牧畜民の村ルブランで、小学生がアチェ・ラモの練習をしているのを見る機会もあった【6-7】。ルブランは、数世代前にブータンのサクテンから移住してきた人々の村で、現在、彼らは指定トライブのモンパとなっている。

　登場人物は、ノルサン王、2人の女神、漁師のニャパとそれを助けるニャロ

第6章　民俗芸能に残る衣装　　169

【6-8a】メラのアチェ・ラモの主要な登場人物。左からニャロ、2人の女神、ノルサン王、ニャパ。ニャパとニャロの2人の漁師の腰からは、黒と白のヤクの毛を撚って作った細いロープが垂れ下がっている。The main characters of *Ache Lhamo* in Merak. From left to right: Nyaro, two goddesses, King Norsang and Nyapa. The thin ropes of twisted black and white yak hair are hanging down from the waist of two fishermen, Nyapa and Nyaro. (【6-8a】,【6-8b】Merak, September 2008)

の5人だが、この登場人物の名前や役割も場所によって異なっている【6-8a, 6-8b】。

　モンユル版の物語は、場所により多様だが、以下が、ノルブ(Tsewang Norbu)がタワンで記録した話を大幅に要約したものである(11)。

　　湖の神ナーガを助けた漁師がお礼にナーガの国へ招かれ、土産に願いが叶う宝珠をもらい、その宝珠を仙人に見せに行った。そこに滞在中に、下界に水浴びをしに降りてきた美しい女神（ラモ）に心を奪われ、なんとかして自分の妻にしたいと思った。宝珠をナーガに返して代わりに特別な投げ縄を入手し、その女神を捕まえることができた。彼は女神を妻にしようとしたが、受け入れられなかった。そこで、彼は仙人のアドバイスによって女神をチョギェル・ノルサン王に献上した(12)。王は、美しい女神を妃として幸せに暮らしていたが、王にはすでに500人の妻がいた。妻たちは、国王を奸計によって他国との戦争に送り出すことに成功した。その留守中に身の危険を感じた女神は、神の国へと去った。戦いから戻ったノルサン

【6-8 b】メラでは、ニャパとニャロの面は若干異なっている。ニャパ（左）の額には赤い太陽と緑の三日月があり、両頬には緑の丸い印がある。ニャロの場合は、その太陽は緑、月は赤、丸い印は赤となっている。In Merak, the masks of Nyapa and Nyaro are slightly different. On the forehead of Nyapa, there is a red sun and a green crescent moon, and on both cheeks, there are green round marks; on Nyaro, the sun is green, the moon is red, and the round marks are red.

　王は女神を探す旅に出て、神の国で、姉の水浴びの水を汲みに来た妻の妹に出会い、ようやく妻と再会し、自国に戻って国を良く治め、2人で幸福に暮らした。

　アルナーチャル・プラデーシュ州のアチェ・ラモについては、エルウィンがルパのシェルドゥクペンのもの、サルカール（Niranjan Sarkar）がタワン県のジャンと西カメン県のリシュのモンパの村のストーリーを、それぞれ採録している(13)。ツェワン・ノルブが聞き書きしたものが比較的新しいものであるが、どこの村のものかは書かれていない。モンパの村々ではアジ・ラム（Azhi LhamuまたはAzhi Lamu）という呼称が一般的であるが、メラやサクテンでは、チベット語同様にアチェ・ラモと呼ばれている。

　興味深いのは、ボット（T. A. Bodt）が、2013年の新年（ロサル）の5日目に採録したリシュ村の向いにあるチュグ谷のアジ・ラムのストーリーである(14)。チュグ谷に住む人々は、指定トライブのモンパであるが、自らをドゥフンビ（Duhumbi）と称している。ボットによれば、ドゥフンビの人々は、1962年の中印国境紛争以前には寄付金集めのためにタワンやディランでもアジ・ラムを演じていたが、チベット難民の人々が流入してきてから、急に演じられなくなったという。面や衣装をチベット難民に売ってしまったという証言があるという。2011年に復活し、それ以降断続的に演じられているという。

　チュグ谷のアジ・ラムの主な登場人物は、聖なる翻訳者ラム・ジャル（Lham Jalu）、2人の兄弟の漁師ニャパとニャロ、2人の女神ラムとラチャ、ボン教の魔術師ンガクパ、仏教僧、父親と母親の扮装をした人々である。先述の「ノル

【6-9a】チュグ谷のアジ・ラムの登場人物の一部、左からニャパあるいはニャロ、ラム・ジャル王子、2人の女神、右端はボン教の魔術師ンガクパ。女神たちの腰から下がっているカラフルな細い紐は、チュグ谷で見られるカード織で織られたものであろう。全員が土地神に捧げるための地酒の入ったカップを手にしている。
Some of the characters of *Azhi Lamu* in the Chug Valley, from left to right, Nyapa or Nyaro, Prince Lham Jalu, the two goddesses, and on the far right the Bonpo magician Ngakpa. The colourful thin cords hanging from the waists of the goddesses are probably woven with the tablet or card weaving technique also found in the Chug valley. Everyone has a cup of local alcohol in their hand as an offering to the local deities. (Photograph by Ismael Lieberherr, Tsangpa village, Chug valley, February 2013)

【6-9b】チュグ谷のアジ・ラムには、他の地域では見たことのない多くの異なる話の筋がある。このシーンは、ンガクパが土地の境界に杭を打っているところである。
There are many different plots in the performance of *Azhi Lamu* in the Chug valley that I haven't seen in any other village. In this scene, Ngakpa is placing the pegs to delimit the area. (Photograph by T. A. Bodt, Tsangpa village, March 2014)

サン法王の伝記」のような物語とは全く異なり、もっと神話的で象徴的な要素が濃い。例えば、このストーリーには、世界の創造や人間の起源、農耕や家畜の始まり、仏教伝来、仏教とボン教との対立など、さまざまな象徴的な問題が暗示されている。このパフォーマンスには、土地神と仏教の神々の両方を喜ばせ、かつ鎮めてその年の幸運や豊作がもたらされ、伝染病や自然災害が起こらないように祈る人々の祈りが込められている【6-9a, 6-9b】。

チュグ谷のような象徴的なストーリーがモンユル由来のもので、それがチベット・オペラに取り入れられて物語化され、モンユルに逆輸入された可能性はないだろうか。しかし、その結論を得るためにはより多くの例証と研

【6-10】ジョンカールのアチェ・ラモの主要キャラクター。宝冠を被った2人の女神はモンパやブロクパの女性が着る上着トトゥンを着ている。両端の2人の漁師の腰からは、白と黒で撚られたロープが吊り下げられている。
The main characters of *Ache Lhamo* in Joenkhar. The two goddesses in crowns are wearing the jackets (*tothung*) worn by the Monpa and Brokpa women. From the waist of two fishermen on the both ends, the black and white twisted ropes are hanging down. (Joenkhar, Trashigang district, August 2007)

究が必要であろう。

モンユルのアチェ・ラモ（アジ・ラム）の衣装は、場所によって異なるが、ニャパとニャロの着けている仮面が大変独特なものであることは共通している。チベットのアチェ・ラモでは板状の平面的な面だが、モンユルのものは、顔はフェルト布に目鼻口を縫い付け、鼻の先に子安貝（宝貝）を下げた立体的なものである。額には、月と星を表す印があり、両頬には丸い印がある。メラの場合は、それらの色の違いがニャパとニャロの違いを示しているが【6-8b】、他の

【6-11a】ゼミタンのアジ・ラムの衣装。白と黒のヤクの毛を撚ったロープが漁師の腰から下がっていて、ズボンは、カラフルなチベット布で作られている。
The costume of *Azhi Lamu* in Zemithang. The thin ropes of twisted black and white yak hair are hanging down from the waist of the fishermen and their trousers are made of colourful Tibetan cloth. (Zemithang, March 2009)

【6-11b】2人の女神の下半身の衣装は、白い長ズボンで、腰から何本かのカラフルな布が下がっている。
The lower part of the costume of the two goddesses consists of white long trousers and some colourful cloths that are hanging down from their waist. (Zemithang, March 2009).

【6-12】メラのニャパとニャロの面は、顔はフェルトに目や鼻などを縫い付けたもので、頭はヤギの皮とその長い毛からできていて、それをすっぽりと被る。
The masks of Nyapa and Nyaro have faces made of felt with eyes and noses sewn onto it, and the heads are made of goat's skin with long hair, which the dancers put over their heads (Merak, August 2007).

【6-13a】カラクタンのボハ村からやってきた一団。彼らの衣装のほとんどは、新しく色鮮やかであった。
The dance troupe from the village of Boha in Kalaktang. Almost all their costumes were new and colourful. (Rama Camp, November 2013)

【6-13b】腰の周りには、女性の上着トトゥンの柄と同様の布の他に、美しいカード織によって織られた、数多くのさまざまな柄の紐が下がっている。
Many beautiful cords of various patterns woven by tablet or card weaving, in addition to the same patterned cloth of the women's jacket (*tothung*), hang down from the waist. (Rama Camp, November 2013)

場所では、同じ色か、頬の色だけが異なっている。頭はヤギの長い毛と皮で作られた立体的な形状で、それを頭から被ると後ろの毛が背中全体まで覆う【6-12】。ほとんどの場所で、ニャパとニャロの腰からは、おそらくヤクの毛であろう黒と白の動物の毛を撚った何本かの細いロープが垂れ下がっている【6-8a, 6-9a, 6-10, 6-11a, 6-13a】。チュグ谷では、ンガクパもこのロープを着けている【6-9a, 6-9b】。ゼミタンでは、漁師たち【6-11a】はカラフルなチベットの布のズボンを着け、2人の女神【6-11b】は長くて白いズボンを穿いて腰から何本かのカラフルな布を垂れ下げている。すべての写真の女神は、頭に宝冠を被っている。

　ラマ・キャンプで演じられていたものは、地元のものではなく、県南西部のカラクタン・サークルのボハ（Boha）村からやって来た一団によるもので、その目的は、彼らの村の寺院の再建資金の勧進のためであった。稲の収穫を終えた後に村を発ち、一カ月以上かけて、毎日西カメン県の異なる村々を巡回しているという【6-13a, 6-13b】。

【6-14】タントン・ギャルポは常に、白髪・白髭の老人が右手に鉄鎖を持った姿で描かれる。
Thangtong Gyalpo is always depicted as an old man with white hair and a beard, holding an iron chain in his right hand. (Trashi Rabten Gompa, Namshu, April 2019)

　チベット・オペラのアチェ・ラモまたはラモには、14世紀にチベットやブータン、モンユル地方に多くの鉄鎖の橋を建設したタントン・ギャルポが、その資金集めのために7人の姉妹からなる歌と踊りのグループ「アチェ・ラモ」を組織して、橋の建設資金を集めたという伝承がある⑴。かつてチュグ谷の人々が遠くタワンまで出かけ、現在もボハ村の一団が寄付金集めに遠くまでやってきてアチェ・ラモを舞うという話は、このタントン・ギェルポの伝説を彷彿とさせる【6-14】。

⑴ タワンや西カメン県のヤク・チャムのストーリーについて［Wangchu 1999］、［Norbu 2008: 108-110］などが英語で記述している。メラのヤク・チャムについては、［Karchung 2013］が詳述している。［脇田 2019: 257-287］がそれらを日本語でまとめている。
⑵ 2011年8月に取材した。
⑶ ［Tilman 2016(1946): 63］。彼らの登山は失敗に終わっている。
⑷ イギリスからキリスト教宣教師として来印したが、ガンディーの思想に傾倒し、キリスト教を捨て、インド市民権を獲得し、アルナーチャル・プラデーシュ州の前身NEFAの人類学顧問となって、部族の文化に関する多くの著作を残した。
⑸ ［Eiwin 1959: 89］。撮影場所は書かれていないが、エルウィンは、シェルガオンとルパのヤク・チャムの物語を書いている［Elwin 1958: 376-377］。シェルドゥクペンも西カメン県の指定トライブの一つである。彼らについては第9章で述べる。
⑹ 3人の息子の名前や兄弟の順番は、場所により異なっている。
⑺ 一説によると、カンドゥ・ドワ・サンモの物語は、モン地方の古い民話を元にゲルク派の高僧が創作したものだという［三宅 2008: 277］。
⑻ ダラムサラを根拠地とするチベット舞台芸術団（TIPA）の東京公演2006年のDVDより。
⑼ ［スタン 1971: 316］。
⑽ ［三宅・石山 2008: 233-235］に「ノルサン法王の伝記」が日本語に訳されている。
⑾ ［Norbu 2008: 110-115］。
⑿ チベット語のチョギェル［chos rgyal］には、「宗教上の王」の意味がある。
⒀ ［Elwin 1958: 122-123］、［Sarkar 1993(1974)：145-149］。
⒁ 詳しくは、https://doi.org/10.5281/zendo.1202204 を参照のこと。
⒂ ［Gerner 2007: 84-85］。この説に関する反論などについては、［三宅 2008: 257-264］を参照されたい。

CHAPTER 6
Costumes in Folk Performing Arts

In general, Cham is a term used to describe religious dances or masked dances based on the Buddhist doctrine. In Monyul which includes the Monyul Corridor and eastern Bhutan, apart from the masked dances performed by monks at festivals of Buddhist monasteries, there are also the folk masked dances such as Yak Cham and *Ache Lhamo* or *Azhi Lhamu*, which are performed in the villages. The costumes of Yak Cham and *Ache Lhamo* vary according to the place where they are performed, and like the traditional costumes, they are not fixed and may change over time. In this chapter, I would like to report on what I have seen and heard in the Monyul area.

Yak *Cham*, a masked dance that tells the origin of yak rearing

I visited Tawang for the first time with friends in February 1999. It was the time of Tibetan New Year, Losar, and as we were leaving Tawang by car, we happened to meet a group of Yak *Cham*(1) performers. The body of the yak was woven from bamboo and covered with a yak hide and a rug woven from yak hair. It had a wooden head and two people inside the body. Around the yak, a group of men wearing dark blue wooden masks and herdsman's costumes were dancing. They would stop passing cars and offer us local wine on the table placed next to them and show us their dance. After enjoying their dance for a while, we gave them a tip and left 【6-1】.

It was not until four or five years later that I learned that this Yak *Cham* was originally a traditional masked play based on a legend. The performance of this play was a special event limited to the New Year days in the case of Gyangkhar village in Tawang. In Gyangkhar, it is performed on the third day of Losar on the village ground, and it lasts a whole day. At that time, dance troupes used to go from door to door in the village and then be served alcohol, but this custom is now disappearing(2).

I have heard that Yak *Cham* is also performed in some villages in the Dirang region of West Kameng, but unfortunately, I have not yet had the chance to see them. In 1939, an English mountaineer Harold William Tilman (1898-1977) and his team visited Rupa in West Kameng, where the Sherdukpen people live, on the way back from Mt. Gori Chen, and took a photograph of Yak Cham(3). In 1950s, Verrier Elwin (1902-1964)(4) also took a photograph of Yak *Cham* in Rupa or Shergaon(5). The yaks in these two photographs are carrying a goddess of calm face on their backs.

The Yak *Cham* is also still being performed in Merak and Sakteng on the

Bhutanese side of the border, as I wrote in Chapter 3. In the case of Merak, it is performed on the last day of the annual Buddhist ritual of fasting and silence called *Nyungne*, which takes place in the 6th to the 7th month of the Bhutanese calendar. This Yak *Cham* is a short version, not a full story.

The yak (*Bos grunniens*) is an important animal for the Monpa and Brokpa people. The yak is used not only for food, such as dairy products and meat, but the hair is also used for making clothing, such as hats, jackets, and raincoats, and for making for household items, such as bags, rugs, tent material and ropes; and the dung is used as fertiliser in fields and dried for fuel.

The Yak *Cham* is a dramatic representation of how the yak came to the lands of the Monpa and Brokpa, with instruments and dances in different scenes. In November 2013, there were a total of five groups performing traditional Yak *Cham* in villages around Tawang, the oldest of which was the group from Gyangkhar village. It is said that it takes nine to ten hours to perform the complete story, but the ones I saw were shortened to two to three hours.

In the case of the short version of the Yak *Cham* that I saw in Gyangkhar village, there are five characters: three sons, including the main character, Thupa Gali, his father and Thupa Gali's servant, Naro(6) 【6-2a】. In addition, there are two other characters: a yak with two people inside, and a Garuda laying three eggs of different colours 【6-2b, 6-2c】. On the back of the yak is the one of the local guardian deities of the region, Sungma Gonpu Maling, with its hands raised 【6-2d】. In the case of Merak, the yak is mounted by the Buddhist dharma-protecting deity Palden Lhamo. She is a wrathful female deity in Tibetan Buddhism, but the female deity on this yak is not a wrathful form but has the face of an ordinary woman. 【3-55, 6-3】.

I was told in Gyangkhar village that the traditional Yak Cham is the one with a deity riding on it, but the yaks in the Yak *Cham* shows performed on stage during events such as the Tawang Festival to promote tourism are yak costumes worn by two people and do not have a deity riding on them. Also, these Yak *Chams* are performed by groups of young Tibetan men. Although it is called the Yak *Cham*, I suspect that this scene is probably derived from a famous scene of a nomadic yak-herding family in one of the Tibetan operas, *Drowa Zangmo*(7) and is called *yak tse*(8) which means 'yak play' or 'yak dance' in Tibetan. It is different from the Yak *Cham* in Monyul, although it is more commonly used at event festivals than the original Monpa Yak *Cham* because of the intensity of the dance and the shorter time it takes to perform on stage. However, no matter whether or not it is a shortened version, it is apparently different from the Yak *Cham* of Monyul. The story the Yak *Cham* of Monyul consists of various long narratives, such as the hero finally getting the yak after a difficult journey, and the scene where the yak emerges from the egg and other parts of the story, which are interspersed with mythological elements in Monyul's Yak *Cham*. In the past, the Gyangkhar group was invited to various events, but they lamented that since the Tibetan Yak *Cham* group 【6-4】 has been adopted for some occasions, there were fewer opportunities to show their traditional Yak *Cham* to the public.

In Merak, a similar yak costume has been used for Yak *Cham* for guests from outside and tourists since around 2012. It is performed by the villagers, who gives a small glimpse of theYak *Cham*, however this yak doesn't carry Palden Lhamo 【6-5】. However, in 2019 the village bought an original yak with Palden Lhamo on the back, and now they use two of them, one in the yak costume and one in the original one.

In all Yak *Cham*, the characters wear typical herdsman's costumes. In the villages of Monpa, white culotte skirts and round portable cushions are all that remain of the Yak *Cham* costume 【6-5】.

Ache Lhamo different from Tibet Opera

The Tibetan opera *Ache Lhamo*, which translates as "sister goddess", is a general term for several operas(9). It is often abbreviated to "*Lhamo*". In the case of Monyul, however, the performance is more like a masked dance or pantomime than a song-and-dance drama, with five or six characters and all male performers. The only musical instruments are a drum and cymbals, which are also played by men. The story is based on a story similar to the Tibetan "Legend of King Norsang(10)".

Ache Lhamo is still performed in several of the villages of the Monyul region, and I saw the performance in Joenkhar and Merak in Trashigang district in eastern Bhutan, in Zemithang in Tawang district in Arunachal Pradesh, and in Rama Camp in Dirang circle in West Kameng district. I also had the chance to see primary school pupils practising *Ache Lhamo* in Lubrang, a pastoralist village in the Dirang circle 【6-7】. Lubrang is a village of people who migrated from Sakteng in Bhutan a few generations ago, but the people now belong to the Monpa Scheduled Tribe.

The five characters are King Norsang, the two goddesses, Nyapa the fisherman and Nyaro who helps him, but the names and roles of these characters also vary from place to place 【6-8a, 6-8b】. The stories in the Monyul version vary according to location, but the following story was collected in Tawang by Tsewang
Norbu and I have summarised it here(11).

> A (Nyapa) fisherman who rescued Naga, the god of the lake, was invited to the land of the Naga to thank him and received a wish-fulfilling gem as a souvenir. He went to show the gem to a hermit, and during his stay there, he fell in love with a beautiful goddess (*Lhamo*) who came down from the land of the Gods to bathe in the water, and he wanted to make her his wife. He returned the gem to the Naga and obtained a special lasso in return, which enabled him to capture the goddess. He tried to make her agree to marry him but failed. On the advice of a hermit, he presented her to the king Choegyal Norsang(12). The king lived happily with the beautiful goddess as his wife, but

he already had 500 wives. The wives succeeded in sending him off to war with other countries by means of a plot. The goddess, fearing for her life in his absence, left for the land of the Gods. After returning from the war, King Norsang set out on a journey to find the goddess and he met his wife's younger sister who had come to fetch water for her elder sister's bathing, and finally the king met his wife again in the land of the Gods. He returned to his own country, ruled it well and they lived happily together.

For the *Ache Lhamo* of Arunachal Pradesh, Elwin has recorded the stories told by the Sherdukpen people of Rupa in West Kameng and Niranjan Sarkhar has collected stories from the Monpa villages of Jang in Tawang and Lish in West Kameng respectively(13). Tsewang Norbu's verbatim record is relatively new, but he does not say which village it was from. In the Monpa villages, the name *Azhi Lhamu* or *Azhi Lamu* is common, but in Merak and Sakteng it is called *Ache Lhamo* as in Tibetan.

It is interesting to note that T. A. Bodt recorded the story of *Azhi Lamu* on the fifth day of the New Year (*Losar*) 2013, in the Chug valley opposite to the village of Lish in Dirang circle(14). The inhabitants of the Chug valley, who belong to the Monpa Scheduled Tribe, call themselves Duhumbi. According to Bodt, before the Sino-India border dispute in 1962, the Duhumbi dance troupe used to perform *Azhi Lamu* in Tawang and Dirang to raise money, but after the influx of Tibetan refugees, they suddenly stopped performing. There are accounts of masks and accessories of characters being sold to Tibetan refugees, but the performance was revived in 2011 and has been performed intermittently since then.

The main characters in *Azhi Lamu* of the Chug valley are the divine interpreter Lam Jalu, the two fisherman brothers, Nyapa and Nyaro, the two female goddesses Lamu and Lacha, the Bonpo magician Ngakpa, the Buddhist Lama, and the father and mother figures. The story is quite different from King Norsang's story shown before and appears to be much more mythical and symbolic. For example, the story implies various symbolic issues such as the creation of the world, the origin of mankind, the start of agriculture and animal husbandry, the introduction of Buddhism and the conflict of Buddhism with Bon. The performance aims to convey the people's prayers to please and appease both the local deities and the Buddhist deities, and thus assure good fortune, good harvests in the year ahead, and avoid epidemics and natural disasters 【6-9a, 6-9b】.

It is possible that symbolic stories such as those of the Chug valley are original to Monyul and that they have been adapted and narrated in Tibetan opera and imported back into Monyul. However, more examples and studies will be needed to reach that conclusion.

The costumes of the Ache Lhamo (*Azhi Lhamu*) of Monyul vary from place to place, but the masks worn by Nyapa and Nyaro are very unique. In the Tibetan *Ache*

Lhamo, the mask is flat and board-like, but in Monyul, the face is three-dimensional with eyes, nose and mouth sewn onto a felt cloth and a small cowry hangs from the tip of the nose. On the foreheads of these two masks there are marks representing the sun and the moon, and on the cheeks, there are round marks. While in Merak the colour of each shows the difference between Nyapa and Nyaro 【6-8b】, in other places they are the same colour, or differ only in the colour of the cheeks. The head is a three-dimensional shape made of the long hair and skin of the goat, and when it is put on over the head, the hair at the back covers the whole back 【6-12】. The several thin ropes of twisted black and white animal hair, probably yak hair are hanging down from the waist of Nyapa and Nyaro in most of the places 【6-8a, 6-9a, 6-10, 6-11a, 6-13a】. In Chug valley, Ngakpa is also wearing these ropes 【6-9a, 6-9b】. In Zemithang, fishermen are wearing trousers which made of colourful Tibetan cloth and the two goddesses are wearing long white trousers and some colourful cloths are hanging down from their waist 【6-11a, 6-11b】. The goddesses in all the pictures are wearing crowns on their heads.

The performances at Rama camp were not local but performed by a group of people from Boha village in Kalaktang circle in the south-west of the district, the purpose of which was to raise funds for the reconstruction of their village temple. They left their village after the rice harvest and spent more than a month travelling daily to different villages in West Kameng district 【6-13a, 6-13b】.

As for the Tibetan opera "*Ache Lhamo*", there is a tradition that in the 14th century, Thangtong Gyalpo who built many iron bridges in Tibet, Bhutan and the Monyul region, organized a song and dance group of seven sisters "Ache Lhamo" to raise funds for the construction of the bridges[15]. The story of the people of the Chug valley who used to travel as far as Tawang, and the group of people from the village of Boha who travel even at present to collect donations and dance the *Ache Lhamo*, is reminiscent of this legend of Thangtong Gyalpo 【6-14】.

(1) The stories of Yak *Cham* in Tawang and West Kameng district have been described in English by [Wangchu 1999], [Norbu 2008: 108-110] and others. The Yak *Cham* of Merak is described in detail by [Karchung 2013]. [Wakita 2019: 257-287] summarises them in Japanese.
(2) I interviewed the group in August 2011.
(3) [Tilman 2016 (1946): 63], their climb was unsuccessful.
(4) He came to India as a Christian missionary from England, but became devoted to the ideas of Gandhi, renounced Christianity, acquired Indian citizenship, became an anthropological advisor to NEFA, the predecessor of Arunachal Pradesh, and wrote many books on tribal culture.
(5) [Elwin 1959: 89]. The photo location was not mentioned but Elwin wrote about Yak *Cham* stories from Shergaon and Rupa [Elwin 1958: 376-377]. The Sherdukpen people are also one of the Scheduled Tribe in West Kameng district, I will write about them in Chapter 9.
(6) The names of the three sons and their order vary from place to place.
(7) Acoording to one theory, *Khandro Drowa Zangmo*'s story is said to have been invented by a high lama of the Gelug school, based on an ancient folk tale of the Mon region. [Miyake 2008: 277].
(8) From a DVD of a 2006 performance in Tokyo by the Tibetan Institute of Performing Arts (TIPA), based in Dharamsala.
(9) [Stein 1972: 277].
(10) The legend of King Norsang was translated into Japanese in [Miyake & Ishiyama 2008: 233-235].
(11) [Norbu 2008: 110-115].

(12) In Tibetan, *Choegyel* means the king of religion.
(13) [Elwin 1958: 122-123], [Sarkar 1993 (1974): 145-149].
(14) Original details by Bodt, see https://doi.org/10.5281/zenodo.1202204.
(15) [Gerner 2007: 84-85], for a refutation of this theory, see [Miyake 2008: 257-264].

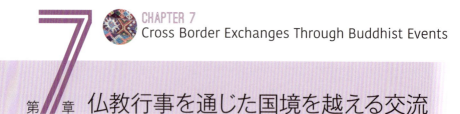

CHAPTER 7
Cross Border Exchanges Through Buddhist Events

第7章 仏教行事を通じた国境を越える交流

　ブータン東部のタシ・ヤンツェ、タシガン、サムドゥプ・ジョンカル3県とインドのアルナーチャル・プラデーシュ州タワン県、西カメン県との間には、10カ所以上の国境があるが、往来は、現地の人々のみに許されている。外国人は、ブータンとインドの東から西、西から東への旅行には、アッサム州を経由しなければならない。その多くは、険しい山道か、道路が一部しか完成していないため、徒歩での国境越えとなっている。中には、牧畜民しか知らない特別なルートも存在する。かつては交易路としても使用されていたこれらのルートも、両国の経済圏がそれぞれ首都ティンプーやアッサム平原へと向かうようになり、車の普及によっても廃れていった。だが、現在でも仏教行事の際には東西の国境を越えて参集する人々の姿が見られる。

　仏教行事の際には、盛装して集まる人が多く、民族衣装を観察する良い機会となる。また、同じように見える衣装が実はそれぞれの出身地や民族集団を示していることも多く、興味深い。

ゴム・コラのツェチュ祭

　ブータン東部のタシ・ヤンツェ県のゴム・コラ（Gom Kora）は、タシガンから北に23 kmの場所にある。チベット語、ゾンカ語の正式名は、ゴムフー・コラ（Gomphu Kora)で、ゴムフーは「瞑想の洞窟」、コラは、「周回」を意味し、ゴム・コラはその短縮形である。この名の由来は、8世紀にチベットのサムエからこの地へ逃げてきた悪霊が、自らを大きな岩の中に閉じ込めたが、それを大聖者パドマサンバヴァ（グル・リンポチェ）が追ってきて、自分も3日間この岩に閉じこもり、瞑想の後にこの悪霊を打ち破ったという伝説である(1)。この岩の周りを時計回りに巡ることによって功徳が得られると信じられている。毎年ブータン暦2月10日にツェチュ祭が行われるが、この祭りには、タワン県

各地からモンパも大勢やってくる。東ブータンの人々は、モンパのことをツァンラ語（シャルチョプ語）でブラーミと呼んでいる。

私がゴム・コラを訪ねたのは1999年11月で、ちょうど寺の修復作業が行われていた。タントン・ギャルポ(14-15世紀)が架けたと伝わるドゥクスムの鉄鎖の吊り橋は、ここから北へ5分ほど走ったところにあった【7-1】。この写真を撮影した時には、一部が破損しながらも橋の姿をとどめていたが、その後、取り外され、鉄鎖は、2006年にパロのタチョガン（またはタムチョガン）の吊り橋の修復のための材料の一部として使われた。そのため、ドゥクスムの橋は現存しない(2)。

この橋は、北から南へ流れるコロン・チュと東から西へ流れるタワン・チュの合流地点のすぐ北にあり、ドゥクスムの町は1976年後半に近隣の村の交易の中心地として作られた。しかし、人々は2016年以来、ケトゥシャンにできた新市街地に移住している(3)。タワン・チュにもタントン・ギャルポが架けたと伝わる橋が現存し、モクトウまでの道路ができるまでは、タワンからサクテンに歩いて行くときに使われていた【7-2】。

2005年3月にゴム・コラのツェチ

【7-1】ドゥクスムの鉄鎖の吊り橋は、タントン・ギャルポによって架けられたと伝わっている。
The iron-chained suspension bridge of Doksum is said to have been built by Thangtong Gyalpo. (Doksum, November 1999)

【7-2】タワン・チュに架けられたこの鉄鎖の橋もタントン・ギャルポによって建てられたと伝えられる。
This iron-chained suspension bridge over the Tawang Chu was also built by Thangtong Gyalpo. (Tawang, August 2010)

【7-3】中央の巨石が、ゴム・コラの伝説に残る岩である。
To the left of the temple is the rock of the legend of Gom Kora. (Gom Kora, March 2005)

【7-4】ゴム・コラのツェチュ祭。第70代ジェ・ケンポ大僧正（中央）の右手後方に、タワンから来たモンパ女性の一群が見える。
The *tshechu* festival in Gom Kora. A group of Monpa women from Tawang can be seen behind the right hand of His Holiness the 70th Je Khenpo. (Gom Kora, March 2005)

【7-5】タワンから2日間歩いてゴム・コラに到着したタワンのモンパ女性たち。彼女たちは、自分たちのシンカとトトゥンはディランで織られたものだと誇らしげに私に語った。
The Monpa women of Tawang who walked for two days from Tawang and arrived in Gom Kora. They proudly told me that their *shinkas* and *tothungs* were woven in Dirang. (Gom Kora, March 2005)

ュ祭を見学した。当時はタシガンにもホテルが少なかったのと、3日間ツェチュを見学するための移動時間を省くために、近くの畑にティンプーから持参したテントを張って3晩過ごした。東のタワン周辺の町や村、ルムラやゼミタンからやってきた人びとを100人ほど見かけた【7-3, 7-4, 7-5】。

　当時は、タワンの町からゴム・コラへは2日から3日かかったが、2010年頃からインド側の国境事務所まで車で行けるようになり、1日でゴム・コラに着けるようになった。そのためか、2015年には300人以上がタワンからやって来たという(4)。

チョルテン・コラとゴルサム・コラの祭り

　ゴム・コラからコロン・チュに沿った道を北上すると、タシ・ヤンツェの町の手前に白いネパール式の仏塔が視界に入ってくる【7-6】。18世紀にンガワン・ロデが建立し、ドゥエロン・チョルテン（「悪魔の谷の仏塔」）と名付けられ、現在はチョルテン・コラ（Chorten Kora）として知られている。この仏塔は、12年かけて建立された。チョルテン・コラは、本来は仏塔の周りを回る祭りの名前であったが、いつの日か人々はこの仏塔とその周辺もチョルテン・コラと呼ぶようになった。落慶法要を執り行ったのは、この地を訪れた第13代ジェ・ケンポのヨンテン・タエ（在位1771-1775）であった。ブータンの文献では、ンガワン・ロデは友人であったタワンの

【7-6】18世紀に建てられたというチョルテン・コラの仏塔。
The stupa at Chorten Kora, said to have been built in the 18th century. (Trashi Yangtse, October 2014)

【7-7】タワン県ゼミタンにあるゴルサム・チョルテン。
Gorsam Chorten on the bank of Nyamjang Chu. (Zemithang, November 2012)

【7-8】ドゥクパ・コラの日にチョルテン・コラを巡るブータンの人々。
Bhutanese people walking around the Chorten Kora on Drukpa Kora day. (Trashi Yangtse, March 2006)

パンチェン地方のラマ・サンポと一緒にネパールのカトマンドゥにあるボーダナートへ巡礼の旅に出かけ、その仏塔の模型を大根に刻んで帰宅し、それを模した仏塔をそれぞれがタシ・ヤンツェとゼミタンのゴルサム村に建立したとされる(5)。

一方、ニュムジャン・チュの川岸にあるゴルサム・チョルテン【7-7】に関する確かな資料はなく、口承で伝わっている限りでは、ンガワン・ロデ、ラマ・サンポ両名の名は出てこない。ゼミタンで入手したパンフレットによれば(6)、建設された時期は明確ではないが、13世紀後半で、建立者は仏塔の近くのカルマン村出身のラマ・プラタールだという(7)。この地域の仏教史を考慮すると、13世紀というのは、仏塔建立の時期としては早すぎる。2つの仏塔がブータンの史料にあるように同時期に建設されたものだとしたら18世紀の可能性もあるが、確証はない。

ゼミタンの仏塔のある場所の語源は、タワン・モンパの言語でゴル・ザム（ゴルは「石」、ザムは「橋」）である。たった一つ、この2つの仏塔の話に共通しているのは、ボーダナートから巡礼者が帰着した時には大根が萎びて縮んでしまったという部分のみである。確かに、これら2つの仏塔の形とサイズは、ネパールにあるものとは異なっている。

チョルテン・コラの祭りは、ブータン暦1月の15日と30日に行われ、前者はダクパ・コラ（モンパの周回）、後者はドゥクパ・コラ（ブータン人の周回）と呼ばれる【7-8】。ダクパ・コラの日には、数百人の人々がタワン各地からやってくるが、その背景には、この仏塔の建設中に、8歳のタワンからやって来た少女が自ら仏塔に入って埋葬されたという伝説がある(8)。少女は、実は天からやって来たダーキニー（空行母）で、すべての生き物の幸福のためにその身を捧げたと信じられている。この伝説は、2005年に『チョルテン・コラ』の題名でブータン人監督ギェム・ドルジによって映画化され、この仏塔と物語は

ブータン内外の多くの人の知るところとなった。

ゴルサム・チョルテンの周回は、毎年チベット暦1月の最終日に行われる。2024年は、3月10日がその日に当たった。3月7日から10日までの間に、高僧による仏教儀礼や、インド軍楽隊の演奏、「廃棄物ゼロの祭り」を掲げるNGOによる清掃活動など、さまざまなイベントが続いた。ブータンからは、約80人がやって来たが、その半数は巡礼者、残りは商いを目的にした人々だという(9)。

トルギャ祭とドンギュル祭

この国境地帯のインド側最大の仏教行事は、タワン僧院（正式名は、ガンデン・ナムギェル・ラツェ・リン）で毎年チベット暦の11月28日から3日間にわたって催されるトルギャ祭（*Torgya*

【7-9】タワン僧院のドンギュル祭。
The *Dungyur* Festival at Tawang Monastery. (Tawang, January 2013)

【7-10】ドンギュル祭の3日目。中央が、伝統的で豪華な衣装を着けて舞う、タワン僧院の守護女尊パルデン・ラモ。
The third day of the *Dungyur* Festival. In the center, Palden Lhamo, the female guardian deity of Tawang Monastery, dances in a traditional and sumptuous costume. (Tawang, January 2013)

第7章　仏教行事を通じた国境を越える交流　187

【7-12】僧院長によって、邪悪なものを象徴するトルマが火に投げ込まれる。右の2人はトルマを運ぶ護衛官アルポ。
A *torma* representing evil thrown into the fire by the chief abbot. The two men on the right are the bodyguards, *arpo*, who carry the *torma*. (Tawang, January 2013)

【7-11】火に投げ込まれる前の邪悪なものを象徴する髑髏を付けたトルマ。
Two *torma* with skulls, representing evil, just before being thrown into the fire. (Tawang, January 2017)

【7-13】ドンギュル祭2日目の僧院長による灌頂（加持）に集まった人々。黒い腰当て布を着けている女性の一群はサクテンやメラの人々。
People gathered to receive the empowerment by the chief abbot on the second day of the *Dungyur* festival. The group of women wearing black back aprons are people from Sakteng and Merak. (Tawang, January 2013)

Festival）である。トルギャとは、「供え物トルマを投げる」という意味で、この祭りは3年に一度タワンのモンパ語でドンギュル祭（*Dungyur* Festival）と名を変えて、より大規模に催される【7-9】。この名は、チベット語で「一億の真言（マニ）を唱える」という意味が込められたトゥンチュル（*dung phyur*）「一億」に由来する。この時には、1カ月前から僧侶によって真言を唱える読経が始まり、併せて僧侶によって特別に加持された丸薬マニ・リルプが手作りされる。この丸薬は、幸福や繁栄、長寿を願い、自然災害などから身を護るために法要の参加者に配られる。ドンギュル祭の踊り手の衣装や仮面は、トルギャ祭より伝統的な豪華なものが使われる【7-10】。

　トルギャ祭、ドンギュル祭のプログラムは、演じられる仮面舞踏などはほぼ同じだが、若干の違いがある。1日目のハイライトは、夕方のトルマ【7-11】を

投げる儀式である。悪魔を表すソル（zor）と呼ばれる髑髏の頭を持つ高さ1ｍほどの2基のトルマを、僧院の西門から外に運び出し、僧院長が焚火の中に投げ込む儀式である【7-12】。

ドンギュル祭の2日目には、本堂に納められていた弥勒菩薩ジャンパ像を輿に乗せて参拝者の周りを巡幸するゲワ・ジャンパ・コラが追加される。この日の夕方、僧院長による法要と説法、および灌頂（ワン）が行われるが、この灌頂を受けるためだけにやってくる地元の人々もいて、長蛇の列となる【7-13】。

3日目の重要なプログラムは、タワン僧院の守護尊として重要な女性の護法尊、パルデン・ラモの登場である。タワン僧院とすべての生き物の繁栄を祈る重要な儀礼となっている。

いずれの祭りにも、地元の人々だけでなくサクテンやメラ、そのほかのブータン東部各地から多くの人びとがやってくる。隣接したタシ・ヤンツェからやってきて、干し魚やオレンジ、ピーナツなどを商うブータン人の露店も見られる。特に参拝者が多いのはトルギャ祭よりもドンギュル祭の時である。西暦でいうと1月の厳冬期に当たるため、サクテンやメラからは雪深い山道を2日から4日以上かけて歩かなければならないが、高齢者もそれをいとわずにやってくる【7-14】。

2011年と2017年のトルギャ祭、2013年のドンギュル祭に参加したが、毎回、極寒の早朝5時半頃から始まる最初のチャムから見学しているのは、地元のモンパではなく、メラやサクテンから来た人々である。彼らはこの祭りをとても楽しんでいるように見える。それは、敬虔であるからというだけではなく、同じような服装をした地元のモンパの人々の中で、居心地が良いからでもあろう。

【7-14】 この70代の夫婦は、ドンギュル祭に参加するために、メラから雪の中を4日間歩いてやって来た。
This couple in their seventies walked for four days in the snow from Merak to attend the *Dungyur* festival. (Tawang, January 2013)

【7-15】 ダライ・ラマ法王14世のインド亡命を伝える『ライフ』誌1959年5月4日号。
Life magazine, May 4, 1959, reporting on the exile of His Holiness the 14th Dalai Lama to India.

ダライ・ラマ法王の公開説法

　ブータンの人々が国境を越えてアルナーチャル・プラデーシュ州へやってくる最も人気がある時期は、ダライ・ラマ法王14世の公開説法がある時である。法王は、1983年から2017年の間にアルナーチャルを7回訪問しているが、そのうち、タワン県と西カメン県の訪問は5回に及ぶ。法王は、訪問の都度、集まった人々の前で、この地域への特別な思いを語っている。それは、このモンユルの回廊地帯こそが、1959年の法王のチベットからの脱出ルートでもあったからである。3月17日にラサを脱出した15日後にインドに入国し、2日目には、ゴルサム・チョルテン【7-7】脇の小さな建物に宿泊した。当時NEFAと呼ばれていたこの地域を、徒歩や馬、最後の2日間のみジープで南下し、19日間かけてアッサムのテズプルに到着している【7-15】。ディランやタワンには、現在でも、その当時のことを覚えている老人たちがいる。

　2017年4月8日からのタワンでの法王による公開説法の際には、5万人近い人々が集まったが、それらの中には地

【7-16】ダライ・ラマ法王14世の公開説法に参加したブータンからの人々。
People from Bhutan at the public teachings of His Holiness the 14th Dalai Lama in Tawang. (Tawang, April 2017)

CHAPTER 7

Cross Border Exchanges Through Buddhist Events

There are more than ten border crossing routes between Trashi Yangtse, Trashigang and Samdrup Jongkhar districts of eastern Bhutan and Tawang and West Kameng districts of Arunachal Pradesh in India, but only local people are allowed to travel through them. Foreigners have to pass through Assam to travel between Bhutan and

元のモンパや内外からのチベット人に混じって、多くのブータン人の姿があった【7-16, 7-17】。主催者によれば、ブータン国籍の人々の数はおよそ2,000人だったという。3日間のプログラムは、毎朝4時過ぎからの会場の場所取りから始まった。法王は8時頃まで登壇しなかったが、それまでには仮設の屋根付きドームの中も野外も人々で埋め尽くされていた。人々は昼頃の法要終了まで、飲食もせず熱心に法王の読経や説法に耳を傾けていた。

【7-17】 ダライ・ラマ法王14世のタワンでの公開説法の会場。
The special venue for the public teachings of His Holiness the 14th Dalai Lama in Tawang. (Tawang, April 2017)

⑴ [Bhutan Times 2008: 372]。グル・リンポチェは、ブータン、チベットやヒマラヤ圏では第二の仏陀として信仰され、ブータンに仏教を伝えたと信じられている。
⑵ タチョガン橋の修復に使われた鉄鎖は、タントン・ギャルポがブータン国内に架けた8カ所の橋から集められたものが使われたという［Wangdi 2008: 8］。
⑶ 2020年2月28日付Kuenselによる。
⑷ 2015年4月1日付Kuenselによる。
⑸ [Chhopel 2002: 1-4]。
⑹ [Managing Committee of Gontse Gaden Rabgyel-Ling Monastery 1997: 7-9]。
⑺ いくつかの資料では、建立者はラマ・サンギェ・テルタールとされている [Tenpa & Tempa 2013: 1]。だが、テルタールは、モンパの名前のプラタールがチベット語化したもので、現地の方言ではプラ (pra)が「猿」を、チベット語ではテル (sprel)が「猿」を意味する（T. A. Bodtの個人的な助言による）。
⑻ [Chhopel 2002: 3]。しかし映画のヒロインは8歳の少女ではなく、タワンの王の16歳の王女で、タシ・ヤンツェの人々の要請を受け入れて、自ら建設中の仏塔に入り、衆生の幸福をその障害から救うべく、身を捧げたことになっている。
⑼ 2024年3月11日付のアルナーチャル・タイムズ・オンラインより。

India from east to west and vice versa. Most of the border crossings are on foot, either because of the steep mountain paths or because the roads are only partially completed. Some are special routes known only to the local pastoralists. These routes, which were once used as trade routes, have fallen into disuse as the economies of both countries have moved towards the capital Thimphu and the Assam plains respectively, and as cars have become more common. Today, however, the people still cross the border to attend the Buddhist events.

During Buddhist events, many people gather in full costume, providing a good opportunity to observe traditional costumes. It is also interesting to note that while many of the costumes look the same or similar, they, in fact, represent different regions and ethnic groups.

Tshechu Festival in Gom Kora

Gom Kora, in Trashi Yangtse district of eastern Bhutan, is 23 km north of Trashigang. The official name in both Tibetan and Dzongkha is Gomphu Kora, where *gomphu* means 'meditation cave' and *kora* means 'circumambulation', and Gom Kora is a shortened form. The name is derived from the legend that in the 8th century, an evil spirit escaped from Samye in Tibet, chased by the great saint Padmasambhava (Guru Rinpoche). The evil spirit trapped itself in a large rock, and the saint defeated him after meditating for three days(1). There is a belief that by walking around the rock in a clockwise direction, one can attain merit and virtue. The *tshechu* festival is celebrated every year on the 10th day of the second month of the Bhutanese calendar and many Monpa people from all over Tawang come to this festival. The people of Eastern Bhutan call them Brami in Tshangla (Sharchop).

I visited Gom Kora in November 1999, when the temple was undergoing restoration work. The iron-chained suspension bridge of Doksum, said to have been built by Thangtong Gyalpo (14th-15th century), was a five-minute drive north from there 【7-1】. When this photo was taken, the bridge was still intact, although partly damaged, but it has since been removed and the iron chains have been used as part of the materials for the restoration of the suspension bridge at Tachogang or Tamchogang, Paro, in 2006. Hence, the bridge is no longer in existence at Doksum(2).

This bridge was located just north of the confluence of the Kholong Chu, which flows southward from the north, and the Tawang Chu, which flows westward from the east. At this confluence, Doksum town was started as a trading center for the neighbouring villages in late 1976. But since 2016, the residents have been relocated to the new township at Khetshang(3). There is another bridge over the Tawang Chu which was also built by Thangtong Gyalpo. This bridge was used when people walked between Tawang and Sakteng, before the road to Mukto was built 【7-2】.

In March 2005, I visited the *tshechu* festival in Gom Kora. As there were not many hotels in Trashigang at that time, and to save the travel time to visit the *tshechu* for three days, I pitched my tent, which I had brought from Thimphu, in a nearby field and stayed there for three nights. I saw about 100 people from the towns and villages around Tawang, Lumla and Zemithang in the east 【7-3, 7-4, 7-5】.

In those days it took two or three days to get from Tawang town to Gom Kora, but since approximately 2010, people can drive from Tawang to the check post on the Indian side and reach Gom Kora in one day. This may be the reason why more than 300 people came from Tawang in 2015(4).

Festival of Chorten Kora and Gorsam Kora

From Gom Kora, heading north along the Kholong Chu road, just before the town of Trashi Yangtse, you will see a white Nepalese style stupa 【7-6】. This stupa was built in the 18th century by Ngawang Loday. While it was originally named Duerong Chorten 'stupa of the valley of demon', and it is now popularly known as Chorten Kora. The stupa took 12 years to build. Chorten Kora was originally the name of the festival that took place around the stupa, but one day people began to call the stupa, and the area around it, by the same, too. The inauguration ceremony was conducted by Yonten Thaye (reigned 1771-1775), the 13th Je Khenpo, who visited the site. According to the Bhutanese literature, Ngawang Loday travelled with his friend Lama Zangpo of the Pangchen area in Tawang to the famous stupa of Boudhanath in Kathmandu, Nepal, for pilgrimage. There, they carved a model of the stupa from a radish and back home they built two stupas in its likeness; one in Trashi Yangtse and the other one in Gorsam village in Zemithang[5] 【7-7】. However, there is no reliable information about Gorsam Chorten on the bank of the Nyamjang Chu, and the names of Ngawang Loday and Lama Zangpo are not mentioned in the local oral tradition there. According to a pamphlet available locally in Zemithang[6], the date of construction of the stupa there is not clear, but it can roughly be estimated to be in the late 13th century. The founder is said to be Lama Prathar[7] from the village of Kharman, which is located near the stupa. Considering the Buddhist history of the area at that time, the 13th century is too early for the construction of the chorten. If these two stupas were constructed at the same time as Bhutanese literature mentioned, it could be in the 18th century, but there is no proof. The original name of the place where the stupa is located in Zemithang was Gor Zam (*gor* 'stone' and *zam* 'bridge') in the Tawang Monpa language. The only thing that the two stories of the stupas have in common is that the radishes had shriveled up when the pilgrims arrived home from Boudhanath. Indeed, these two stupas are different in shape and size from the original one in Nepal.

The festival of Chorten Kora is celebrated on the 15th and 30th day of the first month of the Bhutanese calendar, the 15th day being known as Dakpa Kora (circumambulation of the Monpa) and the 30th day as Drukpa Kora (circumambulation of the Bhutanese) 【7-8】. On the day of Dakpa Kora, hundreds of people come from all over Tawang. The reason behind this is the legend that during the construction of the stupa, an eight-year-old girl from Tawang volunteered to enter the stupa and was buried inside of the stupa[8]. It is believed that she was actually a dākinī from heaven who gave her body for the well-being of all sentient beings. In 2005, the legend was made into the film "Chorten Kora" by the Bhutanese director Gyem Dorji, and both the stupa and story became known to many people inside and outside Bhutan.

The Gorsam Kora is held every year on the last day of the first month in the Tibetan calendar; in 2024, this was on the 10th of March. From 7th to 1oth March, the Gorsam Kora Festival was celebrated and various events took place, including

Buddhist rituals by a high lama, performances by Indian military bands, and cleanup activities by NGO's with the theme 'Zero waste festival'. Around 80 people from Bhutan visited as well, with half of them utilizing the festival for trade(9).

Torgya and *Dungyur* festivals

The biggest Buddhist event on the Indian side of the border is the annual *Torgya* Festival held for three days from the 28th day of the Tibetan calendar at at Tawang Monastery (officially known as Ganden Namgyel Lhatse Ling). The literal meaning of Torgya is "throwing torma". This festival is held on a larger scale every three years, when it is called as the *Dungyur* festival in the Monpa language of *Tawang* 【7-9】. The name is derived from the Tibetan word *dung phyur*, which means "(the chanting of) a hundred million (mantras)". On this occasion, the chanting of mantras by the monks begins a month in advance, along with the preparation of specially blessed handmade pills called mani rilbu by the monks. These pills are distributed to the participants of the ceremony to wish them happiness, prosperity, and long life, and to protect them from natural disasters. During the *Dungyur* festival, the costumes worn by the masked dancers are more traditional and sumptuous that those worn during the *Torgya* festival 【7-10】.

The programme of the *Torgya* and *Dungyur* festivals is almost the same, with a few differences.

The highlight of the first day is the *Torgya* ritual in the evening. Two one-meter tall *tormas*, called *zor* and representing evil, are decorated with skulls are carried out through the west gate of the monastery, where the chief abbot of the monastery throws them into the bonfire 【7-11, 7-12】.

On the second day of the Dungyur festival, there is the addition of the Gyelwa Jampa Kora, in which the statue of Jampa or Maitreya (the Future Buddha), normally kept in the main hall, is carried on a palanquin around the worshippers. On the evening of this day, the chief abbot holds special prayers and public teachings, followed by a long queue of people who have come to the monastery to receive the empowerment (*wang*) 【7-13】.

The third day's important program is the appearance of Palden Lhamo, the female guardian deity of Tawang Monastery. This is an important ritual to pray for the prosperity of Tawang Monastery and all living beings.

Both festivals attract not only local people but also many people from Sakteng and Merak and other places in eastern Bhutan. Small Bhutanese stalls selling dried fish, local orange and peanuts from neighbouring Trashi Yangtse district can also be seen. But we find many more visitors during the *Dungyur* festival than during the *Torgya* fesival. As it is January in the western calendar, the peak of winter, it takes two to four days to get there from Sakteng or Merak, via snowy mountain paths, but even the elderly are willing to come 【7-14】.

I have attended the *Torgya* festival in 2011 and 2017 and the *Dungyur* festival in 2013, and every time it was not the local Monpas but people from Sakteng and Merak who attended from the very first program, which starts at about 5.30 in the freezing cold morning. They seem to be really enjoying the festival. This is not only because of their religious beliefs, but also because they feel at home among the similarly dressed local Monpa people.

Public Teachings of His Holiness Dalai Lama

The most popular time for people from Bhutan to cross the border into Arunachal Pradesh is when His Holiness the 14th Dalai Lama holds public teachings. His Holiness has visited Arunachal Pradesh seven times between 1983 and 2017, including five visits to Tawang and West Kameng districts. On each of his visits, His Holiness has expressed his special feelings for the region in front of the assembled people. This is because the Monyul Corridor was His Holiness' escape route from Tibet to Assam of India in 1959. He entered India 15 days after escaping from Lhasa on 17th March and on the second day, he stayed in a small building beside Gorsam Chorten 【7-7】. It took 19 days from the border of Tibet to reach Tezpur in Assam, after travelling south through the area then known as NEFA on foot, by horse, and only the last two days by jeep 【7-15】. There are some old people in Tawang and Dirang who still remember those days.

Nearly 50,000 people gathered for public teachings by His Holiness from 8th April 2017, and among them were many Bhutanese, mixed with local Monpas and Tibetans from within and outside the state 【7-16, 7-17】. According to the organisers, the number of Bhutanese nationals was about 2000. The three-day programme began each morning with an early start at around 4 am, when people started occupying their place to sit. His Holiness did not take the stage until around 8 am, but by then the temporary covered dome and the surrounding area were packed with people. Without eating or drinking, they listened attentively to His Holiness's sutra recitation and preaching until the end of the service around noontime.

---

(1) [Bhutan Times 2008: 372]. Guru Rinpoche is worshipped in Bhutan, Tibet, and other Himalayan regions as the second Buddha and credited for introducing Buddhism.
(2) The iron chains used for the restoration of the Tachogang bridge were collected from eight different bridges built by Thangtong Gyalpo in Bhutan [Wangdi 2008: 8].
(3) Kuensel, 28th February, 2020.
(4) Kuensel, 1st April, 2015.
(5) [Chhophel 2002: 1-4].
(6) [Managing Committee of Gontse Gaden Rabgyel-Ling Monastery 1997: 7-9].
(7) Some sources give the stupa's founder as Lama Sangay Telthar [Tenpa and Tempa 2013: 16]. But Telthar is the Tibetanised version of the Monpa name, Prathar. In the local Monpa dialect, 'pra' means 'monkey', whereas 'tre' (sprel) means 'monkey' in Tibetan (on the personal advice of Mr. T. A. Bodt).
(8) [Chhophel 2002: 3]. But the heroine in the movie is not an eight year old girl but a sixteen year old princess of the king in Tawang. The princess accepted the request of the people of Trashi Yangtse and voluntarily went into the stupa-under- construction. She thus offered herself to relieve all sentient beings from suffering.
(9) From the Arunachal Times online, 11th March 2024.

CHAPTER 8
Creating a Home Away From Home: Pemakö's Monpa
The original text is in English, and the author is Timotheus A. Bodt

第二の故郷を創る
―ペマコのモンパ―

（本章の原文は英語で、筆者及び写真はティモテユス・A・ボット）

　以下のチベットのペマコ（Pemakö）のモンパの歴史と彼らの衣装に関しての記述は、17世紀あるいは18世紀初頭のブータンの資料［Ngawang 年不詳 1668/1728?］、20世紀初頭のイギリスの探検家の記録、例えば、[Kingdon-Ward 1926][Baily 1957]、20世紀後半と21世紀初頭のの中国の資料、例えば［XSLDZCBZ 1987］[Bāo 2014][MBZBBZ 2016（2008）]など、20世紀後半のブータン資料［Dorji 1986］、欧米の学術資料、例えば［Grothmann 2012］、そして、21世紀初頭に収集したペマコ・モンパやブータン東部の高齢者の口伝などに基づいている。

　17世紀、現在のチベット南部、ブータン東部、アルナーチャル・プラデーシュ州西部の国境地帯であるモンユルは、ヒマラヤの2つの国家が領土を拡大する舞台となった。新たに樹立されたシャブドゥン神政下のブータンとチベットを支配していたガンデン・ポダン（訳註：ダライ・ラマを長としたチベット中央政府）が、権力と領土を巡って張り合った。

　ブータンはモンユル地方の小さな独立領を西から東に、チベットは東から西に併合した。この2つの新勢力は18世紀を通じて争いを続けた。少なくとも8世紀以来続いてきた旧来の氏族を基盤とする社会構造は廃止された。その代わりに新しい中央政府は、地方や地域の権威をさまざまな階層に導入した。彼らはまた、地方住民に重くのしかかる現物税や労働税などの圧政的な税制も確立させた。加えて、17世紀後半から18世紀、19世紀を通してこの地域は、数多くの地震に見舞われ、そのいくつかは破壊的なものであった。

　それゆえ、破れた地方の族長やその一族、時には村全体が、神秘的なベユル（「隠された土地」）の話に魅了されたのも不思議ではない。この隠された土地は、ヒマラヤ東部で少し前に「発見」されたもので、迫害された仏教徒、特にニンマ派「古派」の信者に安全な安息の地と避難所を提供するものだった。こ

の中には、ゲルク派、ドゥック・カギュ派という、それぞれ敵対する宗派を信奉するチベット人とブータン人の猛攻撃に直面したモンユルの人びとも含まれていた。

ペマコのモンパ

隠された土地は、ペマコ「蓮の花の荘厳（しょうごん）」と呼ばれ、モンユルから移住した人びとはペマコ・モンパと呼ばれるようになった。17世紀半ばから20世紀半ばの間に、何度かの連続的な移住があり、その後、親戚や仲間の村人たちが先の移住者に続いて少しずつ移住してきた。移住者の多くはブータン東部、主にモンガルやタシガン上部の地域から来たツァンラ語話者であったが、タシ・ヤンツェのコロントェ[1]（Kholongtö）から来たザラカ語話者もいた。彼らは、今は、すべてアルナーチャル・プラデーシュ州西部にあるディラン地方から来たツァンラ語話者、そしてタワンのさまざまな村から来たパンチェンパ語話者、ダクパ語話者、タワン・モンパ語話者と合流した。これらの移住者の多くは別々の村に定住し、最近まで言語的な区別が保たれていた。

無住の土地ではない

モンパの移住者たちは、誰も住んでいない土地に到着したわけではなかった。ペマコ地方には、アディ（Adi）あるいはタニ系の言語を話すさまざまなグループ（訳註：アルナーチャル・プラデーシュ州のアディ、ガロ、ニシ、アパタニ、タギン、ミシュミなどの指定トライブを指す）が住んでいた。当初、元々の住民と新しい移住者の関係は友好的だった。しかし、徐々にモンパは結婚によっていくつかのアディの集団と同化していった。その他のアディの村は攻撃され、人口が激減した。モンパの移住者が増えるにつれ、緊張も高まっていった。そして、隣接した仏教徒のポウォ（Powo）（訳註：中国語では、波密ボーミ）王国はペマコ地方に経済的チャンスを見出し、仏教徒モンパの移住者に無理のない同盟者を見出した。彼らは力を合わせ、いくつかのアディのコミュニティを暴力的に絶滅させ、その他のコミュニティはヤルンツァンポ（シアン／ブラフマプトラ）川を下り、アディのグループに関連する人々が住んでいた現在のアルナーチャル・プラデーシュ州のシアン渓

谷へと力ずくで追い出された。これによってアディの人口はさらに減少し、国境は南へと移動した。ポウォ、カンパ、その他のチベット人もペマコに定住し、しばしばニンマ派仏教の師を伴っていた。これらすべての人々は、ペマコパとして総称されるようになった。

再びの社会政治的混乱、課税、そして地震

　ポウォによる支配は、主としてモンパやアディのコミュニティから租税を徴収する搾取的な植民地支配であった。それでもペマコの人々は、相対的な自治権を有していた。1905年から1911年にかけて、趙爾豊（Zhào Ěr Fēng）に率いられた清朝軍がチベット東部に侵攻し、ポウォ王国を転覆させると、この状況は一変した。清王朝の崩壊後、中国は撤退した。ラサとデプン僧院のチベット・ガンデン政府がペマコを掌握し、租税と労働税を掛け合わせた圧政を敷いた。

　1950年、大地震がこの地域に広範囲に破壊をもたらし、その災害に対するチベット政府の対応は役に立ったとは言い難いものだった。その1年後、共産主義中国がチベットに侵攻し、1959年に併合した。中国政府は1962年にペマコの大部分を完全に支配下においた。インドの一部となったのは、主にツァンラ語とカムのチベット語を話すほんの一握りの村だけで、これらの人びとは現在、それぞれアルナーチャル・プラデーシュ州上シアン県のメンバ族（Memba）とカンバ族（Khamba）に属し、インドの指定トライブとなっている。ペマコの大部分は現在、チベ

【8-1】竹かごバンチュン3個（左上）、竹かごショマ1個（右下）、乾燥させた数珠玉ポムバリン「ヨブの涙」（学名*Croix lacrima-jobi*）のネックレス（左下）。ペマコの人からのギフト。
Three bamboo *bangchung* baskets, a bamboo *shoma* basket, and necklaces of dried *phombaling* 'Job's tears' (*Coix lacryma-jobi*). Gifts obtained from Pemakö. (Photograph by author. Bayi district, Nyingthri prefecture-level city, Tibet, April 2018)

【8-2】白無地の木綿のカムタマ・チュパを着たモンパ男性。H. T. モーズヘッド著「ペマコのマクティのモンパ7-6-13」の詳細な記述より。
Monpa man wearing a plain white cotton *kamthama chupa*. (Detail from 'Mönba at Makti, Pemakö 7-6-13', by H. T. Morshead. From the collection of F. M. Bailey, British Library India Office Records and Personal Papers, MSS Eur 157, Photo 1083/36(102), with permission)

ット自治区林芝（ニンティ）市墨脱（メト）県に属している。

文化の維持

　モンパは、自分たちの文化や生活様式のすべてを元の故郷からペマコ地方に移植した。彼らは、かつて栽培していた作物の種子、飼育していた家畜の種畜、崇敬していた地元の神々、村の寺院や家にあった仏教経典・仏像・道具類一式を持ち込んだ。彼らはまた、ツァンラ語、ダクパ語、モンケット語（訳註：タワン・モンパ語のこと）、ザラ語、そして伝統的な手工芸で

【8-3】モンパ女性は、破れた広袖の無地の白い木綿のトトゥンの上から縞模様のパガを縞模様の帯（チュダン）で締めて着用し、無地の白い（ただし繕ってあり、汚れた）木綿のメヨクを着用している。H. T. モーズヘッド著「ペマコの墨脱（メト）のモンパ女性 9-6-13」の詳細な記述より。
Monpa woman wearing a striped *paga* fastened by a striped *chudang* over a torn, broad-sleeved plain white cotton *tothung* and a plain white (but mended and dirty) cotton *meyok*. (Detail from 'Mönba woman at Meto, Pemakö 9-6-13', by H. T. Morshead. From the collection of F. M. Bailey, British Library India Office Records and Personal Papers, MSS Eur 157, Photo 1083/36(111), with permission)

第8章　第二の故郷を創る―ペマコのモンパ―　　199

ある竹製のバンチュン（*bangchung*）「弁当箱」や竹の「運搬籠」フロクパ（*phrokpa*）、「貯蔵籠」ショマ（*shoma*）を編んだり【8-1】、竹製の水桶を作ったり、舞踊用の仮面を含む木彫りの品々を作ったり、家を建てたり、そして最後になったが、布を織ったりもした。ペマコのモンパは、綿の種、綿繰り器、梳き具、糸紡ぎ器、機織りなどの道具、綿花栽培や染料植物に関するノウハウを、遠く離れた故郷から持ち込んだのだ。

服飾品

20世紀初頭にイギリスの探検家が撮影したペマコ・モンパの古い写真、1950年代半ばに中国の軍隊や研究者が撮影した写真や記述、そして20世紀半ばに生まれたペマコ・モンパの記憶による補強を基に、20世

【8-4】天然の植物染料で染色された手織り木綿のパガの細部。
Detail of a handwoven cotton *paga* dyed with natural plant dyes. (Photograph by author from personal collection, August 2024)

紀初頭から半ばにかけて着用されていた「一般庶民の服装」(2)カムン（*khamung*）を再現することができる。

　ペマコ・モンパの男性は、白い木綿織のチュパ「長上衣」カムタマ・チュパ（*kamthama chupa*）、「織られた木綿の長上衣」【8-2】、または「白無地の木綿織の長上衣」カムタック・カルキャン・チュパ（*kamthak karcang chupa*）と呼ばれる、太ももと臀部を覆い、大腿部の途中まであるものを着ていた。彼らは、ブータン人がゴ（*go*）「長上衣」を着るように、チュパを下の方まで着ることはなく、ブータン人のようにチュパの背中の部分をきれいに整えることもなかった。ペマコ・モンパのチュパのカナン「前ポケット」カナン（*Khanang*）は大きかった。彼らはチュパを赤い茜染めや白い木綿の「帯」チュダン（*chudang*）で結んでいた。ペマコ・モンパの男たちは、寒い季節でも履物を履かないのが

普通だった。下着も身に着けなかった。時には、仕事中に炎天下から身を守るために平たい籐製の帽子を被ることもあった。森に出かけるとき、モンパ男性は、成長したゴーラル属のカモシカ、バシャ（*basha*）（学名*Naemorhedus goral*）の皮2枚、またはケムニャク（*kemnyak*）「ターキン」（学名*Budorcas taxicolor*）の子供の皮2枚に頭を入れる穴を作って縫い合わせた防護用のパクツァ（*paktsa*）「皮の貫頭衣」を着用していた。これは、今でもブロクパやモンパが着ているものとよく似ている。

　ペマコ・モンパの女性の主な服装はメヨ（*meyok*）とパガ（*paga*）だった【8-3】。白い木綿のメヨ「下半身を覆う衣」は、無地の木綿の樽型のスカートを腰で結んで膝、あるいはその下まで丈を伸ばしたものである(3)。このメヨの上に女性は木綿のパガ「貫頭衣」を着る。パガは白無地もあるが、赤と青みがかった黒と細い白の縦縞が交互に入っているのが一般的だった【8-4】。パガは中央の1枚の細長い布と両サイドの2枚の布で構成され、肩と脚の部分が広く、中央のあたりが狭い砂時計型をしていた。パガは中央に頭を入れる穴があり、両側は縫われていない。パガはチュダン「ベルト」で結ばれ、男性のチュダンと素材も色も似ているが、幅が広い。女性は、特に暑く湿気の多い夏には、パガの下には、何も着ないことが多かった。パガの脇が開いているため、上半身が日差しや虫にさらされることが多く、パガの下に真っ白な綿のトトゥン（*tothung*）「シャツ」あるいはノンコ（*nongko*）（後述）を着る女性もいた。ノンコは、寝間着として、または冬や高地へ旅する際の下着としても着られた。男性同様、ペマコ・モンパの女性も履物を履く習慣はなかったが、仕事をする時は、平らな籐製の帽子を被っていた。

　ペマコ・モンパの中でも裕福な人々は、この非常にシンプルだが機能的な日常着に加えて、祝祭

【8-5】20世紀半ばのコサンパ布（左）とコンガパ布（右）。
Mid-20th century *kosampa* (left) and *kongapa* (right) cloth. (Photograph by author, Ramjar, Trashi Yangtse, Bhutan, April 2007, and from personal collection)

用の服も持っていた。男性用の木綿のモンデ・チュパ（mondre chupa）「長上衣を作るために裁断されたモンパ布」には2つのバージョンがあった。それは、コサンパ（kosampa）「3つの扉」とコンガパ（kongapa）「5つの扉」のチュパで、白地に赤と青みがかった黒の縦線が交互に描かれている【8-5】。コ（ko）とは「ドア」のことで、繰り返される縞模様の数を表している。例えば、コサンパの場合は3つ（赤－黒－赤白、黒－赤－黒白）、コンガパの場合は5つ（赤－黒－赤－黒－赤白、黒－赤－黒－赤－黒白）である。

時間に余裕があったり、織り手を雇う余裕があったりする裕福なペマコ・モンパの女性は、無地の白い木綿のメヨではなく、青・緑・赤の帯が入ったユルタ（yulthra）「田舎風の色とりどりの布」、または青み

【8-6】色とりどりのメヨと絹のトゥトゥンの上に、銀のバックル式ベルトを締めた伝統的なパガを身に着けた2人の女性。
Two women wearing the traditional *paga* fastened by silver buckle belts over a multicoloured *meyok* and silk *tothung*. (Photograph by DR, Metok township, Pemakö, Tibet, May 2022)

がかった黒と赤の縞が入ったモンタ（monthra）「モン地方の色とりどりの布」(4)と呼ばれるカラフルな布のメヨを着ていた。これらの布はいずれも、ジャディマ（jadrima）「虹模様」と呼ばれる多色（一般にオレンジ、緑、白、青みがかった黒、またはピンクがかった赤）の縦縞がデザインされている。彼女たちのパガには錦織の裏地がついていたり、時にはチベットのコンポ地方の女性たちも着ている、より厚手で重い、こげ茶色の毛織物のゴシュプ（goshup）という貫頭衣を着たりすることもあった。パガの内側には、白・ピンク・水色などの上質な絹製のトゥトゥンを着て、チュダンの上には銀のバックルがついた革のベルトをしていた。これらのベルトの多くは、先祖代々のモンユルの家から持ってきた家宝である【8-6】。

自家製コットン

　ペマコ・モンパの服飾品はすべて、地元で栽培されたモンガン「綿」（学名

【8-7】綿糸生産に使われる2つの器具、綿繰り機ティティ（左）とかせとり棒ジナン（右）。
Triti (left) and jinang (right): two devices used in cotton yarn production. (Photograph by author, Folk Heritage Museum, Thimphu, Bhutan, March 2007)

Gossypium spp. ワタ属）と、周囲の森から入手したツォス（tshos）「染料」を使って伝統的に作られてきた。綿の種は、チベット暦の2月に土地を耕した後に蒔かれ、発芽するまで4〜15日かかる。苗が30cmほどの高さに達すると、剪定して間引く。高さ90 cmから1.2 mになると花が咲き、3〜5週間後に綿の実が成長し、収穫できる。霜が降りない生育期間が4〜6カ月、日照時間が長く、十分な水分が必要だが、土と根は再び乾燥させる必要がある。そのため、ペマコの低地は綿花栽培に理想的だった。植物は1シーズン以上生き延びることができる。

綿糸は、モンユルの故郷で使われていたのと同じ、労働集約的な工程を経て採取された。綿は晩秋から初冬にかけて綿の木から収穫され、籠に集められる。その後、ペマコ・モンパ女性たちは11月から2月の農閑期を利用して

【8-8】ソンダリンを使って綿糸を玉にする。
Using a sondaring to make cotton yarn into a ball. (Photograph by Tshering Phuntsho, Chongshing, Pemagatshel, Bhutan, November 2019)

【8-9】後帯機で木綿のシャルダン・タラを織る。
Weaving a cotton *shardang thara* on a backstrap loom.
(Photograph by Tshering Phuntsho, Chongshing, Pemagatshel, Bhutan, November 2019)

綿糸を準備し、布を織る。2枚の木の板からなるティティ（*triti*）と呼ばれる簡単な綿繰り機【8-7】で綿を通し、種は残す。これは「綿から種子を分離する」モンガン・ダン・ルン・ブライベ（*mongan dang lung braibe*）の工程として知られていた。綿は洗って、乾かされた。それからその綿を梳かねばならなかった。つまり、きれいにして、「空に浮かぶ雲のような小片」に引き抜いた。これは通常、小さな竹の弓を使ってワタの塊を撃つ方法で行われ、綿はどんどん増えていき、白いほこりを創り出す。この作業は、モンガン・リ・ガフニ・ティフェ（*mongan li gaphni thiphe*）「弓でワタを撃って梳く」として知られていた。この綿をヨクパ（*yokpa*）（紡錘）を使って紡いで糸にしたのがクッパ・ロンメ（*kutpa lomme*）（紡績）である。この糸はジナン（*jinang*）「かせとり棒（*niddy-noddy*）」を使って綛（かせ）にし、最後にソンダリン（*sondaring*）と呼ばれる器具で玉状に丸めて織る準備をした。これを「ソンダリンで糸をかせにする」ソンダリン・ギ・クッパ・ルム・コトゥペ（*sondaring gi kutpa lum cotpe*）と呼ばれた【8-8】。

　無地の白い綿糸は、洗って乾かされ、地元で採れる植物染料、例えば、ヤンカクパ（*yangkhagpa*）、あるいはヤンシャバ（*yangshaba*）と呼ばれる「アッサム藍」（学名*Strobilanthes cusia syn. S. flaccidifolius*）で、青みがかった黒色を発色させたり、ラニメト（*lanimeto*）あるいは、ラニル（*laniru*）と呼ばれる、ピンクがかった赤色を発色させる「アカネ科アカネ属の植物」（学名*Rubia cordifolia*）などである。また、色を保つための媒染剤として、ケ・コプタン（*khe khoptang*）（クルミの皮で学名*Juglans regia*、黒糸のみ）、コマン（*khomang*）「ボ

【8-10】若いペマコ・モンパの女性たち。新デザインのキラとジャケット（中央と右）と、ピンクのシルクのトトゥンと白いメヨ（左）の上に錦織のアップリケをあしらった伝統的なパガを着ている（左）。
Young Pemakö Monpa women wearing the newly designed *kira* and jacket (centre and right) and a more traditional *paga* with brocade appliques over a pink silk *tothung* and white *meyok* (left). (Photograph by PC, Dezhing township, Pemakö, Tibet, March 2018)

ケ」（学名 *Chaenomeles speciosa syn. Ch. lagenaria*)、あるいは、ロプタンシン（*roptangshing*）（訳註：白膠木〈ぬるで〉の木に虫が寄生してできる虫こぶ）（学名 *Rhus chinensis syn.R.semialata*）にも浸した。

ほとんどのペマコ・モンパは一組の服しか持たず、それを毎日毎晩（夜はベルトを緩めて）着用し、時々洗濯する。穴の開いた服はボロ布になるまで繕われ、その頃には新しい服が後帯機【8-9】で織られ、着られるようになってい。通常、この新しい衣服一式は冬の終わりまでに出来上がり、チベット暦12月1日に当たるソナム・ロサル（*sonam losar*）「農民の新年」に着ることができる。

20世紀半ばと後半の変化

中国がペマコ地方を併合してからの数十年間、この地域は、人里離れた、アクセスしにくい、低開発の地のままであった。1950年代から1960年代初頭にかけて、中国政府は国内のすべての民族について調査を行い、南チベットに住む主に仏教徒でありながら非チベット族とみなされる人々に、「門巴族」（Ménbāzú メンバ族）として「少数民族」の地位を与えた。この少数民族には、錯那（ツォナ）県のモンパ（パンチェン・モンパやタワン・モンパに近い言語を話す）とメト県のモンパ（主にツァンラ語を話し、わずかにパンチェン・モンパ語、ザラ語、タワン・モンパ語を話す）が含まれる。このように、これらの人々は蔵族（Zàngzú）の「チベット族」とは明確に区別されている。2023年3月から、モンパ族は中国の全国人民代表大会（全人代）において、ペマコ・モンパ女性1名が代表を務めている。

1960年代から70年代にかけての文化大革命で、モンパの文化的・宗教的伝統や習慣の多くが廃止された。男性はチュパを着なくなり、中国や西洋の服装

を取り入れた。年配の女性たちはパガを着続けたが、若い世代はカム・チベット族のチュパと西洋の服装を取り入れた。かつて有名だった織物の技術は急速に失われていった。

21世紀に入ってから、ペマコでは多くの変化が起こった。電気や携帯電話、インターネット・サービスの提供、2013年にはポウォから、2022年にはコンポから、(ほぼ)通年開通する道路の開通、学校の建設と義務教育の実施、産業用の木材の伐採と水力発電開発の開始、自然保護区の設

【8-11】ペマコ・モンパの改良ドレスを着た老夫婦。多色の伝統的なメヨと多色のトトゥンの上に、伝統的なパガだが、錦織のアップリケを施したもの(左)と、現代的な機械織りのチュパ(右)。
Elderly couple wearing modified Pemakö Monpa dress: a traditional *paga* but with brocade appliques on a multicoloured *meyok* and multicoloured *tothung* (left) and a modern machine-woven *chupa* (right). (Photograph by DR, Metok township, Pemakö, Tibet, February 2022)

立とモンパ住民の再定住、町の設立、モンパ族以外(漢民族や回族やチベット族)の移民の流入など、すべてがペマコのモンパの人々とその文化に大きな影響を与えている。

同時に、モンパは独自のアイデンティティを再確認した。さらに最近では、民族衣装を一新した。男性は古いジャドリマの柄を大まかに踏襲したデザインのチュパを着用し、女性は、同じデザインのキラを大まかに踏襲した巻き付ける衣服に、それを引き立てる飾り帯と帽子を着用するようになった【8-10】。近年、これらの服装はむしろポピュラーになったが、パガやメヨクを着る女性は減少の一途をたどっている。2018年現在、ペマコでパガを織ることができるのは、高齢の女性2人だけである【8-11】。

亡命先での復興

中国がチベットを併合したとき、カムやポウォから多くのチベット人がペマ

コ地方を通ってインドに逃れた。ペマコ・モンパを含む多くのペマコの住人も彼らに加わった。彼らは最終的に、アルナーチャル・プラデーシュ州、オディシャ州、カルナータカ州にあるいくつかのチベット難民居住区に移動した。2010年以降、アルナーチャル・プラデーシュ州の入植地から1,000人以上の難民がカナダに再定住した。

インドの入植地では伝統的なペマコ・モンパの服装は姿を消し、カム・チベット族の標準的な服装や西洋やインドの衣服に取って代わられているが、カナダのペマコ・モンパの間では女性の服装がいくらか復活している。ソナム・ロサルやダライ・ラマの誕生日を祝うような公式の場では、彼女たちは白無地のメヨク、錦の縁取りのある赤無地のパガ、空色のトトゥンを着て踊りを披露する【8-12】。

比較および結論

ペマコのモンパは、17世紀半ばから19世紀半ばにかけて彼らの故郷を離れた。当時、故郷のツァンラ語を話す人々が着ていた服装は、その後、ブータンではゴやキラ、アルナーチャル・プラデーシュ州西部ではシンカといった他の服装に取って代わられた。ブータン東部では20世紀半ばまで、男性でもカムタマ・チュパやモンデ・チュパを日常的に着用していたことが、年配の人々との対話で確認されている。いくつかの古い布も残されている。また、パガとノンコ と呼ばれる女性用の衣服が以前に存在していたことも、同じ高齢者たちによって確認されている。キラは、ツァンラ語ではタラ（*thara*）と呼ばれ、20世紀に入ってから服飾

【8-12】白い無地のメヨとスカイブルーのトトゥンの上に、錦織のアップリケが付いた赤い無地のゴシュプという復活された服を着た亡命ペマコ・モンパの女性たち。
Exile Pemakö Monpa women wearing the revived dress: a plain red *goshup* with brocade appliques over a plain white *meyok* and sky blue *tothung*. (Photograph by TN, Toronto, Canada, January 2022)

品になった。村の一般の女性は、シャルダン・タラ（*shardang thara*）「東の輝きのある織布」のようなシンプルなデザインの純綿の服を着ていた。

ブータン東部のパガは、袖のない一枚の長い布で、真ん中に頭を入れる穴があり、両脇は縫われておらず、通常は白無地の木綿で作られていたという。このパガは、明らかにペマコ・モンパのパガやチベットのゴシュプに似ている。ゴシュプはチベット中央部のコンポ地方で着用され、茶色のウールで織られている。同じゴシュプは、アルナーチャル・プラ

【8-13】コンポ・スタイルのグーシを着て銀製のバックル式ベルトをしたメンチュカのメンバ女性。下には、メヨは着けず、袖なしのフメイ（チベット女性のチュバと同じ）とピンク色のトトゥンを着ていた。以前はフメイの下に下着としてメヨを着ていた。しかし、現在ではメヨを着る人はほとんどいない。
This Memba woman in Menchukha is wearing a Kongpo-style *gushi* fastened by a silver buckle belt. Under the *gushi*, she is wearing a sleeveless *fumey* (same as the Tibetan *chuba*) and pink *tothung*. Before they used to wear a *meyok* as underwear for *fumey*. However, nowadays, very few people wear a *meyok*. (Photograph by Michiko Wakita, Menchukha, September 2010)

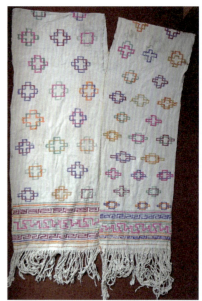

【8-14】ブータンの 貫頭衣ノンコ。
A tunic dress *nongko* from Bhutan. (photograph by author from personal collection, August 2024).

【8-15】肩に刺繡が施された赤いレウシンカを着用しているクルトェ地方の女性たち。
Kurtō women wearing red *leushingka* with embroidered shoulders. (Photograph by Ugyen Pelgen, Tangmachu, Lhuentse, Bhutan, January 1998).

デーシュ州シー・ヨミ県メンチュカ谷のメンバ(Memba)も着用している。しかし、彼らは、それをグーシ（*gushi*）と呼んでいる【8-13】。メンチュカのメンバは、行政上は上シアン県のメンバと同じ指定トライブに属するが、ブータン東部、タワン、主にコンポ地方を含むチベット中央部の一部から来た出自が混じった人々である。言語はチベット語の一種であり、チベットの服を着ていた。

ブータン東部のノンコ（ノンノンマと呼ばれることもある）は、パガと同様、袖のない貫頭衣である。しかし、パガとは異なり、脇の下の両脇が縫い合わされており【8-14】、これはタワンやディランのブロクパやモンパの野生絹や木綿のシンカ（第2章、第3章を参照）、タシ・ヤンツェやルンツェのウールのレウシンカ（*leushingka*）【8-15】やンゴウシンカ（*ngoushingka*）、そしてクルトェ地方やブムタン地方のクシュン（*kushung*）と類似のものである。ノンコは、無地のイラクサの繊維か木綿で作られ、通常は、幾何学模様が施されていた。20世紀中頃までは、ブータン女性は、キラの下に下着として、寝間着としてシンプルなノンコを着ていた。より精巧なノンコは、宗教的な行事の際の衣装として保存されてきた。

(1) コロントェは、コロン・チュ（川）渓谷上部の地域全体の旧名なので、ブムデリンを含むタシ・ヤンツェ県のほとんどに当たる。
(2) これは、通常チベット貴族の服装と同等の服を着ていた高位のペマコ・モンパの衣服を除外し、通常一般的なチベットの僧や在家の僧の衣服である宗教修行者の衣服も除外したものである。
(3) メヨに似たスカートは、ブータンでは現在でも僧侶の下着として着用され、また一部の儀式的な踊りの際にも着用されている。
(4) ゾンカ語でユル・タムは「田舎で織られた布」、モン・タムは「モンパが織った布」である。

第8章 第二の故郷を創る―ペマコのモンパ― 209

CHAPTER 8
Creating a Home Away From Home: Pemakö's Monpa
Written by Timotheus A. Bodt

The following history of the Pemakö Monpas in Tibet and description of their dress is based on various sources, including a late 17th century or early 18th century Bhutanese source (Ngawang n.d. [1668/1728?]), early 20th century British explorer's records (e.g., Kingdon-Ward 1926, Bailey 1957), late 20th and early 21st century Chinese sources (e.g., XSLDZCBZ 1987, Bāo 2014, MBZBBZ 2016[2008]), a late 20th century Bhutanese source (Dorji 1986), western academic sources (e.g., Grothmann 2012), and oral accounts of elderly Pemakö Monpas and eastern Bhutanese collected in the early 21st century.

In the 17th century, Monyul, the border area of what is now southern Tibet, eastern Bhutan, and western Arunachal Pradesh, became the scenery for two Himalayan nations to expand their territory. The Bhutanese, under the newly established Zhabdrung's theocracy, and the administration of the Ganden Phodrang, that had taken control in Tibet, vied for power and territory. While the Bhutanese annexed the small, independent fiefdoms in the Monyul region from the West eastwards, the Tibetans did the same from the East westwards. The two new powers continued to contest each other throughout the 18th century. The old clan-based social structure that had evolved at least since the 8th century was abolished. Instead, the new central governments installed various layers of local and regional authority. They also established an oppressive taxation system with in-kind taxes and labour duties that weighed heavily on the local population. In addition, during the late 17th and throughout the 18th and 19th century, the area saw numerous earthquakes, some of which were very destructive.

Hence, no wonder that the defeated local chiefs and their clansmen, sometimes entire villages, were attracted by stories of a mystical *beyül* (Tib. sbas-yul) 'hidden land'. This hidden land had recently been 'discovered' in the eastern Himalayas and was to provide a safe haven and refuge for persecuted Buddhists, in particular the followers of the Nyingmapa (Tib. rnying-ma-pa) 'old order'. Among them were the people of Monyul facing the onslaught of the Tibetans and Bhutanese, who followed the rival sects of Gelukpa (Tib. dge-lugs-pa) and Drukpa Kagyü (Tib. 'brug-pa bka'-rgyud), respectively.

The Pemakö Monpa

The hidden land was called Pemakö (Tib. pad+ma-bkod) 'array of the lotus', and the people who migrated there from Monyul became known as the Pemakö Monpa (Tib. pad+ma-bkod mon-pa). Between the mid-17th century and the mid-20th century, there were several successive batches of migrations followed by a trickle of relatives and fellow villagers who followed earlier migrants. Most of the migrants were Tshangla speakers from areas of eastern Bhutan, mainly in Monggar and upper Trashigang, but there were also Dzalakha speakers from Kholongtö[1] in Trashi Yangtse. They were joined by Tshangla speakers from the Dirang area, and Pangchenpa, Dakpa and Tawang Monpa speakers from various villages in Tawang, now all in western Arunachal Pradesh. Many of these migrants settled in separate villages where linguistic distinctions were maintained until recent times.

No empty land

The Monpa migrants did not arrive in an empty land. The Pemakö area was inhabited by various groups of Adi (Tani) people. In the beginning, the relations between the original inhabitants and the new settlers were cordial. But slowly, the Monpas assimilated some Adi communities through marriage. Other Adi villages were attacked, and their population was decimated. As the number of Monpa migrants increased, tensions increased, too. Then, the neighbouring Buddhist Powo (Tib. spo-bo) kingdom saw economic opportunities in the Pemakö region and found natural allies in the Buddhist Monpa settlers. Through their combined strength, they violently annihilated several Adi communities, while others were driven out by force, down the Yarlung Tsangpo (Siang/Brahmaputra) river into what is now the Siang valley of Arunachal Pradesh, which was already inhabited by related Adi groups. This further reduced the Adi population in Pemakö and extended the border southward. Powo, Khampa and other Tibetans settled in Pemakö, too, often accompanying Nyingmapa Buddhist masters. All these people became collectively known as the Pemaköpa.

Socio-political upheaval, taxation, and an earthquake, again

The Powo rule was largely an extractive colonial rule, taxing the Monpa and remaining Adi communities. Still, the Pemakö people had relative autonomy. This changed when, between 1905 and 1911, the Qīng Chinese army led by Zhào Ěrfēng invaded eastern Tibet and overthrew the Powo kingdom. After the fall of the Qīng empire, the Chinese retreated. The Tibetan Ganden administration from Lhasa and Drepung monastery took over control of Pemakö and established an oppressive taxation system with a multiplication of taxes and corvee duties.

In 1950, a massive earthquake caused widespread destruction in the region, and the Tibetan response to the disaster was far from helpful. A year later, Communist China invaded Tibet, annexing it in 1959. The Chinese established full control of most of Pemakö in 1962. Only a handful of villages, mainly inhabited by Tshangla and Kham Tibetan speakers, became part of India, and these people now belong to the Memba and Khamba Scheduled Tribes of Upper Siang district of Arunachal Pradesh, respectively. The majority of Pemakö is now part of Metok county, Nyingthri prefecture-level city, Tibet Autonomous Region.

Maintaining culture

The Pemakö Monpa people transplanted their entire culture and livelihood system from their original homeland to the Pemakö region. They brought the seeds of the crops they used to grow, a breeding stock of the animals they used to rear, the local deities they used to revere, and the Buddhist scriptures, statues, and paraphernalia their village temples and homes contained. They also brought their languages, Tshangla, Dakpa, Monket and Dzalakha, and their traditional handicrafts, such as weaving bamboo *bangchung* 'lunch boxes' and bamboo *phrokpa* 'carrying baskets' and *shoma* 'storage baskets' 【8-1】, making bamboo water pails, carving wood items including dance masks, constructing houses, and, last but not least, weaving cloth. The Pemakö Monpas had brought the cotton seeds, the ginning, carding, spinning and weaving equipment, and the know-how about cotton cultivation and dye plants from their far-away homeland.

Dress items

Based on old photographs of Pemakö's Monpas taken by British explorers in the early years of the 20th century and the photographs and descriptions of Chinese troops and researchers in the mid-1950s and augmented by the memories of Pemakö Monpas born in the mid-20th century, we can reconstruct the *khamung* 'dress' of the ordinary people(2) as it was worn in the early to mid-20th century.

The Pemakö Monpa men wore a plain white cotton *chupa* 'gown' called *kamthama chupa* (Tib. kam-thag-ma phyu-pa) 'woven cotton gown' 【8-2】 or *kamthak karcang chupa* (Tib. kam-thags dkar-rkyang phyu-pa) 'plain white woven cotton gown' that covered the thighs and buttocks and reached down mid-way the upper legs. They did not wear their *chupa* as low as the Bhutanese wear their *go* (Tib. bgo) 'gown', and neither did they adjust the back part of the *chupa* as neatly as the Bhutanese do. The *khanang* 'front pocket' of the Pemakö Monpa *chupa* was large. They tied their *chupa* with a red-madder dyed and plain white cotton *chudang* 'belt'. The Pemakö Monpa men usually did not wear any footwear, even in cold weather circumstances. Neither did they wear any underwear. Sometimes, they would wear a flat cane hat to protect themselves from the scorching sun while out at work. When heading out into the forest, they would wear a protective *paktsha* (Tib. pags-tshag) 'skin tunic' made from two adult *basha* 'goral' (*Naemorhedus goral*) or two *kemnyak* 'takin' (*Budorcas taxicolor*, Tib. skyin-g.yag) calf skins sewn together with a hole for the head on top, similar to the *paktsha* still worn by the Brokpa and Monpa people.

The Pemakö Monpa women's main dress items were the *meyok* and the *paga*

【8-3】. The white cotton *meyok* (Tib. smad-g.yog) 'undercover' was a plain cotton barrel skirt tied around the waist that reached till the knees or a little lower(3). Over this *meyok* the women would wear a cotton *paga* 'tunic'. The *paga* could be plain white, but more commonly it had alternating red and bluish-black and thinner white vertical stripes 【8-4】. The *paga* consisted of a single middle panel with two side panels on each side and was in an hourglass shape, wider at the shoulders and legs and narrower around the middle. The *paga* had a hole for the head in the middle and was not stitched on the sides. The *paga* was tied with a *chudang* 'belt', similar in material and colours to the men's *chudang*, but wider. Under the *paga*, women would often wear nothing at all, especially in the hot, humid summer. Because the sides of the *paga* wear open, this would often expose their upper body to the sun and insects, so some women would wear a plain white cotton *tothung* (Tib. stod-thung) 'shirt' or a *nongko* (see below) under the *paga*. The *nongko* was also worn as nightgown, and as underwear in winter and when traveling to higher altitudes. Like the men, the Pemakö Monpa women were not accustomed to footwear, but they would wear a flat cane hat while at work.

In addition to this very simple but functional daily wear, the more well-to-do among the Pemakö Monpas also had a festive dress. For the men, there were two versions of the cotton *mondre chupa* (Tib. mon-dras phyu-pa) 'Monpa cloth cut for making a gown': the *kosampa* 'three doors' and *kongapa* 'five doors' *chupa*, with alternating red and bluish-black vertical lines on a plain white background 【8-5】. The *ko* 'doors' referred to the number of repetitive stripe patterns: three in the case of *kosampa* (red-black-red white black-red-black white) and five in the case of *kongapa* (red-black-red-black-red white black-red-black-red-black white).

Rather than the plain white cotton *meyok*, well-to-do Pemakö Monpa women, who had time to spare or could afford to employ weavers, would wear a *meyok* made of the colourful cloth called *yulthra* (Tib. g.yul-khra) 'multicoloured (cloth) from the rural area', having blue, green and red bands, or *monthra* (Tib. mon-khra) 'multicoloured (cloth) from Mon'(4), featuring blueish-black and red bands. Both these cloths were designed with a multicoloured (commonly orange, green, white, bluish-black and/or pinkish-red) warp striping called *jadrima* (Tib. 'ja'-sgrig-ma) 'rainbow pattern'. Their *paga* could have brocade linings, or sometimes they would even wear the thicker, heavier, dark brown woollen *goshup* (Tib. mgo-shubs) 'tunic' also worn by women in the Kongpo region of Tibet. And inside the *paga*, they would wear a finer silk *tothung*, often in the colour white, pink, or sky-blue. They would wear a leather belt over the *chudang* with silver buckles. Many of these belts were heirlooms brought from their ancestral Monyul homes 【8-6】.

Home-produced cotton

All the Pemakö Monpa dress items were traditionally made from locally grown *mongan* 'cotton' (*Gossypium spp.*) and *tshos* 'dyes' obtained from the surrounding forest. The cotton seeds were sown in the second month of the Tibetan calendar after ploughing and tilling the land and would take four to 15 days to germinate. After the plants reached a height of around 30 centimetres, they would be pruned and thinned. After reaching a height of around 90 centimetres to 1.20 meters, the plants would flower and then after three to five weeks the balls would develop which could then be harvested. In total it would require a frost-free growing season of four to six months and a lot of sunshine as well as enough moisture, but the soil and roots should be allowed to dry again. This made the lower-lying parts of Pemakö ideal for cotton cultivation. The plants would survive for more than one growing season.

The cotton thread was extracted through the same labour-intensive process that was used in the Monyul home region. The cotton would be harvested from the cotton trees in late autumn or early winter and collected in baskets. The Pemakö Monpa women would then use the agricultural slack season between November and February to prepare the cotton thread and weave the cloth. A simple ginning device called *triti* (Tib. dkris-ti) consisting of two wooden planks would allow the cotton to move through whereas the seeds would be left behind 【8-7】. This was known as the process of *mongan dang lung braibe* 'to separate the seeds from the cotton'. The cotton was then washed and dried. Then it had to be carded: purified and plucked into 'small pieces similar to the clouds in the sky'. This was usually done by using a small bamboo bow to shoot in the mass of cotton, which would then become more and more and create a white dust. This was known as *mongan li gaphni thiphe* 'carding the cotton by shooting with a bow'. The cotton was then spun into yarn, a process called *kutpa lomme* 'spinning the yarn' by making use of a *yokpa* 'spindle'. This yarn was made into a skein by using a *jinang* 'niddy-noddy' and finally made ready for weaving by rolling it into a ball with a device known as a *sondaring* (Tib. son-mda'-ring), called as *sondaring gi kutpa lum cotpe* 'making a skein of yarn with the *sondaring*' 【8-8】.

The plain white cotton yarn was then washed, dried, and coloured with locally available plant-based dyes: *yangkhagpa*, also called *yangshaba* 'Assam indigo' (*Strobilanthes cusia syn. S. flaccidifolius*), which gives a bluish-black colour, and *lanimeto*, also called *laniru* 'madder' (*Rubia cordifolia*), which gives a pinkish-red colour. The yarn was also soaked in *khe khoptang* (the peel of the walnut, Juglans regia, only for black yarn), *khomang* 'Chinese flowering quince' (*Chaenomeles speciosa syn. Ch. lagenaria*) or *roptangshing* 'Chinese sumac gallnut' (*Rhus chinensis syn. R. semialata*) in order to retain colour.

Most Pemakö Monpas would have only a single set of clothes, that would be worn on a daily and nightly (with the belt loosened) basis and occasionally washed. Holes would be mended till the dress became a rag, by which time a new dress set would be woven on the backstrap loom and ready to be worn 【8-9】. Usually, this new set of clothes would be ready by the end of winter and could be worn on *sonam losar* (Tib. so-nam lo-gsar) 'agricultural new year', coinciding with the first day of the twelfth month of the Tibetan calendar.

Mid- and late-20th century changes

In the first few decades since the Chinese annexation of the Pemakö region, the area remained remote, inaccessible, and underdeveloped. During the 1950s and early 1960s, the Chinese administration conducted research on all the ethnic groups in the country, and subsequently conferred the status of *shǎoshù mínzú* 'minority nationality' as the Ménbāzú 'Monpa nationality' on the mainly Buddhist but what they considered as non-Tibetan people living in southern Tibet. The Ménbā ethnic minority includes the Monpa of Tshona county (who speak a language closely related to Pangchen and Tawang Monpa) and the Monpa of Metok county (primarily Tshangla speakers, and a few Pangchen, Dzalakha, and Tawang Monpa speakers). Thus, these people were clearly differentiated from the Zàngzú 'Tibetan nationality'. Since March 2023, the single representative in China's National People's Congress, is a Pemakö Monpa woman.

During the Cultural Revolution in the 1960s and '70s, many Monpa cultural and religious traditions and customs were abolished. Men stopped wearing the *chupa* and adopted Chinese and western dress. While elderly women continued to wear the *paga*, the younger generation adopted the Kham Tibetan chupa, and western dress. The once so famous weaving skills were rapidly lost.

Since the start of the 21st century many changes have taken place in Pemakö. The provision of electricity and mobile phone and internet services, the opening of an (almost) all-year road from Powo in 2013 and from Kongpo in 2022, the construction of schools and enforcement of compulsory education, the inception of industrial logging and hydropower development, the establishment of nature reserves and resettlement of the Monpa inhabitants, the establishment of towns and the influx of non-Monpa (Han and Hui Chinese and Tibetan) migrants have all had major impacts on the Monpa people of Pemakö and their culture.

At the same time, the Pemakö Monpa people reasserted their unique identity. More recently, they completely reinvented their ethnic dress. Men started wearing a *chupa* with a design broadly based on the old *jadrima* pattern, while women started wearing a wrap-around loosely based on the *kira* with the same design and a sash and cap to complement it 【8-10】. While these dress items became rather popular in recent years, there has been a continued decline in the number of women wearing the *paga* and *meyok*. By 2018, only two elderly women in Pemakö were still able to weave the *paga* 【8-11】.

Revival in exile

When China annexed Tibet, many Tibetans from Kham and Powo fled to India through the Pemakö region. Many Pemaköpa also joined them, including many

Pemakö Monpa. They eventually moved to several Tibetan refugee settlements in Arunachal Pradesh, Odisha, and Karnataka. Since 2010, over 1,000 of the refugees from the settlements in Arunachal Pradesh have been resettled in Canada.

While the traditional Pemakö Monpa dress has disappeared in the settlements in India, being replaced by standard Kham Tibetan, western, and Indian dress, there is some revival of the women's dress among the Pemaköpa in Canada. During official occasions, such as the celebration of *sonam losar* and the Dalai Lama's birthday, they will perform dances wearing a plain white *meyok*, a plain red *paga* with brocade borders, and a sky blue *tothung* 【8-12】.

Comparison and conclusion

The Monpa of Pemakö left their original homeland between the mid-17th and mid-19th centuries. The dress that the Tshangla people of the home region wore at that time was later replaced by other dresses, such as the go and *kira* in Bhutan and the *shingka* (see Chapter 2) in western Arunachal Pradesh. Discussions with elderly people confirm that until the mid-20th century, even men in eastern Bhutan used to wear the *kamthama* and *mondre chupa* on a daily basis. Even some antique examples of the cloth are available. And the same elderly people also confirm the previous existence of two dress items for women, called the *paga* and the *nongko*. The *kira*, in Tshangla called *thara*, only became a dress item around the turn of the 20th century. The common village women would wear pure cotton dress in simple designs, like the *shardang thara* (Tib. shar-mdangs thags-ras) 'eastern radiant woven cloth'.

The *paga* of eastern Bhutan is described as a sleeveless, single piece of long cloth with a hole for the head in the middle and not stitched on the sides, usually made of plain white cotton. This *paga* is clearly similar to the Monpa *paga* and the Tibetan *goshup*. The *goshup* is worn in the Kongpo region of Central Tibet, where it is woven of brown wool. The same *goshup* is also worn by the Memba of Menchukha valley of Shi Yomi district of Arunachal Pradesh 【8-13】. While the Memba of Menchukha administratively belong to the same Scheduled Tribe as the Memba of Upper Siang district, they have a mixed origin from eastern Bhutan, Tawang, and parts of Central Tibet, including mainly the Kongpo region. Their language is a variety of Tibetan, and they wear Tibetan dress.

The *nongko*, sometimes called *nongnongma*, of eastern Bhutan is, like the *paga*, a sleeveless tunic. But unlike the *paga*, the sides of the *nongko* below the armpits are stitched together 【8-14】, similar to the raw silk or cotton *shingka* of the Brokpa and Monpa of Tawang and Dirang (see Chapter 2,3), the woollen *leushingka* 【8-15】 and *ngoushingka* of Trashi Yangtse and Lhüntse, and the cotton or nettle fibre *kushung* of the Kurtö and Bumthang regions. The *nongko* was made of plain nettle fibre or cotton and usually decorated with geometric designs. Until the mid-20th century, women in Bhutan would wear the simple *nongko* under the *kira* as a type of underwear and as a night dress. More elaborate versions of the *nongko* were preserved as dress item during religious functions.

(1) Kholongtö is the old name of the entire upper region of the Kholong chu river valley, so most of Trashi Yangtse district, including Bumdeling.
(2) This excludes the dress of high-ranking Pemakö Monpas, who usually wore clothes comparable to Tibetan aristocrat's dresses, and this also excludes the dress of religious practitioners, which usually was standard Tibetan monk's or lay monk's dress.
(3) A skirt similar to the meyok is still worn as undergarment by monks and in some ceremonial dances in Bhutan.
(4) In Dzongkha *g. yul-thagm* 'rural woven [cloth]' and *mon-thagm* 'Monpa woven cloth'.

CHAPTER 9
Traditional Attires of the Neighbours of the Monpa in West Kameng district
第9章 西カメン県のモンパの隣人たちの民族衣装

【9-1a】サロク祭で撮られたこのフルソ（アカ）の男性は、銀製の帽子を被り、模様の入った洋風のジャケットの下に民族衣装を身に着けている。口にはパイプをくわえ、帯には剣を差している。
This Hruso (Akha) man, photographed at the *Sarok* festival, wears a silver hat and a traditional attire under a western-style jacket. He has a pipe in his mouth and a sword in his sash. (Photograph by David Sangtam, Thrizino, January 2012)

2024年2月、西カメン県東部と東カメン県西部の一部から新しくビチョム（Bichom）県が創設されたが、まだ詳細な地図が入手できておらず、訂正が間に合わなかったため、本書では、西カメン県に、現在のビチョム県の一部も含んでいる。

指定トライブのモンパは、アルナーチャル・プラデーシュ州のタワン県、西カメン県の多数派を占める民族集団で、人口は2011年の国勢調査に基づく統計では60,525人である。ただし、これには、2021年8月に別のトライブとして認められたサルタン（Sartang）も含まれている。

西カメン県を主たる居住地としているモンパ以外の民族集団としては、フルソ（アカ）、サジョラン（ミジ）、ブグン（コワ）、シェルドゥクペンなどが挙げられる。いずれも人口1万人に満たない少数派の民族集団であり、モンパと隣接した地域に住んでいる(1)。彼らもモンパ同様、すべてアルナーチャル・プラデーシュ州の指定トライブである。居住地は標高150mから1,500mの間で、夏は暑く、雨も多いが、冬は温暖である。

本章では、これらの集団の民族衣装についても触れておきたいが、いずれの居住地でも滞在期間が短かったため、表面的な観察しかできなかった。

【9-1b】このフルソ女性たちはサロク祭のために盛装している。
These Hruso women are dressed up for the *Sarok* festival.
(Photograph by David Sangtam, Thrizino, January 2012)

　しかし、アルナーチャル・プラデーシュ州の他の集団と同じように、人々の日常着は洋装が主流で、民族衣装は、特別な行事の際にのみ着用されるようになってきている。また、すでに見られなくなった衣装もある。そのため、1990年代から現在までの記録としても残しておこうと思う。

　個々の集団の移動と定住の歴史、そして彼らの言語がどのように発展してきたかについては、既存の研究があるが、紙面の都合上、本章ではその詳細の一部を簡単に述べるにとどめる(2)。

フルソ（アカ）

　アカ（Aka）は、彼らに顔を塗る風習があったことから「塗られた」という意味でつけられたアッサム平原の人々からの他称で(3)、自称はフルソ（Hruso。あるいは、フルッソHrussoと綴る）である(4)。彼らの居住地は、西カメン県南東部にあるスリジノ（Thrizino）、ジャミリ（Jamiri）、バルクポン（Bhalukpong）の各サークルで、人口は、8,167人である（2011年統計）。

　1913年にこの地を訪れたイギリスの軍医、ケネディ（R. S. Kennedy）は、アカの男性の服装について、「粗い木綿の布を体に巻き付け、小さな竹のピンで肩に留めている。その衣服は幅の広い帯を腰の周りで締め、その下はいわば短いスカート状になっていて、膝の少し下まである。その上に、腰まである上

着を着る。(中略)彼らは皆、彼らの住む丘陵部にたくさんいるダムディム・バエ(学名*Simulium indicum*)(5)から身を守るために、足に脚絆を着けている」と記述している。ケネディはまた、アカの女性の服装について、「男性が着るものと似ているが、くるぶし近くまであり、アッサム・シルクであることが多い。アッサム・シルクの上着は、男性の上着よりやや長い。髪は例外なく後頭部で結ばれている。裕福な女性は、頭の周りに銀の鎖でできた、とても印象的でかわいらしいヘアバンドを着けている。耳には大きな壺型の銀のイヤリングがあり、首には無数のカラービーズのネックレスが巻かれている。(中略)女性は原則として、男性と同じような脚絆を着用している」と述べている(6)。

　1962年に出版されたシンハ(Raghuvir Shinha)の著書によれば、伝統的に男性の上半身は、小さな一枚布を肩から下げて覆う。また、肩から膝までの長いコートの一種を掛けて、特別な時には、ムサルガ(*musarga*)と呼ばれる円筒形の竹製の帽子を被るという。女性は、肩からくるぶしまである長い衣服を身に着けるが、男性用より丈が長く、色は濃い赤が一般的であると述べている。しかし、著書に収められている写真の女性の衣服は、モノクロ写真ではあるが、白色であると思われる。シンハもまた、男女ともにふくらはぎを覆う虫除けの円筒形の脚絆グドゥ(*gudu*)を着用していると記述している(7)。

　1847年にジョン・バトラー(John Butler)が描いたタギ・ラジャとその兄弟の絵に描かれた脚絆は、プリーツの装飾が施されたファッショナブルなものであった(8)。2012年に撮られた【9-1a】の男性は、この絵でタギ・ラジャが被っているものに似た帽子を被っている。サムビョ(Dusu Sambyo)によれば、ワガ(*wagha*)と呼ばれるこの銀製の帽子は、貴族が被るものだったという(9)。

　【9-1b】は、【9-1a】と同じ時期に撮影されたものである。女性たちは、ケネディの報告にあるような銀製のヘアバンドをしているが、一枚布ではなく、白い貫頭衣を着ている。私が2013年にジャミリ村で見た女性の民族衣装も、白いエリ・シルクまたは木綿の貫頭衣ウーソゲ(*wusoge*)と、モンパのものとよく似た臙脂色の上着サショポル(*sashopol*)である。この上着には襟が付いていた【9-2a】。銀製品などのさまざまな装身具を身に着けるが、【9-2b】の中央にある大きな銀製の首飾りは、メルー(*melu*)、その奥の銀製のヘアバンドは、レンツィ(*lentsi*)と呼ばれる。

　これらの衣装は、現在では祭りやイベントなど特別な際にのみ着用されてい

【9-2a】このフルソの少女が来ている上着には、襟が付いている。
The jacket that this Hruso girl is wearing has a collar. (Jamiri, November 2013)

【9-2b】写真【9-2a】の少女の家族が所有する女性の装身具。
Women's ornaments owned by the family of the girl in photograph 【9-2a】. (Jamiri, November 2013)

る。

サジョラン（ミジ）

　ミジ（Miji）というトライブ名は、フルソからの他称で「火をくれた人」という意味がある。ミジの言語は、少なくとも以下の3つの自称を持つ集団に分かれるという。ナフラ・サークルではサジョラン（Sajolang）、ジャミリ・サークルではダンマイあるいはディンマイ（Dhammai/Dimmai）、隣の東カメン県周辺の人々はナムライ（Namrai）がそれぞれの自称であるという(10)。総人口は、2011年統計ではフルソよりやや少ない8,127人であった。

　2004年11月にナフラ・サークルのアッパー・ザン（Upper Dzang）村で行われていたチンダン（Chindang）という儀礼を見る機会があった。チンは「祈りの儀式」、ダンは「いけにえを捧げること」だという(11)。毎年10月から12月の間に行われるが、日時は占いによって決める。この儀礼は太陽・月・山・川などに住む神々に動物を供犠して豊作を祈り、悪霊を追い払う伝統的な儀礼で

ある。司祭を務める男性は、伝統的な白い一枚布を巻き付けた衣装グレイ・モンドン（*grey mongdong*）に、脚絆ライロ（*lailo*）を着け、頭には円筒形の竹製の帽子シュポタン（*shupotang*）を被って、ビーズの首飾りヴロ（*vulo*）を着けている【9-3a】。赤いジャケットは、アルナーチャル・プラデーシュ州の各地の村長（ガオンブラ）が着ているものと同じようであることから、彼は村長であったかもしれない。近年、キリスト教や仏教に改宗するミジの人々が増えている。

　私が見た儀礼の場には、女性はおらず、代わりに少年が女性の衣装を着て銀製のヘアバンドをしていた【9-3b】。2005年8月15日のインド独立記念日のボムディラでの式典で、各民族の踊りが披露されたが、その時にミジの少女たちが着ていた民族衣装を見た。モンパのシンカと同じような形状の白い貫頭衣ギブルン（*gibulung*）【9-4a】を着て、その上にサショリ・パンロウ（*sashori panglho*）

【9-3a】チンダンという儀礼の場で、赤い上着を着た村長と思われるサジョラン（ミジ）男性は、フルソと同じような白い衣装に、竹製の帽子を被り、脚絆を着けている。
This Sajolang (Miji) man, possibly the village chief, wears a red jacket and a white costume similar to that of the Hruso, a bamboo hat and leg covers at a ritual called *Chindang*. (Upper Dzang, November 2004)

【9-3b】理由は確かめることができなかったが、このサジョランの少年は女性の衣装を着ていた。
For reasons that could not be identified, this Sajolang boy was dressed in a woman's costume. (Upper Dzang, Nafra, November 2004)

【9-4a】インド独立記念日祝賀会で、サジョラン（ミジ）女性の踊り手は白い貫頭衣を着ていた。The Sajolang(Miji) women dancers at the Indian Independence Day celebrations wore white tunic dress. (Bomdila, August 2005)

【9-4b】これから踊りを披露するサジョラン（ミジ）女性たちの衣装。Costumes of the Sajolang(Miji) women who will be performing the dance. (Bomdila, August 2005)

という赤い上着を着ていた【9-4b】。この上着もモンパのトトゥンによく似てはいるが、素材はエリ・シルクではなく化学繊維で、柄もモンパの物と比べると大きめで色鮮やかである。ギブルンも木綿か化学繊維のようであった。黄色やブルー、赤褐色のビーズのネックレスを何重にも重ねて下げていた。正装では、女性は銀のヘアバンドを着けるが、この時のダンサーたちは、ヘアバンドはしていなかった。私の友人によると、2013年11月のチンダン祭のイベントには、多くの男女が帽子やヘアバンドを着けて盛装して参加していたという【9-4c】。

ブグン（コワ）

ブグン（Bugun）は、西カメン県の指定トライブの中では、人口1,432人と少数の

【9-4c】2013年のチンダン祭のイベントで盛装したサジョランのカップル。A couple of the Sajolang, dressed up for the event at the *Chindang* Festival in 2013. (Photograph by T. A. Bodt, Nafra town, November 2013)

第9章 西カメン県のモンパの隣人たちの民族衣装

【9-5】ニンマ派に属する仏教寺院シンチュン・ゴンパ。
Singchung Gompa, a Buddhist temple belonging to the Nyingma school, in the Bugun village of Sinchung. (Singchung, November 2013)

集団である（2011年統計）。コワ（Khowa）とも他称されているが、その名を嫌い、自称はブグンである。居住地は、シンチュン（Singchung）、ジャミリ、ルパ（Rupa）の3つのサークルにある12の村で、北をサルタン、南をフルソ、西をシェルドゥクペン、東をサジョランなどの民族集団に囲

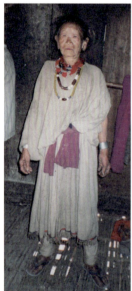

【9-6】1999年に私が会ったこのブグン女性は、この衣服を普段着として着ていた。
This Bugun woman I met in 1999 wore this garment as her daily wear. (In a village near Tenga Market, February 1999)

【9-7a】このブグン女性は、シンチュン・ゴンパでの法要に参加するためにやって来た。
This Bugun woman came to attend a ceremony at Singchung Gompa. (Singchung, November 2013)

【9-7b】同じ女性は、背中に大きなスカーフをマントのように着ている。
The same woman wears a large scarf on her back like a cape. (Singchung, November 2013)

【9-8a】寺院で出会ったブグン女性が、こちらが正式な民族衣装だと着替えてくれた。
A Bugun woman I met at the temple changed her clothes, saying that this was the Bugun's traditional attire for women. (【9-8a】-【9-8c】: Sinchung, November 2013)

【9-8b】彼女の家族の一人も、銀製のヘアバンド、筒状のイヤリング、何重もの首飾りを着けて盛装してくれた。
One of her family members also dressed up, wearing a silver headband, tubular earrings and multiple necklaces.

【9-8c】その上着の背面には三角の布が下がっている。
There is a triangular piece of cloth down the back of the jacket.

まれて暮らしている。サジョランと同様に、動物供犠を伴う儀礼や川・山・樹木などを対象とした自然崇拝などの伝統的な土着信仰を持っていた(12)。

　だが、ブグンが多く住むシンチュンには、近年になって仏教を受け入れた人々も多く、チベット仏教ニンマ派に属する寺院も建てられている【9-5】。また、キリスト教に改宗した人々もいる。

　ブグン女性の伝統的な衣装は、フルソやサジョランとほとんど同じである。1999年に私が初めて出会った年配のブグン女性【9-6】は、エリ・シルクの白い貫頭衣に白い脚絆を履いていたが、これは普段着として着られている様子だった。シンチュン・ゴンパで会った女性【9-7a, 9-7b】は、寺では赤いジャケットを着て、背中に大きなスカーフをマントのように着けていた。このスカーフはイービオウ（ibiow）と呼ばれている。寺には若い女性も来ていたが、この女性のような衣装を着ている人は少なかった。彼女の自宅に招かれて、他の家族

も交えて、盛装してもらった【9-8a, 9-8b, 9-8c】。白い貫頭衣はエリ・シルク製でシンカウ（shingkau）、帯はラトゥン（ratung）、ジャケットはパダック（padak）、銀製のヘアバンドはマトン（matong）、筒状のイヤリングは、ミヘン（mihen）、脚絆はラナ（rana）と呼ぶという。男女ともこの円筒形の脚絆をダムディム・バエ(13)除けのために着けている。

　男性の民族衣装を見る機会はなかったが、パンディ（B. B. Pandey）は、フルソやサジョランと同様で、肩から膝くらいまで一枚布をまとい、帯を締め、下衣は腰巻スタイルで、円筒形の竹の帽子を被ると書いている。金持ちはアッサムのエリ・シルクだが、そうでない人は工場で大量生産された布を使用するという(14)。

シェルドゥクペン

　シェルドゥクペン（Sherdukpen）は、19世紀のイギリス植民地政府の記録では、ルパのブーティア（Bhutia）、シェルガオン（Shergaon）のブーティアなどと記されている。ブーティア、あるいはボーティアは、インド北部に住むチベット文化の影響を受けた人々に対する呼称である。シェルドゥクペンの名前の由来は、シェルガオン、ルパという現存する彼らの2つの居住地名に由来する。チベット統治時代の旧名はシェル（Sher）とトゥクペン（Tukpen）で、住民の民族名はそれぞれセンジ（Senji）とトンジ（Thongji）であった。この2つの地名を組み合わせた名前がシェルドゥクペンとなったが、彼ら自身は、シェルトゥクペンと発音し、シェルガオンの人びとは、モー（Möö）、ルパの人びとはメー（Mee）という自称を好んでいる(15)。

　シェルドゥクペンの名称は、1961年の国勢調査のリストには見られるが、インド独立前の記録には出てこない。1935年にシェルガオンに滞在したイギリスの植物収集家のキングドン・ウォード（F. Kingdon Ward）は、その住民をシェルチョクパ（Sherchokpa）と記し、1939年にチベットとの国境の山ゴリ・チェン（Gori Chen）登頂を目指す旅の途中でルパを訪れたイギリス人のティルマン（H. W. Tilman）も、同じくシェルチョクパと書いている(16)。ブータンでは、東部のツァンラ語を話す人々をシャルチョップ（Sharchop）と呼んでいる。シェルチョクパもシャルチョップも、意味は「東の人」である。だが、シェルドゥクペンの言語は、ツァンラ語とは発生起源的にも近似関係になく、

【9-9】チョスコル祭で民族衣装サペに身を包んだシェルドゥクペンの男性たち。
Sherdukpen men in traditional dress *Sape* at the *Choskor* festival. (Photograph by Neten Dorjee Thongdok, Shergaon, May 2010)

【9-10】このシェルドゥクペンの男性は、仏教寺院のイベントにやって来たが、その帽子には白い花飾りは付いていなかった。
This Sherdukpen man came to an event at a Buddhist temple, but his hat had no white flowers on it. (Rupa, March 2004)

むしろサルタンの言語に近いという(17)。

　シェルドゥクペン男性は、祭りや特別な行事の際には、民族衣装サペ（*sape*）を着る【9-9】。シャルマ（R. R. P. Sharma）によると、サペは、幅1.5ヤード（約137㎝）、長さ2.5ヤード（約228cm）の布で、それを身体の膝下くらいまで巻き付けて両肩で布の端を銀製のピンで留めるスタイルである。寒い時には、腰を覆う長さの長袖のジャケットをサペの上から着て、もう1枚腰巻のスタイルの布を巻くか、時には、ズボンを穿く。

　シェルドゥクペンの帽子はヤクの毛をフェルト状にしたもので、グルダム（*gurdam*）という(18)。ただし、ルパ出身の現在70歳代の男性は、このヤクの毛の帽子をチクパ・グトゥン（*chikpa guthung*）と呼んでいた。グトゥン（*guthung*または*gthung*）は「帽子」を意味し、チクパは「ヤクの毛」を意味するツィパ（*tsitpa*）の彼らの発音である。帽子には、4本の房があり、【9-9】のように、しばしば白い花飾りが付けられていて、周囲をカラフルなテープ状のベルトで囲んでいる。この帽子を被っている人も稀で、私が出会った人たちの帽子には、白い飾りは付いていなかった【9-10】。

　現在の女性の民族衣装は白い貫頭衣で、シンク（*singku*）と呼ばれる。だが、

【9-11a】このシェルドゥクペン女性は、貫頭衣シンクの上に花柄のある上着を着ている。
This Sherdukpen woman wears a floral-patterned jacket over a tunic dress *singku*. (Jigaon, March 2004)

【9-11b】シェルドゥクペン女性のシンクの背面は大きく開いている。
The back of the Sherdukpen women's *singku* is wide open. (Jigaon, March 2004)

モンパやフルソ、サジョラン、ブグンのものと比べると幅が倍ほどあり、かなり広く、正面のギャザーも7〜8本ある。襟の開き方がV字型で、特に背中が大きく開いている。素材はエリ・シルクもあるが、木綿や化学繊維が多い。帯はマカック（*makhak*）と呼ばれ、臙脂色に柄が織り込まれたモンパと同じような布を使っているが、腰当て布はしない【9-11a, 9-11b】。

白い長めの上着を着ることもある。無地のものはリディック（*lidik*）、柄のあるものはリディック・アラン（*lidik aran*）と呼ぶ。アランは、花のことである。寺院の法要などに出かける際には、スナップ（*snap*）と呼ぶ大きなスカーフをマントのように背中に掛ける【9-12】。

だが、1960年に出版されたシャルマの著書には、女性の服は膝丈までで、男性と同じように、ダムディム・バエから守るために布をふくらはぎの周りに着けていたと書かれている。当時の女性の服は、現在のように長くて幅広いものではなかったことが、その本所収の写真からもわかる(19)。

まとめ

以上を総括すると、これらの集団に共通しているのは、男性の衣装が、一枚布で上半身または全身を覆って、肩で留めるスタイルであること、女性の衣装が白い貫頭衣であること、それには腰当て布は着けないこと、男女ともに虫除

【9-12】シェルドゥクペン女性は、寺院での行事などに出かける時には、大きなスカーフをマントのように掛ける。
The Sherdukpen women wear a large scarf over their backs like a cape when they go to the events at temple. (Rupa, March 2004)

【9-13】ニシの民族衣装は、男女ともに一枚布を身体に巻き付ける。
The traditional attire of the Nyishi is a single piece of cloth wrapped around the body for both men and women. (Tago, Lower Subansiri district, November 2012)

けの脚絆を着けていたことなどである。名称は集団によって異なるが、シェルドゥクペン以外は、ほぼ同じような衣服である。各集団の女性の衣装が現在と同じだったかどうかは不明だが、フルソの場合のように、男女とも一枚布をまとっていた時代があったかもしれない。現在、各集団が、それぞれの違いを強調するために服装を微妙に変えている可能性もある。

　モンパのトトゥンに似た臙脂色の上着の起源についてはあまりわかっていない。貫頭衣については、タワンのモンパとブータンのブロクパが、エリ・シルクの貫頭衣以前にはウールの貫頭衣を着ていたことから、より暖かい低地に住む他の集団がモンパとブロクパのエリ・シルクの貫頭衣を真似たのではないかと推測している。素材は、エリ・シルクの他に、イラクサや木綿が使われていた。現在見られる各集団の臙脂色の帯に、モンパとの共通点が見られるが、どの集団が最初に身に着けたのかは不明である。しかし、隣接して暮らす集団が、互いの衣装や装身具を真似たり、自らに取り入れたりすることはごく自然のことなのではないだろうか。

【9-14】一枚布の衣を両肩で結んでいるこのニシ男性には、道端でたまたま出会った。彼の衣装は、2012年に見たものとは、だいぶ着方が異なっている。
In 1995, I happened to meet this Nyishi man by the roadside, who was wearing a single piece of cloth robe tied around both shoulders. He wore the garment differently from the way of wearing it later, in 2012. (Itanagar, March 1995)

【9-15】ブータン女性の国民服、キラ。一枚布を身体に巻き付け、両肩で留める。
Kira, the national dress of Bhutanese women. A single piece of cloth is wrapped around the body and pinned at both shoulders. (Tokyo, April 2022)

【9-16】このブータン南西部のロプ（ドヤ）の男性は、伝統的な衣服パキを着ている。
This Lhop (Doya) man in south-western Bhutan is wearing the traditional garment *pakhi*. (Photograph by Keiko Yamamoto, in a village near Amochu river, Samtse district, Bhutan, December 2002)

　一枚布の民族衣装に焦点を当てると、西カメン県に隣接した東カメン県や他の県に住むニシ族（Nyishi）の民族衣装も、男女ともに一枚布をまとうスタイルである【9-13】。写真【9-14】は、私が1995年にたまたま出会ったニシ男性の服装である。このような服装を、祭り以外の場で、日常的に見ることはほぼなくなった。

　ブータン女性の標準的な民族衣装のキラ（*kira*）も一枚布で身体を覆い、両肩で留めるスタイルだが、各地で織られたカラフルな手織り布である【9-15】。

　だが、ブータン南西部のサムツェ県の少数民族ロプ（Lhop）あるいはドヤ（Doya）と呼ばれる人々の伝統的な服装も一枚布をまとう形である。この服は、

パキ（*pakhi*）[20]と呼ばれる長方形の白い布で、かつてはイラクサの繊維で織られ、現在はインドの綿織物で作られる。首の後ろで結び、後ろで2つのプリーツに折り、ベルトの上にブラウスのようにたるませて、膝丈にする【9-16】。女性の場合は、同じ長さの布を肩で結び、ベルトを締め、足首までの長さにする[21]。

ブータン中央部のトンサ県とワンデュ・ポダン県にまたがるブラック・マウンテンと呼ばれる地域に住むモンパ（Monpa）の男女も、かつてはイラクサで織った類似の一枚布からなる衣服を着ていて、その名称はパゲイ（*pagay*）という[22]。ブラック・マウンテンのモンパには、アルナーチャル・プラデーシュ州のモンパやメンバ、チベットの門巴族との民族集団としての直接的な関係はないと思われる[23]。この地域のモンパの古老は、彼らがブータンにもっとも古くから住んでいて、モンパという呼称は、ブータンの中部、東部の言語の一部で、「古い」という意味のあるマン・パ（man-pa）に由来していると主張しているという[24]。

現在は、ロプ、モンパの二つの集団ともに、民族衣装はブータンの国民服であるゴやキラに同化して、ほぼ失われてきている。

(1) 本章に記した人口は、2011年の国勢調査をもとに作成されたインド部族問題省のデータを使用して計算した。
(2) 各集団の言語や集団の移動の歴史に関しては、[van Driem: 2001]、[Bodt 2012, 2014a, 2014b]、[Lieberherr and Bodt 2017] などの報告がある。
(3) [Sinha 1988 (1962): 4, 30-31]。
(4) [Elwin 1958: 435]。
(5) このハエはブユ（ブヨ）のことで、ダムディム（*damdim*）[Kennedy 1914: 4-5]、[Grewal 1997: 107, 123]、[Dusu 2013: 69] と書いているものと、ディムダム（*dimdam*）[Sinha 1988 (1962): 27]、[Sharma 1988 (1960): 19] と書いているもの、ダムダム（*damdam*）[Pandey 1996: 43] と書いているものなどがある。
(6) [Kennedy 1914: 4-5]。
(7) [Sinha 1988 (1962): 27]。
(8) [Elwin 1959: 7]。
(9) [Dusu 2013: 68]。
(10) [Bodt 2014a: 229]。
(11) [Chaudhuri S. K. 2004: 230]。
(12) [Pandey 1996: 81-82]。
(13) [Pandey 1996: 43]。
(14) [Pandey 1996: 42-43]、および所収の写真による。
(15) [Bodt 2014a: 222]。
(16) [Kingdon-Ward 1941: 18]、[Tilman 2016 (1946): 27]。ティルマン隊の遠征は失敗に終わった。
(17) [Bodt 2014a: 222]。
(18) [Sharma 1988 (1960): 17]。
(19) [Sharma 1988 (1960): 19]。
(20) シャルマ(Sharma B. Deben)は、ロプの衣服をパキではなく、ゴダ（*go-da*）と記述している [Sharma B. D. 2005: 50]。
(21) [Myers 1994: 129]。[山本 2001: 142]。
(22) [Giri 2004: 33-34]。
(23) 彼らの言語は、以前はタワンのモンパと同じく東ボデーシュ語に分類されていたが、古い形だという [van Driem 2001: 918]。その正確な位置付けは未解決のままである。
(24) [Phuntsho 2013: 3]。

CHAPTER 9
Traditional Attires of the Neighbours of the Monpa in West Kameng district

In February 2024, the new Bichom district was created from the eastern part of West Kameng and the western part of East Kameng district. As detailed maps were not yet available and corrections could not be made in time, in this book, when speaking of West Kameng district, it includes parts of what is now called Bichom district.

The Monpa Scheduled Tribe forms the majority ethnic group in Tawang and West Kameng districts of Arunachal Pradesh. The group has a population of 60,525 according to the 2011 census. However, this also includes the Sartang, who were recognised as a separate tribe in August 2021. Ethnic groups other than the Monpa whose main residence is in West Kameng district include the Hruso (Aka), Sajolang (Miji), Bugun (Khowa) and Sherdukpen. All are minority ethnic groups with a population of less than 10,000 that live in areas adjacent to the Monpa[1]. Like the Monpa, they are all the Scheduled Tribes of Arunachal Pradesh. Their settlements are located between 150 m and 1500 m, with hot and rainy summers but mild winters. Some of the traditional costumes of these groups will be shown in this chapter, but due to the short duration of my stay in all the settlements, only superficial observations could be made. As with other groups in Arunachal Pradesh, people's daily wear is increasingly dominated by western clothing, with traditional dress being worn only on special occasions. Some costumes are also no longer seen already. For this reason, I will keep a record of the period from the 1990s to the present. There is existing research on the history of migration and settlement of the various groups and how their languages have progressed, but due to space limitations, I will only briefly describe some of these details in this chapter[2].

The Hruso (Aka)

The people of the plains of Assam called these people *Aka* meaning 'painted', as they had the custom of painting their faces profusely[3]. They refer to themselves as Hruso (also spelled Hrusso)[4] and live in Thrizino, Jamiri and Bhalukpong circles in the south-east of West Kameng district, with a total population of 8,167 (2011 census).

R. S. Kennedy, a British military doctor who visited the area in 1913, described the Aka man's dress as follows: "it consists of the coarse cotton cloth which is wound round his body and pinned over his shoulders with little bamboo pins. The garment is bound round the waist by a cummerbund and below it forms, as it were, a short skirt, which reaches a little below the knees. Over this he wears a jacket, which reaches to the hips. ...They all wear gaiters on their legs as protection against the *damdim* flies (*Simulium indicum*)(5) which abound in their hills". Kennedy also described the Aka woman's dress as being "is similar to that worn by men, except that it reaches almost to the ankles and is often Assamese silk. She wears jacket of Assamese silk, rather longer than a man's jacket. Her hair is invariably tied at the back of the head. Round her head, a well to do Aka woman wears a very striking and pretty fillet of silver chain work. In her ears are large vase-shaped silver earrings, while innumerable necklaces of coloured beads encircle her neck. ...As a rule, the women wear gaiters just like those worn by men"(6).

According to a book by Raghuvir Shinha, published in 1962, men traditionally wear a small garment, that hangs below the shoulders, and covers the upper body. Men also wear a kind of long coat which hangs from the shoulders to the knees, and on special occasions they wear cylindrical bamboo hats, called *musarga*. Sinha also described that women wear a long garment over the body which hangs from the shoulders up to the ankles. It is longer than the men's garment, and is usually coloured dark red. However, the women's dress in the photographs in his book appears to be white, although they are monochrome. Sinha also described that men and women wear cylindrical lower leg covers (*gudu*) covering their calves, which is said to protect their skin from insects(7).

A drawing of Tagi Raja and his brother by John Butler in 1847 shows that these lower leg covers were fashionable with pleated decorations(8). The man in the photo [9-1a], taken in 2012, is wearing a hat similar to the one worn by Tagi Raja in this drawing. According to Dusu Sambyo, the silver hat called wagha was initially worn by the aristocrats(9).

The photo 【9-1b】 was taken at the same time as 【9-1a】. The women wear silver headbands as reported by Kennedy, but instead of a single piece of cloth, they wear a white tunic dress. Women's traditional attire as I saw it in Jamiri village in 2013 consists of a white *eri* silk or cotton tunic dress called *wusoge* and a dark red jacket called *sashopol*, similar to the *tothung* of the Monpa. Her jacket had a collar 【9-2a】. They wear a variety of ornaments, including silverware, but the large silver necklace in the centre of the picture is called *melu* and the silver headband above it is called *lentsi* 【9-2b】.

These costumes are now only worn during festivals and events.

The Sajolang (Miji)

The tribe name 'Miji' is the name given by the Hruso, meaning 'the ones who gave fire'. The language of the Miji is said to be divided into at least three distinct groups: Sajolang in Nafra Circle, Dhammai or Dimmai in Jamiri Circle and Namrai for the people in neighbouring East Kameng District(10). The total population of the Miji was 8,127 according to the 2011 census, slightly less than the Hruso population.

In November 2004, I had the opportunity to observe a ritual called *Chindang* being performed in the Upper Dzang village in Nafra Circle. *Chin* means worship and dang means offerings of sacrifices(11). It takes place every year between October and December, with the date and time determined by a fortune-teller. The ritual is a traditional ceremony in which animals are sacrificed to the deities of the sun, moon, mountains, and rivers. These are offered for a good harvest and to exorcise the evil spirits. The man who officiates wears the traditional *grey mongdong*, a costume wrapping of a single piece of white cloth, with a pair of cylindrical lower leg covers called *lailo* and a cylindrical bamboo cap called *shupotang* on his head. He wears a beaded necklace (*vulo*) 【9-3a】. He may have been a Gaon Burah (village head), as his red jacket looks like those worn by Gaon Burah in various parts of Arunachal Pradesh. In recent years, an increasing number of the Miji people are converting to Christianity and Buddhism.

Other than a boy who was wearing a woman's costume and a silver headband 【9-3b】, I saw no women. During the Indian Independence Day ceremony in Bomdila on 15th August 2005, traditional dances of various tribal groups were performed. At the ceremony, I saw the traditional costume worn by the Sajolang girls. They were wearing white tunic dress called the *gibulung* 【9-4a】, which has the same shape as the Monpa's *shingka*, and over this they wore a red jacket called *sashori panglho* 【9-4b】. This jacket is also similar to the Monpa's *tothung* but it is made of synthetic fibres rather than *eri* silk, and the pattern is larger and more colourful than the Monpa version. The *gibulung* also appeared to be made of cotton or synthetic fibres. They wore yellow, blue, reddish-brown, and white beaded necklaces with layers of beads around their necks. In formal dress, women wear silver headbands, but the dancers did not wear headbands at this time. According to a friend of mine, many men and women wore hats and headbands at the *Chindang* festival event in November 2013 【9-4c】.

The Bugun (Khowa)

The Bugun is a small Scheduled Tribe in West Kameng district with a population of 1,432 (2011 census). The Bugun are also known by the exonym Khowa, but they don't like this name and refer to themselves as Bugun. They live in 12 villages in three circles: Singchung, Jamiri and Rupa, and are surrounded by the Sartang in the north, the Hruso in the south, the Sherdukpen in the west and the Sajolang in the east. Like the Sajolang, they uphold indigenous practices such as rituals involving animal sacrifices and nature worship of rivers, mountains, and trees(12). However, many people in Singchung, where the majority of the Buguns live, have embraced Buddhism in recent years, and several temples belonging to the Nyingma school of Tibetan Buddhism have also been built 【9-5】. Some of the Bugun people converted to Christianity too.

The traditional dress of the Bugun women is almost the same as that of the Hruso and the Sajolang. The elderly Bugun woman I first met in 1999 wore a white tunic dress of *eri* silk and white cylindrical lower leg covers, which seemed to be worn as casual wear 【9-6】. A woman I met the temple at Singchung wore a red jacket and a large scarf on her back like a cape 【9-7a, 9-7b】. This scarf is called an *ibiow*. Young women also came to the temple, but only a few were wearing a dress like this woman. I was invited to her home, and she dressed up with other family members 【9-8a, 9-8b, 9-8c】. The white tunic dress is made of *eri* silk and called *shingkau*, the sashes are called *ratung*, the jackets are called *padak*, the silver head bands are called *matong*, the tubular earrings are called *mihen* and the cylindrical lower leg covers are called *rana*. Both men and women still wear these lower leg covers to protect the legs from *damdim* flies(13).

Although I did not have the opportunity to see the men's traditional dress, B.B. Pandey writes that they wear a single piece of cloth from the shoulders to about the knees, and a sash, that the lower garment is in a loincloth style and that they wear a cylindrical hat, similar to the Hruso and Sajolang. The rich people wear Assamese eri silk, while the rest use mass-produced cloth from factories(14).

The Sherdukpen

The Sherdukpen are described in 19th century British colonial government records and are called the Bhutia of Rupa and the Bhutia of Shergaon. Bhutia or Bhotia is a designation for the people of northern India that are influenced by Tibetan culture. The name Sherdukpen is derived from the names of their two existing settlements, Shergaon and Rupa. During the Tibetan rule, their Tibetan names were Sher and Tukpen, while their endonyms are Senji and Thongji, respectively. The name Sherdukpen combines the two place names as Sherdukpen, which they themselves pronounce as Shertukpen, and they prefer to call themselves Möö in Shergaon and Mee in Rupa(15). The name Sherdukpen appears in the 1961 census list but does not appear in pre-independence records of India. F. Kingdon Ward, a British plant collector who stayed in Shergaon in 1935, called its inhabitants Sherchokpa. H. W. Tilman, a British mountaineer who visited Rupa in 1939 on a journey to the summit of Mt. Gori Chen, on the border with Tibet, also referred to the inhabitants as Sherchokpa(16). In Bhutan, the Tshangla-speaking people of the east are known as Sharchop. Both Sherchokpa and Sharchop mean 'easterner'. However, the origin and settlement history of the Sherdukpen is distinct from the Tshangla speaking groups and their language is not closely related to the Tshangla language in terms of origin or proximity but it is rather closer to the language of the Sartang(17).

Today the Sherdukpen men rarely wear their traditional costume, the sape, except during festivals and special occasions 【9-9】. According to R. R. P. Sharma, the *sape* is a piece of cloth 1.5 yards (about 137 cm) wide and 2.5 yards (about 228 cm) long, which is wrapped around the body to just below the knees and fastened at both shoulders with silver pins at the cloth ends. In cold weather, a long-sleeved jacket covering the waist is worn over the *sape*, and another piece of cloth in the style of a loincloth is wrapped around the body. Sometimes trousers are worn instead.

The Sherdukpen hats are made of felted yak hair and are called *gurdam*(18). However, a man from Rupa, now in his 70s, referred to this yak hair hat at as *chikpa guthung*. *Guthung* or *gthung* means 'hat', *chikpa* is their pronunciation of *tsitpa* 'yak hair'. Each hat has four tassels, often with a decoration of white flowers, and is surrounded by a colourful taped belt. The hats of those people I met did not have white decorations 【9-10】.

The current traditional attire of women is a white tunic dress. It is called *singku*. However, it is twice as wide as those of the Monpa, Hruso, Sajolang and Bugun, and has seven or eight pleats in the front. The collar has a V-shaped opening, especially at the back. The material used for the dress is often cotton or synthetic fibres, although *eri* silk is also used. The belt is called *makhak* and is made of a dark red cloth with a pattern woven into it, similar to the Monpa's belt, but they don't wear a back apron 【9-11a, 9-11b】.

Sometimes women wear a white jacket. A plain one is called *lidik*, while a patterned one is called *lidik aran*. *Aran* means flower. When going to temple services, a large scarf, called a *snap*, is draped over the back like a cape 【9-12】.

However, Sharma's book, first published in 1960, states that women's clothes were knee-length, and like men, they wore cloth around their calves to protect them from the *damdim* flies. The photographs in the book show that women's clothes then were not as long and broad as they are today(19).

Conclusion

In summary, what these groups have in common is that the men's attire is a single piece of cloth covering the upper body or the whole body fastened at the shoulders while the women's attire is a white tunic dress, without a back apron. Both men and women wore cylindrical lower leg covers to protect against insects. Although the names vary across the different groups, the garments are almost identical. It is not known whether the women's attire of the various groups was the same in the past as they are today, but there may have been a time when both men and women wore a single piece of cloth, as is the case with the Hruso. It is possible that currently each group might be making subtle changes in their attire to emphasise the differences between the different groups.

Not much is known about the origin of the dark red jackets similar to the Monpa's *tothung*. In terms of the tunic dress, the Monpa in Tawang and the Brokpa in Bhutan wore woollen tunics before *eri* silk ones, and I speculate that other groups living in the lower warm lands may have adopted the Monpa and Brokpa's tunics. The materials used were nettles and cotton as well as eri silk. The similarities with the Monpa dress items can be seen in the deep-red sashes of the various groups seen today, but it is not known which group wore them first. However, it may be quite natural for groups living adjacent to each other to copy and adopt each other's costumes and accessories.

Speaking of single-piece traditional attires, both men and women of the Nyishi tribe in the neighbouring district of East Kameng and many other districts of Arunachal Pradesh also wear a single piece of cloth 【9-13】 Photo 【9-14】 shows the dress of a Nyishi man I happened to meet in 1995. At present, it is almost impossible to see this kind of dress worn on a daily basis other than during festivals.

The *kira*, the standard national costume of Bhutanese women, also covers the body with a single piece of cloth and fastens at both shoulders, but it is a colourful hand-woven cloth woven in different regions 【9-15】.

However, the traditional dress of the Lhop or Doya minority people of Samtse district in south-western Bhutan is also in the form of a single piece of cloth. This garment is a rectangular white cloth called *pakhi*[20], once woven from nettle fibre and now made from Indian cotton fabric. It is tied behind the neck, folded into two pleats at the back, and sagged like a blouse over a belt to make it knee-length. For women, the same length of cloth is tied at the shoulders and belted to ankle length[21] 【9-16】.

Monpa men and women living in the area known as the Black Mountains, an area which straddles Trongsa and Wangdue Phodrang districts in central Bhutan, also used to wear garments made of a similar single piece of cloth woven from nettles, known as *pagay*[22]. The Monpa of the Black Mountains[23] have no direct affiliation with the Monpa or Memba of Arunachal Pradesh or the Menba of Tibet. According to Karma Phuntsho, some Monpa elders in the region claim that they are the earliest inhabitants of the country and argue that the word Monpa comes from man pa, the word for 'old' in some central and eastern Bhutanese languages[24].

Today, both the Lhop and the Monpa people in Bhutan have changed their traditional attires and their old garments are rarely worn. Their subcultures have been assimilated into the larger Bhutanese culture. Many of the Lhop and Monpa people in Bhutan now were the national dress, the go and *kira*.

(1) The populations noted in this chapter were calculated using data from the Ministry of Tribal Affairs of India, based on the 2011 census.
(2) There are reports on the language of each group and the history of group migration, including [van Driem: 2001], [Bodt 2012, 2014a, 2014b] and [Lieberherr and Bodt 2017].
(3) [Shinha 1988 (1962): 4, 30-31].
(4) [Elwin 1958: 435].
(5) This fly is a gnat, written as *damdim* [Kennedy 1914: 4-5], [Grewal 1997: 107, 123], [Dusu 2013: 69], and *dimdam* [Sinha 1988 (1962): 27] [Sharma 1988 (1962): 19] and some wrote as *damdam* [Pandey 1996: 43].
(6) [Kennedy 1914:4-5].
(7) [Sinha (1962) 1988: 27].
(8) [Elwin 1959:7].
(9) [Dusu 2013: 68].
(10) [Bodt 2014a: 229].
(11) [Chaudhuri S. K. 2004: 230].
(12) [Pandey 1996: 81-82].
(13) [Pandey 1996: 43].
(14) [Pandey 1966: 42-43] and photographs in the same book.
(15) [Bodt 2014a: 222].
(16) [Kingdon-Ward 1941: 18], [Tilman 1946 (2016): 27]. The Tilman expedition was unsuccessful.
(17) [Bodt 2014a: 222].
(18) [Sharma 1988 (1960): 17].
(19) [Sharma 1988 (1960): 19].
(20) Sharma B. Deben describes Lop garments as *go-da*, not *pakhi* [Sharma B. D. 2005: 50].
(21) [Myers 1994: 129], [Yamamoto 2001: 142].
(22) [Giri 2004: 33-34].
(23) Their language was earlier classified as an East Bodish language, like the Monpa of Tawang, but is an older form [van Driem 2001: 918]. Its exact position remains unresolved.
(24) [Phuntsho 2013: 3].

CHAPTER 10
Handmade Papermaking in Tawang

第10章 タワンの手漉き紙作り

　これまで民族衣装について書いてきたが、アルナーチャル・プラデーシュ州タワン県のモクトウ（Mukto）で、モンパの人々によって現在も続く手漉き紙作りについても書き加えておこうと思う。

　モンパの紙作りについては、西カメン県のシェルガオン近くで取材された1959年の記録がある(1)。また、最近まで、モクトウ以外のタワンの町の周辺でも紙漉きが行われていたと聞く。一方、農政部門の役所の支援を受けて、ディラン・サークルのチュグ村で、2021年から女性たちによる紙作りが始まっているという話を耳にした。技術を指導したのは、もともとタワン出身の人だという。

　モンパの人びと以外では、州東部のナムサイ県のタイ・カムティ族も手漉き紙を漉いていたというが、詳細は不明である(2)【10-1a, 10-1b】。

　他にも、現在、紙漉きを行っている人々がいるかもしれないが、州内で長年にわたり伝統的な手

【10-1a】タイ・カムティ、シンボー博物館兼研究センターに陳列されている、手漉き紙に書かれた文書類。Documents written on handmade paper displayed at the Tai Khamti-Singpho Museum-cum-Research-Center. (Chongkham, Namsai, January 2020)

【10-1b】タイ・カムティの手漉き紙は、このインドワタの木と呼ばれるキワタ科の高木 (学名 Bombex ceiba) の樹皮から作るという。
The raw material for the handmade paper of the Tai Khamti was said to be the bark of this tall tree, Indian cotton tree (Bombex ceiba). (Chongkham, Namsai, January 2020)

漉き紙製作を続けているのは、恐らくモクトウの人々だけであろう。

私が初めてモクトウの手漉き紙を目にしたのは、1999年にタワンのクラフト・センターを訪ねた時だった。その時に購入した紙は、知人の日本画家が、そ

【10-2】谷の南向きの斜面に建てられた紙漉き小屋。
Papermaking huts built on the south-facing slope of the valley.
(Langateng, Mukto, January 2013)

れに水墨画を描いたところ、少しざらざらした質感だが、墨によくなじむ紙だとの評価だった。ただし、紙にゴミのようなものが混じっていたり、薄さが均一でなかったりするものもあり、隣国のブータンのものと比べると、品質としては劣る。だが、何よりもその値段の安さに驚いた。1枚当たり2ルピー（当時日本円で約6円）ほどだった。2024年4月時点では1枚20ルピー（現在約38円）だが、物価の変動と比べると決して高価ではない。

しかし、タワンの人々ですら、この手漉き紙がどのように作られているかを知る人は少ない。モクトウ村は、タワンの町の中心地から南東約60 kmの地点に位置する。道路は山道で、以前は片道3時間かかったが、道路整備が進んだ現在は、2時間以内で着けるようになっている。

モクトウ村の外れ、地元住民だけが通行できるインドとブータンの境界地点の一つであるニンサン・ラ（Ningsang La）に向かうと、紙漉き小屋が点在するランガテン（Langateng）という場所がある【10-2】。2013年には、ランガテンとその東の山腹に合計11軒の小屋があった。手伝いの家族が来る小屋もあるが、ほとんどの小屋のオーナーは、一人ですべての工程をこなしていた。11軒の中には、女性が一人で作業している小屋が4軒含まれていた。2024年4月現在も11軒の紙漉き小屋があったが、そのうち毎日作業をしているのは、3軒のみであった。

手漉き紙の用途

モクトゥでの紙作りがいつ頃始まったのかはわかっていないが、1930年代生まれの人々の中に、祖父から紙漉きを習ったという人がいるので、1800年代にはすでに紙漉きが行われていたと思われる。モンパが漉く紙は、かつてはチベットとの交易品であった。2013年現在、ランガテンで紙漉きを続けていた1937年生まれのリンチン・カンドゥ【10-3】と、1939年生まれのソナム・ワンチュの二人も、1962年の中印国境紛争以前には、しばしばチベットのツォナ（錯那）に紙を売りに行っていたと語っていた。

チベットやその隣接地域における手漉き紙の用途は、主として文書や仏教経典用である【10-4】。経典に使う場合は、1枚では薄すぎるので、何枚かを小麦粉で作った糊で貼り合わせて厚くする。大小の円筒形のマニ車の中に収める「オム・マニ・ペメ・フム」という真言をプリントした紙の場合は、紙の端を糊付けして長い巻紙にする【10-5】。リンチン・カ

【10-3】2013年現在、リンチン・カンドゥ（1937-2016）は最高齢の紙漉き人だった。
In 2013, Rinchin Khandu (1937-2016) was the eldest papermaker. (Langateng, October 2013)

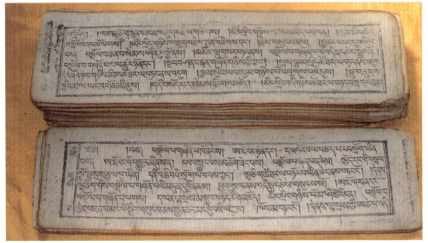

【10-4】手漉き紙に印刷された文書。
Documents printed on handmade paper. (Tawang, December 2011)

【10-5】古くなって一部が破れたマニ車。真言の書かれた巻紙が見える。Old, partially torn mani wheel. A handmade paper scroll with mantras is visible. (Old Dirang, July 2012)

【10-6】祈りを込めてファンを吊るす。白いファンは、手漉き紙製、カラフルなものは大量生産の紙。Hanging *phan* flags with prayers. White *phan* flags are made of handmade paper; colourful ones are made of mass-produced paper. (Mukto, January 2013)

【10-7】手漉き紙で作られた旗、ケーラー・ファン。*Ke lha phan*. (Seru, Tawang, January 2013)

ンドゥによると、ブータンのタシガン県ポンメから寺のマニ車用に2400枚の大量注文が入り、馬で運びに来たことがあるという。後述するように、東ブータンのタシ・ヤンツェ県でも紙漉きが行われているが、値段はモクトウのもののほうが安い(3)。

　他に、モンパの居住地でよく見かけるのが、この紙を切って細い短冊を作り、糸で木の枝に括り付けた旗「ファン（*phan*）」である【10-6】。健康や長寿、家内安全、就職などを祈願するのが目的である。タワンでは、他にもある特定の地域で生まれたすべての人々を守る土地の守り神ケー・ラー（*ke lha*）に供えるケー・ラー・ファン【10-7】や、家庭の安全を祈願する儀礼の際に供える小さな紙製の傘などに用いられている【10-8】。いずれも、信仰や宗教と切り離せ

ないものである。しかし、10年ほど前から便箋や封筒などの商品化を試みる人が現れている。自家用のプリンターでこの紙に印刷することも可能だからである【10-9】。だが、紙を裁断する機器も印刷所もないタワンの場合、すべてアッサムへ持って行って商品を作らなければならず、利益をもたらすビジネスとして成立するためには課題が多い。

作業小屋・原材料・作業工程

モクトウの村の中心地の平均標高は2,385 mで、そこから約100 m下がった谷間の南向きの斜面がランガテンである。このあたりは、タワン県の他の地域に比べ、標高が低く、温暖なので、野外作業に適している。水道はないが、山から湧き出る水をビニール製の管で作業小屋まで引いている。ランガテンそのものは、村の所有地で、誰もが無料でこの土地を利用して紙漉きができる。

彼らの自宅はモクトウ村の中心部にあるので、メインの紙漉き小屋は、雨風をしのげるだけの簡素なものである。小屋には、原料や出来上がった紙を保存したりするスペースと、原料を煮るかまどがある。外には、屋根だけを覆った小さな紙漉き場と紙を天日干しにするスペースがある。多くの紙漉き人は、100 ㎡前後の土地を確保している。

紙漉き場には、地面を掘って作ったコンクリート製の水槽

【10-8】儀礼に使われた粉をこねて作った人形と紙の傘。
A dough figure and a paper umbrella used in rituals. (Tawang, January 2013)

【10-9】モクトウの手漉き紙から作られた便箋と封筒だが、まだあまり出回っていない。
Letterheads and an envelope made from handmade paper of Mukto. These products are not yet widely available. (Tawang, October 2013)

【10-10】リンチン・カンドゥの仕事場、彼の死後、息子の妻が紙漉きを続けている。
Rinchin Khandu's worksite. Since his death, his son's wife has continued to make paper. (Langateng, October 2013)

【10-11】タワン周辺でよく見かけるジンチョウゲ。Common daphne around Tawang. (Langateng, March 2009)

（漉き舟）ショー・カン（*sho kang*）があり、雨除けのためにトタン屋根で覆われている。この紙漉き場は、シュグ・チュカン（*shug chukhang*）と呼ばれている【10-10】。

紙は近くに自生するジンチョウゲ科（学名*Thymelaeaceae*）のジンチョウゲ属の植物（学名*Daphne papyracea*）【10-11】の樹皮から作られる。タワンのモンパは、この植物を「紙の木」を意味するシュグ・シェン（*shug sheng*）と呼ぶ。チベット語では、ショク・シン（*shog shing*）と呼ばれるが、1902年に発行されたチャンドラ・ダース（S. Chandra Das）著の『蔵英辞書』には、「ダフネ、その樹皮から紙を作る植物」と説明されている(4)。ジンチョウゲ科ミツマタ属の植物（学名*Edgeworthia chrysantha*）もやはりショク・シンと呼ばれている。ジンチョウゲ科の植物には多くの種類があるが、本章では、ジンチョウゲ属の植物を総称してダフネと書く。

ダフネは、紙漉き人が自ら近くの共有林へ行って採集することもあるが、高齢で採集作業がきつい場合には、採集したものを他人から譲り受け、漉いた紙の半分を渡すという。このシステムを現地の言葉でグランマ（*grangma*）というが、製品や収穫物を「分かち合う」シェアリング・システムのことだという。

【10-12】ダフネの外皮を削って、靱皮を取り出す。
Removing the outer skin of the daphne and taking out the bast. (Langateng, March 2009)

田畑の耕作を他人に任せた時に、その収穫物を土地の所有者と耕作者とで半分ずつ分け合うなど、農業や牧畜などにもさまざまな例がある。紙漉き人の場合には、元気なうちは、自分で原料を採集に出かけるが、年老いたら、たとえ収入が半分になっても他人の力を借りて原料を供給してもらうことによって紙漉きを継続してゆけるのである。

　ダフネは、3月に採集すると最も外皮をむきやすいという。彼らが採集するのは、樹齢5〜6年の幹である。私は、2003年から2023年までの間、モクトウに行くたびに紙漉きを見学してきたが、工程はどこの紙漉き小屋もほぼ同じで、変化はない。

　以下が、ランガテンの紙漉きの行程である。

① ダフネの外皮を小刀で削り、靱皮（内皮）だけにする。それを2日間天日に干して乾かす【10-12】。
② 灰を作るために薪を燃やしてできた木灰に水を入れて濾す。灰は、1回しか使えないが、良い木の灰であれば、それを家庭の囲炉裏で出た灰など他の灰に混ぜて使うこともある。良い灰を作るための木の選定は、大変重要である。良い灰が得られるのは、樫の木の中の3種類だという【10-13】。
③ 乾かした靱皮を流水で洗い、ゴミや色のついた部分を取り除く。さらに水に浸して柔らかくし、できるだけ細かく切る。
④ 大鍋に水を満たし柄杓一杯分の木灰を入れ、靱皮を煮る。人によって、2時間、4時間、一晩と、時間には差がある【10-14】。
⑤ 煮た靱皮を平らな石の台の上に置き、木槌ルイ・トン（*rui tong*）で叩いてペースト状にし、直径20 cm、厚さ10 cmほどの円筒状の塊を作る。大鍋1杯分の靱皮から8個ぐらいの紙料の塊ができる。8個作るには4時間かかる。強い力

を込めて何度も叩くこの作業が紙漉きの工程の中でもっとも重労働だという【10-15】。

⑥ 地面に掘って作ったコンクリート製の長方形の漉き舟ショー・カン（*sho kang*）に水が張ってある。その上に、木枠に蚊帳用のナイロン製の網を張った漉き桁ショー・シェン（*sho sheng*）を浮かべ、その上に小さな竹籠に入れた紙料を竹製の紙料攪拌用の道具ショク・ボル（*shok bor*）を使って溶かし入れ、手で漉き桁に均一に広げて漉き上げる。平均的なサイズは、漉き舟が縦100 cm、横80 cm、漉き桁の内径は縦65 cm×横50 cmである【10-16a, 10-16b, 10-16c】。

⑦ 小屋の周りの日当たりの良い場所に漉き桁を棒に立てかけて天日で紙を乾燥させる。晴れていれば6時間から7時間で乾くが、曇りの日には10時間以上かかる。雨季には小屋の中の焚火で干すこともあるが、その場合には、紙に煙の臭いが残る。乾いたら1枚ずつ剥がす【10-17】。

　平均すると1日で100枚を漉くことができるという。作業に使われる道具は、すべて手作りのシンプルなものである【10-18】。

　この紙漉き法は、日本でも一般的に行われている溜め漉き法(5)（dipping

【10-13】木灰を入れた缶に水を入れて濾す。
Straining the wood ash with water. (【10-13】–【10-15】 Langateng, October 2013)

【10-14】大鍋に水を満たし、柄杓一杯分の濾した木灰を入れ、その中で靱皮を煮る。
Filling a large pot with water, adding a ladleful of strained wood ash, and boiling the bast.

【10-15】煮て柔らかくなった紙料を木槌で叩いてペースト状にする。この工程が肉体的に最もきつい。
The boiled and softened pulp is beaten with a mallet to make a paste. This is the most physically demanding process.

第10章　タワンの手漉き紙作り　245

method）とは異なっている。溜め漉き法の場合には、漉き舟の中に紙料を入れて、その中に漉き桁を沈めて紙料を均等にすくい上げる。この漉き桁には、竹ひごや葦を編んで作った漉き簀（す）が乗せられている。

世界各地の製紙法を調査したハンター（Dard Hunter）は、上から紙料を入れる前者の方法を流し込み型（pouring type）(6) と呼び、日本やインドのカシミール、そしてベンガル地方で一般的な溜め漉き法とは異なる、タイ、ミャンマー、ネパール、ブータン、チベットにある原始的な技法だとしている(7)。

【10-16a】漉き舟の上に漉き桁を置き、その上から小さな竹籠に入れた紙料を溶かしながら入れる。
The mould is kept floating in a vat. In a small basket, the pulp is dissolved with a churning stick and then poured into the mould.
（【10-16a】〜【10-16c】 Langateng, March 2009）

【10-16b】漉き桁の上に溶かし入れた紙料を手で均一に広げる。
Spreading the dissolved pulp evenly over the mould by hand.

【10-16c】紙料を均一に広げた漉き桁を漉き上げる。
Straining the water from the mould with the pulp spread evenly.

溜め漉き法の場合は、漉き簀から紙を剥がして重ねて水分を切り、後で乾燥させるが、流し込み型の場合には、漉き桁ごと乾燥させるので、1枚につき1枚の漉き桁が必要になる。

実は、かつては、ランガテンでも溜め漉き法が行われていたという。2013年当時、最長老のリンチン・カンドゥの話では、彼が紙漉きを始めた1970年代に短期間溜め漉き法が残っていたが、やがて流し込み型に変わっていったという。ランガテンの溜め漉き法は、竹ひごを編んだ竹の漉き簀を使い、木の板

の上に紙を重ね、その上に板を乗せて重さが平均になるように石を置いて水を切るというやり方だったという。この方法だと厚い紙を漉くことができるが、板や岩の上など1枚ずつの紙を乾かす場所が必要になるので、漉き桁を立てかけて乾かす現在の流し込み型の方が便利だという。

ブータンの手漉き紙

モクトウで行われているのと同様の製法による紙漉きは、ネパール(8)、シッキム(9)、ブータンなどを含む、ヒマラヤ南麓の地域に存在し、一部は現在も継続されている。その紙は、シッキム、ブータン、タワン県や西カメン県一帯のモン地方から来ているため、チベット語ではしばしば「モンの紙」を意味する、モン・ショク（*mon shog*）と呼ばれている(10)。ブータンのゾンカ語では手漉き紙をジンチョウゲ科の植物デーシン（*deshing*）から作る紙という意味で、デーショ（*desho*）と呼んでいる。

ブータンでは、紙は政府に対して税として納められるものの一つで、かつチベットへの重要

【10-17】紙は漉き桁の上で天日に干される。
The paper is dried in the sun within the mould. (Langateng, October 2013)

【10-18】紙漉きに使う小道具はすべて手作りである。上段左は、紙料を入れる籠（ショクツァク）、右は靱皮を叩くための石の台（グドーまたはショー・ドゥン・ドー）、その下は木槌（ルイ・トンまたはショー・トン）、白いプラスチックの容器は、1枚分の紙料を入れる小さな竹籠（ショー・ボル・ションバ）の代用品である。その右は、鍋の中の紙料をかき回すための棒（ショー・ギャ）、棒の先が割れている竹の道具は、紙1枚分の紙料を両手で撹拌するための（ショー・ボル）、その右は竹製のトング（ショク・カンプ）である。
All the small tools for paper making are handmade. In the upper row, left, is a basket for keeping pulp (*shok-tsak*); to the right is a flat stone for beating bast (*gudo* or *sho-dung do*); below it is a wooden mallet (*rui-tong* or *sho-tong*); the white plastic container is a substitute for a small bamboo basket for the pulp for one sheet of paper (*sho-bor-shomba*). To the right is a stick for stirring the pulp in the pot (*sho-gya*), the bamboo tool with the split end of the stick is for churning the pulp with both hands (*sho-bor*) and to the right is a pair of bamboo tongs (*shok kamp*). (Langateng, October 2013)

な輸出品の一つでもあった。そのため、過去には、多くの家庭が紙漉きをしていた。

ブータンの伝統的な紙漉きについては、今枝由郎が1989年に書いた英文の報告が参考になる(11)。当時、ブータンの紙漉き職人は、工房を持たず、各地を転々として、きれいな渓流が流れ、近くに紙の原料となる木が生い茂る場所に工房を構えていたという【10-19】。彼らは2種類の低木を使用した。一つは、ゾンカ語で「黒いダフネの木」と呼ばれるジンチョウゲ属のデーシン・ナプ（*deshing nap*）で、もう一つは「白いダフネの木」と呼ばれるミツマタ属のデーシン・カプ（*deshing kap*）である。

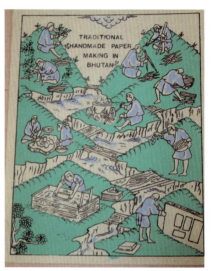

【10-19】ブータンで売られていた、手漉き紙作りの工程を描いたグリーティングカード。
A greeting card depicting the process of handmade papermaking sold in Bhutan. (Thimphu, early 2000s)

漉き桁の上から紙料を流し込む方法の場合、この漉き桁には木綿の布が張られているため、縦糸と横糸が紙に模様として残るので、レショ（*resho*）「木綿布の紙」と呼ばれる。一方、漉き舟に溜めた水に紙料を溶かし入れ、漉き簀をその中に水平に浸して漉き上げる溜め漉き法の場合には、漉き簀には、竹ひごを編んだものが使われる。こうして漉かれた紙は、ツァルショ（*tsharsho*）「竹の紙」と呼ばれる。この方法は、チベットでは見られないという(12)。ツァルショの場合には、厚手の紙を漉くことができる。

現在のブータンでは、ティンプーにある紙漉き工房で、日本の技術指導による溜め漉き法が用いられている。紙を重ねて圧縮して水を切る機械や、ヒーターを使って電動で紙を乾燥する機械などが導入されている。この工房では、日本語でネリと呼ばれる、トロロアオイ（学名*Abelmoschus manifoto*）の根の粘液も使っている。ネリは、紙料が水槽の底に沈むことを防ぎ、均等に分散させ、出来上がりをきれいにするものである。ネリは、また、乾燥される前の重ねられた紙を1枚ずつ剥がしやすくする。

島根県浜田市三隅町は、1969年に日本の重要無形文化財に指定され、2009

年にはユネスコの「人類の無形文化遺産の代表的な一覧表」に記載された手漉き和紙「石州半紙」の産地である。町は、1986年以来、ブータン政府の要請を受けて研修生を受け入れる一方、専門家を送って技術指導を行い、製紙機材を供与するなどの国際協力事業を行ってきた。

日本国際協力機構（JICA）も、三隅町から和紙技術の専門家を派遣している。首都ティンプーにある紙漉き工房の一つは、かつて三隅町で研修を受けた人がオーナーとなり、一部は機械の供与も受けて品質も向上し、順調な運営を続けているという。久保田彰は、三隅町で紙漉き工房を営む熟練紙漉き職人の一人である。彼は研修生の指導やブータンでの指導の経験がある。彼の報告書によると、ブータン政府は伝統的な手漉き紙製作を産業化し、世界市場で通用する品質に高めたいと強く望んでいて、日本からの協力は、それに応えたものであるという(13)。外国人観光客が土産にできるように、レターセットやノート、バッグをはじめ、さまざまな製品が生みだされ、ティンプーの工房は、観光客で賑わっている。

【10-20】東ブータンのツァルショ作り。背後に三角錐の乾燥機が置かれている。
Tsharsho making in eastern Bhutan. A triangular pyramid paper dryer is placed behind.
(【10-20】-【10-22】Bumdeling, October 2014)

【10-21】多くの工房には、紙料の繊維を叩解する機械がある。
Many workshops have machines for beating the pulp to separate the fibres.

【10-22】ブータンでもレショの場合には、流し込み型の製法が用いられ、漉き桁ごと紙を干す。
In eastern Bhutan, the pouring method is also used in the case of *resho*, where the paper is dried inside the moulds.

一方、東ブータンのタシ・ヤンツェ県ブムデリン周辺では、現在も、伝統的な流し込み型による紙作りが行われている。ここで技術指導をした経験を持つ久保田によると、レショ紙製造の注意点として、山水を利用するため、水に不純物が混入しやすいので、それを防ぐこと、原料のダフネを腐らせないように風通しの良い高床で保管すること、原料に付着しているゴミなどをよく取り除くことなどが必要だという(14)。

【10-23】ブータンでは、聖俗を問わず、昇進祝いなどさまざまな祝い事の際に友人たちが贈答品を持ち寄る。それらは手漉き紙で包装されている。
In Bhutan, friends, both religious and secular, bring gifts for various celebrations such as promotions. They are wrapped in handmade paper. (Thimphu, October 2014)

私がブムデリンの工房のいくつかを訪ねた際に見たレショの紙漉きの工程は、モクトウとほぼ同じだが、ツァルショを漉いている工房もあった。水道水を使える場所もあり、紙料を叩いて繊維を潰す機械やツァルショを乾燥させるパネル式の機械のある工房もあった。電力が安定的に供給されていることと、個人の機械購入にも政府の援助があることが、モクトウとの

【10-24】タワンのクラフト・センターの棚に置かれて売られているモクトウの手漉き紙。
Handmade paper from Mukto sold on the shelves of Craft Centre of Tawang. (Tawang, October 2013)

大きな違いである【10-20, 10-21, 10-22】。

　ブータンには、13の芸術・工芸「ゾリグ・チュスム」(Zorig Chusum) というものがあって、織物や木工などと並んで、製紙もその工芸のうちの一つとして、政府が文化遺産として保護・育成を図っている。誰かに品物を贈る場合には、品物を布や紙で包装するという「包む文化」のあるブータンでは、包装紙も手漉き紙の需要を支えている【10-23】。包む文化に加え、ブータンでは、環境保護のため、1994年4月にプラスチック袋の使用禁止が政府によって発表さ

れた。布袋や輸入されたナイロンや紙製の袋などさまざまな代用品があり、手漉き紙もその一つだが、水に触れることで破れてしまうという性質が弱点である(15)。プラスチック袋禁止令はいまだに解除されていないが、実際には、市場での食料品の販売に相変わらずプラスチック袋が使われていて、禁止令の影響は大きいとは言えない。

モクトウの紙漉きの将来

　ランゲテンの場合も、政府が紙漉き人たちをラジャスタン州の紙漉き工場の見学に派遣したり、一部の機械を導入したりしたこともあった。だが、紙漉き人たちのニーズとは合わず、うまくいかなかった。

　タワンの人々が祈りに使うファンも、次第に工場製の紙に取って代わられてきている。僧院の経典や仏教関係の文献は、ダラムサラから印刷されたものが送られてきている。マニ車用の紙も常に注文が入るわけではないだろう。紙漉きの現状を維持するためにも、新たな需要が生まれる必要がある。

　近年、タワンを訪れるインド各地からの観光客が増えている。クラフト・センターや町のいくつかの商店では、モクトウの紙が折り畳まれて10枚1束で積み重ねられて売られている【10-24】。詳しい説明が書かれていれば、この紙がダフネから100％手作業で作られているという価値が伝わるのではないだろうか。誰かが率先して紙を売り込めば、「タワンの手漉き紙」というブランドを創出できるだろう。

⑴ [Elwin 1959: 70, 192]。
⑵ 2020年1月、ナムサイ県のチョンカムにある「タイ・カムティ、シンポー博物館兼研究センター」で、手漉き紙に書かれた文書を見た。しかし、かなり前に紙漉きは絶えているとのことで、製法を知る人には出会えなかった。原料は、インドワタの木と呼ばれるキワタ科の高木（学名 *Bombax ceiba*）の樹皮であるとのことだった。
⑶ ブータンの紙の方がサイズはやや大きいが、2012年のブムデリンでのレショの価格は、1枚10~12ルピー、モクトウでは、同じ製法の紙が6ルピーと半額であった。
⑷ [Das 1902: 1246]。
⑸ 「溜め漉き法」は「流し漉き法」とも呼ばれるが、「流し込み型」と紛らわしいので、本章では、「溜め漉き法」とする。
⑹ [Hunter 1978（1947）: 78]。
⑺ [Hunter 1978: 111]。
⑻ ネパールの製紙に関しては、多くの研究報告がある。例えば、[Hodgson 1832]、[Trier 1972]、[Konishi 2013] である。
⑼ シッキムのゾング (Zongu) のレプチャが2種類のジンチョウゲ科の植物から紙漉きをしていたという報告がある [Gorer 1938: 60-61]。
⑽ [Bodt 2012: 5]。
⑾ [Imaeda 1989: 409-414]。
⑿ [Imaeda 1989: 412-413]。
⒀ [久保田　1999]。
⒁ [久保田　2001]。
⒂ ブータンのプラスチック禁止問題と手漉き紙の環境への影響や経済的な問題点などについては、[Bodt 2001] が詳しく報告している。

CHAPTER 10
Handmade Papermaking in Tawang

So far, I have written about traditional costumes, but I would like to add a note about the handmade papermaking craft that is still practiced by the Monpa people in Mukto, Tawang district, Arunachal Pradesh. There is a record of papermaking by Monpa people in 1959 near Shergaon in West Kameng district(1). It is also said that papermaking was practised elsewhere in the Tawang area, besides Mukto, until recently. Meanwhile, I have heard that women have started papermaking in Chug village in Dirang Circle in 2021, with the support of the Agriculture Department. The person who taught them the technique is said to originally have come from Tawang. Apart from the Monpa, people from the Tai Khamti tribe in Namsai district in the eastern part of the state are also said to have made handmade paper, but details are not available(2) 【10-1a, 10-1b】. There may be other people making paper today, but the Mukto people are probably the only ones who have continued traditional handmade paper production in the state for many years.

    I first saw Mukto handmade paper when I visited the Craft Center in Tawang in 1999. The paper I bought was described by my acquaintance, a Japanese painting artist, as having a slightly rough texture but blending well with ink when used for ink painting. However, the quality was inferior to paper from neighbouring Bhutan, as some of the paper contained dust and was not uniformly thin. Most surprising was the low price: each sheet cost around 2 rupees (then about 6 Japanese yen). As of April 2024, each sheet costs 20 rupees (now about 38 Japanese yen) which is not expensive when taking price inflation into account.

    However, even few Tawang people know how this handmade paper is made. Mukto village is located at a travel distance of about 60 km to the southeast of Tawang town centre. The road crosses mountainous terrain and used to take 3 hours one way, but now that the road has improved, it takes less than 2 hours to reach the village.

    On the edge of Mukto village, towards Ningsang La (pass), one of the India-Bhutan border points accessible only to locals, is a place called Langateng, dotted with paper-making huts 【10-2】. In 2013, there were a total of 11 huts in Langateng and on the mountain slopes to the east. In some huts, there were family members who had come to help, but most hut owners did the whole process themselves. The 11 huts included four huts where women were working alone. In April 2024, there still were 11 papermaking huts, but in only three of them the owners were working on a daily basis.

The uses of handmade paper

It is not known when papermaking in Mukto began, but it is likely that papermaking was already practised in the 1800s, as some people born in the 1930s say they learnt to make paper from their grandfathers. Paper made by the Monpa people used to be a trade product with Tibet. In 2013, Rinchin Khandu, born in 1937, and Sonam Wangchu, born in 1939, who were still making paper in Langateng, at that time, also said that before the Sino-Indian border conflict in 1962, they often walked to Tshona, Tibet, to sell paper 【10-3】.

The main use of paper in Tibet and the adjacent regions is for documents and Buddhist scriptures 【10-4】. When used for scriptures, a single sheet is too thin, so several sheets are pasted together with glue made from flour to make the paper thicker. For paper printed with the mantra 'Om Mani Padme Hum', which is placed inside a large or small cylindrical mani wheel, the edges of the paper are pasted together to make a long roll 【10-5】. According to Rinchin Khandu, once he received a bulk order of 2,400 sheets from Phongme, Trashigang district, Bhutan, for the temple's mani wheel, and the buyer brought his horse to carry them. As mentioned later, papermaking is also practised in Trashi Yangtse district in eastern Bhutan, but the price in Mukto is lower(3).

Another common sight in Monpa settlements is the flag (*phan*), which is made of thin strips cut from the handmade paper and tied to tree branches with thread 【10-6】. The purpose is to pray for good health, long life, family safety and employment. In Tawang, it is also used for the *ke lha phan* 【10-7】, which is offered to the local guardian deity *ke lha* who protects all people born in a certain vicinity, and for small paper umbrellas offered during rituals to pray for family safety 【10-8】. All of these traditional uses are inextricably linked to faith and religion. However, some people have been trying to commercialise letterheads and envelopes for about 10 years, because it is possible to print on this paper with a home printer 【10-9】. But because there is no paper cutter or printing press in Tawang, everything has to be taken to Assam to be made into products, and there are many challenges to turning this into a profitable business.

Work hut, raw material and working process

The average elevation of the village center of Mukto is 2,385 meters above sea level, and Langateng is on the south-facing slope of the valley, about 100 meters lower. This area is suitable for outdoor work because of its lower elevation and warmer climate compared to other areas in Tawang district. There is no running water connection, but water from the mountain streams and springs is drawn to the work huts by plastic pipes. The land of Langateng itself is owned by the village, and anyone can use the land for papermaking free of charge.

The home of the papermakers is located in the centre of Mukto village, so the main papermaking hut is just enough to shelter them from the wind and rain. The hut has a space for storing raw materials and completed paper, as well as a cooking stove for boiling the raw materials. Outside, there is a small papermaking area covered only by a roof, and there is space for drying paper in the sun. Most papermakers occupy around 100 square meters of land. The papermaking area has a concrete water tank (*sho kang*) dug out of the ground and covered with a tin roof to protect it from the rain. This papermaking area is called *shug chukhang* 【10-10】.

The paper is made from the bark of a plant from the family *Thymelaeaceae*, the genus Daphne (*Daphne papyracea*), which grows wild nearby. The Monpa of Tawang call this plant *shug sheng*, meaning 'paper tree' 【10-11】. In Tibetan, it is called *shog shing*, which is explained in S. Chandra Das's Tibetan-English Dictionary published in 1902 as 'the daphne plant, the plant from the bark of which paper is made'(4) Plants of the genus *Edgeworthia* (*Edgeworthia chrysantha*) in the family *Thymelaeaceae* are also called *shog shing*. Although there are many species of daphne plants in the daphne family, in this chapter, daphne is written as a generic term for all plants in this genus.

Daphne is sometimes collected by the papermakers themselves by going to the nearby community forests, but if they are too old to do the work of collecting daphne stems themselves, they take them from others and give them half of the paper they make. This system is called *grangma* in the local language, which refers to a system of 'sharing' a product or harvest. There are various examples of this in agriculture and livestock farming, such as sharecropping, when the cultivation of a field is entrusted to someone else than the owner, and the harvest is shared between the landowner and the cultivator. In the case of the papermakers of Langateng, they go out to collect the raw material themselves while they are still healthy, but when they become old, they can continue to make paper by getting help from others to supply them with raw materials, even if this means that their income is halved.

The outer bark of daphne is most easily peeled off when collected in March. The papermakers collect stems of trees that are 5-6 years old. I observed papermaking every time I visited Mukto between 2003 and 2023, and the process is almost the same in all the papermaking huts, with no changes.

The following is the papermaking process in Langateng.

1) The outer skin of the daphne is torn off with a small knife to leave only the bast (inner bark). This is then dried in the sun for two days 【10-12】.
2) Wood ash is made by burning wood and water is strained through the ash. The ash can only be used once, but if it is good wood ash, it may be mixed with other ash, like from the fireplace at home. The selection of trees for good ash is very important. The papermakers say that good ash can be obtained from three types of oak tree 【10-13】.
3) The dried bast is washed under running water and any debris or coloured parts are removed. It is again soaked in water to soften it and then cut as small as possible.
4) A large pot is filled with water and a ladleful of wood ash is added and the bast is

boiled. The time varies from two hours, four hours, or overnight, depending on the person 【10-14】.

5) The boiled bast is placed on a flat stone and pound into a paste with a wooden mallet (*rui tong*) to form a cylindrical lump about 20 cm in diameter and 10 cm thick. About eight lumps of pulp material can be made from a large pot of bast; it takes four hours to make eight lumps. This step of beating repeatedly with force is said to be the hardest part of the paper-making process 【10-15】.

6) A concrete rectangle vat (*sho kang*) is dug into the ground and filled with water. On top of it floats a mould called a *sho sheng*, a wooden frame covered with nylon netting used for mosquito nets. On this *sho sheng*, pulp brought in small bamboo baskets is poured using a *shok bor*, a bamboo pulp-stirring tool, then the pulp is spread evenly by hand on the mould and then the water is strained. The average size of the vat is 100 cm long by 80 cm wide and the inner size of the mould is 65 cm long by 50 cm wide 【10-16a, 10-16b, 10-16c】.

7) The paper is dried in the sun, with the mould propped up on a stick in the area surrounding the hut. On sunny days the paper dries in six to seven hours, but on cloudy days it takes more than 10 hours. During the rainy season, the paper is sometimes dried near the heat of a fire in the hut, which leaves the smell of smoke on the paper. Once dry, the sheets are removed one by one 【10-17】.

On average, 100 sheets can be made in a day. The tools used in the process are all simple and handmade 【10-18】.

This papermaking method differs from the dipping method commonly used in Japan, where it is called *tamesuki* method[5]. In the dipping method, the pulp is placed in a vat and a mould is sunk into it to scoop up the pulp evenly. A screen made of woven bamboo strips or reeds is placed on this mould.

Dard Hunter, who surveyed papermaking methods around the world, called the former method, in which the pulp is poured over the mould, the 'pouring method'[6]. He considered this a primitive technique found in Thailand, Myanmar, Nepal, Bhutan, and Tibet, that differed from the dipping method' common in Japan, and in Kashmir and Bengal in India[7].

In the case of the dipping method, the paper is peeled off from the screen, piled up and drained of water, and later dried, but in the case of the pouring method, the entire mould is dried, so one mould is needed for each sheet.

In fact, the dipping method was once used in Langateng as well, and according to the eldest papermaker, Rinchin Khandu, the dipping method was still used for a short period in the 1970s when he started papermaking, but this method was eventually replaced by the pouring method. The dipping method in Langateng involved using a bamboo screen with woven bamboo strips, layering the paper on top of the wooden board, then placing a stone on top of the board so that the weight of the paper was averaged out and drained off. This method can make thick paper, but it requires a place to dry each sheet of paper on boards or rocks, so the current pouring method of drying paper in the standing mould is more convenient.

Handmade paper in Bhutan

Papermaking using similar methods to those still practised in Mukto exists in the southern Himalayan foothills, including Nepal(8), Sikkim(9) and Bhutan, and in some places, it continues at present. Because the paper comes from the Mon region of Sikkim, Bhutan, and Tawang and West Kameng districts in Arunachal, the paper is often called *mon shog* in Tibetan, meaning 'Mon paper'(10). In the Bhutanese Dzongkha language, handmade paper is *de sho*, meaning paper made from shrubs of daphne family (*deshing*). In Bhutan, paper was one of the taxes paid to the government and it was one of the most important export products to Tibet as well. Therefore, in the past, many families were involved in papermaking.

A 1989 report in English by Yoshiro Imaeda is informative about traditional papermaking in Bhutan(11). According to the report, at that time, Bhutanese papermakers did not have a fixed workshop and they shifted from one place to another. They established the workshop in a place where a clean mountain stream was running and trees which provided fibers for paper were growing in proximity 【10-19】. They used two shrubs, one is daphne, which in Dzongkha is called *deshing nap* or 'black *de* tree' and the other one is *Edgeworthia*, which is called *deshing kap*, or 'white *de* tree'. In the case of the pouring method, the paper is poured over a mould lined with cotton cloth, so the warp and weft threads remain as a pattern on the paper, which is called *resho* (cotton cloth paper). On the other hand, in the case of the dipping method, in which paper material is dissolved in water collected in a tub and a bamboo screen is horizontally immersed in it to make the paper, a woven bamboo screen is used. Paper made in this way is called *tsharsho* (bamboo paper). This method is said not to be found in Tibet(12). In the case of *tsharsho*, thicker paper can be made.

In Bhutan today, the dipping method is used at a paper-making workshop in Thimphu, under Japanese technical guidance. Machines have been introduced to compress the paper in layers and drain the water, and to dry the paper using electric heaters. This workshop also uses the mucilage of the root of the *aibika* plant (*Abelmoschus manifot*), known as *neri* in Japanese. The *neri* prevents the paper material from sinking to the bottom of the water tank and distributes it evenly, making the finished product beautiful. The *neri* also makes it easier to peel off the layers of paper one by one before they are dried.

Misumi Town, Hamada City, Shimane Prefecture is the home of the handmade paper '*Sekishu-banshi*', which was listed as an Important Intangible Cultural Property of Japan in 1969. It was also placed on UNESCO's Representative List of the Intangible Cultural Heritage of Humanity in 2009. The town has been involved in international cooperation projects since 1986. Some examples include receiving trainees at the request of the Bhutanese Government, sending experts for technical guidance, and providing paper making equipment.

The Japan International Cooperation Agency (JICA) has also dispatched experts in Japanese handmade paper technology from Misumi Town. The papermaking workshop in the capital Thimphu is now owned by a person who once received training in Misumi Town. The workshop is said to be running smoothly, with some equipment also being provided to improve quality. One of the skillful papermakers is Akira Kubota who runs a papermaking workshop in Misumi Town. He has experience in training trainees and teaching in Bhutan. According to his report, the Bhutanese Government has a strong desire to industrialise traditional handmade paper production and raise the quality to a level acceptable in the global market. The Japanese cooperation was a response to this aim(13).Various products, including letter sets, notebooks, and bags, have been produced for foreign tourists to take as souvenirs, and the workshops in Thimphu are crowded with tourists.

Meanwhile, in the Bumdeling area of Trashi Yangtse in eastern Bhutan, the traditional method of making paper using the pouring method is still practised. Kubota also has experience of providing technical guidance there, and according to him several precautions are necessary for *resho* paper production. These include preventing impurities in the mountain water that is used; storing the raw material, daphne, on a well-ventilated high floor to prevent it from rotting; and carefully removing any dust attached to the material(14).

The papermaking process for *resho*, which I saw during my visits to some of the workshops in Bumdeling, is almost identical to that of Mukto, although some workshops also made *tsharsho*. Some places had access to tap water, and some workshops had machines for beating the pulp to crush the fibres and panel machines for drying the *tsharsho*. The stable supply of electricity and government support for purchases of machinery are the main differences with Mukto 【10-20, 10-21, 10-22】.

Bhutan has 13 arts and crafts known as '*Zorig Chusum*', and along with textiles and woodworking, papermaking is one of the crafts that the government is trying to protect and foster as cultural heritage. In Bhutan there is a 'wrapping culture', where goods are wrapped in cloth or paper when given as a gift, and therefor, wrapping paper also supports demand for handmade paper 【10-23】. In addition to the wrapping culture, the Government of Bhutan announced ban on plastic bags in April 1994 to protect the environment. Various alternatives are available, including cloth bags and imported nylon and paper bags, and handmade paper is one such alternative, but its weakness is its tendency to be torn by water(15). The plastic bag ban is still in place, but in practice plastic bags are again commonly used to sell food in markets and the ban has not had a significant impact.

The future of papermaking in Mukto

In the case of Langateng in Tawang, the government also sent papermakers to Rajasthan to visit papermaking workshops, and they introduced some machinery. However, this did not work as it did not match the needs of the papermakers.

The *phan* flags used by the people of Tawang for prayers are gradually being replaced by factory-made paper. Monastic scriptures and Buddhist literature are printed and sent from Dharamsala. It is also unlikely that paper for Mani wheels will continue to be ordered. New demand has to be generated to maintain the current level of papermaking.

In recent years, the number of tourists visiting Tawang from all over India has increased. In the Craft Center in Tawang and in some shops in the town, Mukto paper is sold folded and stacked in bundles of 10 sheets 【10-24】. A detailed description on the bundle conveys the message that this paper is 100% handmade from daphne. If someone took the initiative to market the paper, the brand 'Tawang Handmade Paper' could be created.

---

(1) [Elwin 1959: 70, 192].
(2) In January 2020, I saw documents written on handmade paper at the "Tai Khamti-Singpho Museum cum Research Centre" in Chongkham, Namsai district. However, I was told that papermaking had ceased a long time ago, and I did not meet anyone who knew how it was made. The raw material was said to be the bark of a tall tree, the Indian cotton tree (*Bombax ceiba*).
(3) Although Bhutanese paper is slightly larger in size, in 2012, the price of *resho* in Bumdeling was 10 to 12 rupees per sheet, while in Mukto, paper of the same production method cost only half that amount, i.e., 6 rupees.
(4) [Das 1902: 1246].
(5) In Japanese, '*tamesuki* method' is also referred to as the '*nagashisuki* method' but since this may cause confusion with the '*nagashikomi* type', this chapter will use the term '*tamesuki* method'.
(6) [Hunter 1978（1947）: 78].
(7) [Hunter 1978（1947）: 111].
(8) Many studies have been reported on paper production in Nepal, for example, [Hodgson 1832], [Trier 1972], [Konishi 2013].
(9) There are reports that the Lepchas of Zongu in Sikkim made paper from two species of daphne [Gorer 1938: 60-61].
(10) [Bodt 2012:5].
(11) [Imaeda 1989: 409-414].
(12) [Imaeda 1989: 412-413].
(13) [Kubota 1999].
(14) [Kubota 2001].
(15) The issue of Bhutan's plastic ban and the environmental impact of handmade paper and economic factors as an alternative to plastic are reported in detail in [Bodt 2001].

参考文献／References

〈英語・日本語・チベット語・中国語　English , Japanese, Tibetan, Chinese〉

Aris, Michael. 1989. *Hidden Treasures and Secret Lives: A Study of Pemalingpa (1450-1521) and the Sixth Dalai Lama (1683- 1706)*. London: Kagan Paul International Limited.

―― 1994 *The Raven Crown: The Origins of Buddhist Monarchy in Bhutan*. London: Serindia Publications.

―― 2009. *Sources for the History of Bhutan*. New Delhi: Motilal Banarsidass Publishers.

Bailey, Frederic Marshman. 1914. Exploration on the Tsangpo or Upper Brahmaputra. *The Geographical Journal*, 44(4): 341-360.

―― 1957(1968). *No Passport to Tibet*. London: The Travel Book Club. フレデリック・M・ベイリイ『ヒマラヤの謎の河』(*Mysterious River of the Himalaya*) 諏訪多栄蔵・松月久左訳 (translated into Japanese by Taezo Suwata and Hisasuke Matsuzuki), 東京：あかね書房 (Tokyo: Akane Shobo).

Bāo Lùfāng 包路芳. 2014.『门巴族』(*Menba Ethnic Group*) 中国少数民族人口丛书 北京：中国人口出版社 (Beijing: China Pupulation Publishing House).

Bhutan Times. 2008. *Sacred Monasteries & Religious Sites of Bhutan*. Thimphu: Bhutan Times Ltd.

Bodt, Timotheus A. 2001. *Economic and environmental effects of plastic ban and deysho production in Bhutan*. Wageningen University: unpublished M.Sc.thesis. https://doi.org/10.5281/zenodo.2427181

―― 2012. *The New Lamp Clarifying the History, Peoples, Languages and Traditions of Eastern Bhutan and Eastern Mon*. Wageningen: Monpasang Publications.

―― 2014a. Ethnolinguistic Survey of Westernmost Arunachal Pradesh: A Fieldworker's Impressions. *Linguistics of the Tibeto-Burman Area*, 37: 2, 198-239.

―― 2014b. Notes on the Settlement of the Gongri River valley of Western Arunachal Pradesh. *Bulletin of Tibetology*, 50 (1&2): 153-190.

―― 2018. *Duhumbi Storybook*. Arnhem: Monpasang Publications.

―― 2020. *Duhumbi Dictionary: An illustrated Duhumbi- English dictionary with etymological notes and a reverse wordlist*. Arnhem: Monpasang Publications.

―― 2021. Sartang (West Kameng district, Arunachal Pradesh, India)-Language Contexts. *Language Documentation and Description*, Vol. 20, 162-188.

Britting, Vera & Györgyi Fajcsák (eds.). 2016. *Nagas, Birds, Elephants: Traditional Dress from Mainland Southeast Asia*. Budapest: French Hopp Museum of Asiatic Arts.

Chand, Raghubir 2004. *Brokpas: The Hidden Highlanders of Bhutan*. Nainital: PAHAR.

Chaudhuri, S. K. 2004. Understanding Sajolang Religion: A study of persistence and change. In Tomo Mibang and Sarit K. Chaudhri (eds.), *Understanding Tribal Religion*. pp.223-234, New Delhi, Mittal Publications.

Chen, Liming & Zhang, Yuan 陈立明, 张媛. 2014. 『门巴族』 (*Menba Ethnic Group*), 沈阳; 辽宁民族出版社 (Shenyang: Liaoning Nationality Publishing House).

Chhophel, Kezang. 2002. A brief History of Rigsum Goenpo Lhakhang and Choeten Kora in Trashi Yangtse. *Journal of Bhutan Studies*, 6: 1-4.

Choden, Karma. 2014. *Phallus: Crazy Wisdom from Bhutan*. Thimphu: Butter Lamp Publishers.

Chowdhury, J. N. 1983. *Arunachal Pradesh: From Frontier Tract to Union Territory*. New Delhi: Cosmo Publications.

Clausen, Lucy W. 1962 (1972). *Insect Fact and Folklore*. New York: Collier Books. ルーシー・W・クラウセン 『昆虫と人間』(*Insects and Humans*) 小西正泰・小西正捷訳, (translated into Japanese by Masayasu Konishi and Masataka Konishi) 東京：みすず書房 (Tokyo: Misuzu Shobo).

Cooper, R. E. 1933. Bhutan: Tailed People: 'Daktas'—People with a Tail in the East Bhutanese Himalaya. *Man*, 33, 125-128.

Driem, van, George. 2001. *Languages of the Himalayans: An Ethnolinguistic Handbook of the Greater Himalayan Region*. Vols. 1 & 2. Leiden : Brill.

Das, Sarat Chandra. 1902. *A Tibetan-English Dictionary with Sanskrit Synonyms*. Calcutta: The Bengal Secretariat Book Depot.

Dorji, Tenzin. 1986. rgyal-ba'i byung-rabs gsal-ba'i sgron-me'brug sharphyogs 'khor-lo rtsibs-brgyad-gyi lo-rgyus (*The lamp illuminating the victorious history of the eight spokes of the eastern regions of Bhutan*). Unpublished manuscript.

——2008. *Flute of Diza: Marriage Customs and Practices among the Brogpa of Merak and Sakteng*. Thimphu: Bhutan Times.

Dusu, Sambyo. 2013. *The Akas of Arunachal Pradesh: A Historical Study (Till 1947 A.D.)*. Unpublished Ph.D. thesis for Rajiv Gandhi University, Itanagar, Arunachal Pradesh.

Edmunds, Tom Owen. 1988. *Bhutan: Land of the Thunder Dragon*. London: Elm Tree Books.

Elwin, Verrier. 1958. *Myths of the North-East Frontier of India*. Shillong: North-East Frontier Agency.

—— 1959 *The Art of the North-East Frontier of India* . Shillong: North-East Frontier Agency.

Fraser-Lu, Sylvia. 1988. *Handwoven Textiles of South-East Asia*. New York:

Oxford University Press.

Gait, Edward. 1926(1945). *A History of Assam*. Calcutta and Simla: Thacker, Spink & Co. エドワード・ゲイト『アッサム史』(*A History of Assam*). 民族学研究調査部訳 (translated into Japanese by Department of Ethnological Studies) 東京：三省堂 (Tokyo: Sanseido).

Gerner, Manfred. 2007. *Chakzampa Thangtong Gyalpo: Architect, Philosopher and Iron Chain Bridge Builder*. (translated from German by Gregor Verhufen) Thimphu: The Centre for Bhutan Studies.

Ghosh, G. K. & Shukla Ghosh. 2000. *Textiles of North Eastern India*. Calcutta: Firma KLM.

Giri, Seeta. 2004. *The Vital Link: Monpas and Their Forests*. Thimphu: The Centre for Bhutan Studies.

Gorer, Geoffery. 1938. *Himalayan Village: An Account of The Lepchas of Sikkim*. London: Michael Joseph Ltd.

Grewal, D. S. 1997. *Tribes of Arunachal Pradesh: Identity, Culture and Language* Vol.1. Delhi: South Asia Publications.

Grothmann, Kerstin. 2012. Population History and Identity in the Hidden Land of Pemako. *Journal of Bhutan Studies* Vol. 26, 21–52.

Hodgson, B. H. 1832. On the Native Method of making the Paper, denominated in Hindustan, Nepalese. *The Journal of the Asiatic Society of Bengal*, 1: 8–11.

Huber, Toni. 2015. Naked, Mute and Well Hung: A Brief Ethnographic Comparison of *Kengpa* and Related Ritual Performers in the Eastern Himalayas and Beyond. In Olaf Czaja and Guntram Hazod (eds.) *The Illuminating Mirror. Tibetan Studies in Honour of Per K. Sorensen on the Occasion of his 65th Birthday*. pp.219-242, 592-595. Wiesbaden: Dr. Ludwig Reichert Verlag.

——2020a. *Source of Life: Revitalisation Rites and Bon Shamans in Bhutan and the Eastern Himalayas*, Vol. I. Vienna: Austrian Academy of Sciences Press.

——2020b. *Source of Life: Revitalisation Rites and Bon Shamans in Bhutan and the Eastern Himalayas*, Vol. II. Vienna: Austrian Academy of Sciences Press.

Hunter, Dard. 1978(1947). *Papermaking: The History and Technique of an Ancient Craft*. New York: Dover Publications.

Imaeda, Yoshiro. 1989. Papermaking in Bhutan. *Acta Orientalia Academiae Scientiarum Hungaricae*, Vol. 43, 2/3, 409-414.

Inthavong, Chanthasone チャンタソン・インタヴォン. 2006.『ラオスの布を楽しむ』(*Enjoy Lao Textiles*). 東京：アートダイジェスト (Tokyo: Art Digest).

Karchung, Gengop. 2011. Diminishing Cultures of Bhutan: Costume of Merag Community. *SAARC CULTURE*, 2: 17-43.

——2013 *From Yak-Herding to Enlightenment: The Legend of Thöpa Gali: A Heritage Narrative of the Merak-Sakteng Community*. Thimphu: National

Library & Archives of Bhutan.
Kennedy, R. S. 1914. *Ethnological Report on the Akas, Khoas and Mijis and the Monbas of Tawang*. Shillong: Assam Secretariat Press.
Kinga, Sonam. 2009. *Polity, Kingship and Democracy: A biography of the Bhutanese state*. Thimphu: Bhutan Times.
Kingdon Ward, Frank. 1926. *The riddle of the Tsanpo gorges*. London: Edward Arnold & Co.
――1941 *Assam Adventure*. London: Jonathan Cape.
Konishi, A. Masatoshi 小西正捷. 2013. *Hāth-Kāghaz: History of Handmade Paper in South Asia*. Shimla: Indian Institute of Advanced Study / New Delhi: Aryan Books International.
Kubota, Akira 久保田彰. 1999.『ブータン王国の手すき紙―1998年9月7日〜10月22日報告書』(私家版) (*Handmade Paper of the Kingdom of Bhutan: Report from 7 September to 22 October 1998*) (private edition)
――2001.『ブータン王国手すき和紙製造技術指導報告書』(私家版) (*Report on the Technical Guidance for the Production of Handmade Japanese Paper in the Kingdom of Bhutan*) (private edition)
Kusakabe, Keiko 日下部啓子. 2019.『カード織を理解するために：ヨーロッパにおけるカード織研究・百年の足跡』(「月刊染織α」2006年302〜306号より抜き刷り). (*Understanding Card Weaving: One Hundred Years of Card Weaving Research in Europe*) (offprint from *the Monthly Magazine Sen Shoku Alfa*, 2006, No. 302-306). 埼玉：トラジャ・テキスタイル・アーツ(Saitama: Toraja Textile Arts).
Lange, Diana. 2020. *An Atlas of the Himalayas by a 19th Century Tibetan Lama: A Journey of Discovery*. Leiden/Boston: Brill.
Lazcano, Santiago. 2005. Ethnohistoric Notes on the Ancient Tibetan Kingdom of sPo Bo and its Influence on the Eastern Himalayas. *Revue d'Etudes Tibétaines*, 7, 41-63.
Leach, E. R. 1954(1987). *Political Systems of Highland Burma: A study of Kachin Social Structure*. London: University of London. E. R. リーチ『高地ビルマの政治体系』(*Political Systems of Highland Burma*) 関本照夫訳 (translated into Japanese by Teruo Sekimoto), 東京：弘文堂 (Tokyo: Koubundou).
Lieberherr, Ismael and Timotheus A. Bodt. 2017. Sub-grouping Kho-Bwa based on shared core vocabulary. *Himalayan Linguistics*, 16(2): 26-63.
Mackenzie, Alexander. 2001(1884). *The North East Frontier of India*. New Delhi: Mittal Publications.
Ménbāzú Jiǎnshǐ Xiūdìng Běn Biānxiě Zǔ (MBZBBZ) 门巴族简史修订本编写组(编写). 2016(2008).『门巴族简史』(*A Brief History of the Menba People*)北京:民族出版社 (Beijing: Publishing House of Minority Nationalities).
Miyake, Shinichiro & Ishiyama Natsuko 三宅伸一郎・石山奈津子訳、2008.『天翔ける祈りの舞―チベット歌舞劇アチェ・ラモ三話』(*The Heavenly*

Prayer Dance: Three Stories of the Tibetan Opera Ache Lhamo) (translated from Tibetan into Japanese by Shinichiro Miyake and Ishiyama Natsuko) 京都：臨川書店 (Kyoto: Rinsen Book Co.).

Miyake, Shinichiro 三宅伸一郎. 2008.「解説：チベットの歌舞劇アチェ・ラモ概観」『天翔ける祈りの舞―チベット歌舞劇アチェ・ラモ三話』（三宅伸一郎、石山奈津子訳、pp. 239-285、Shinichiro Miyake（Explanation: An Overview of the Tibetan Opera Ache Lhamo, in *The Heavenly Prayer Dance: Three Stories of the Tibetan Opera Ache Lhamo*, pp. 239-285）京都：臨川書店 (Kyoto: Rinsen Book Co.).

Myers, Diana K. 1994. Women, Men, and Textiles. In Diana K. Myers and Susan S. Bean (eds.), *From the Land of the Thunder Dragon: Textile Arts of Bhutan.*, pp. 81-141. New Delhi: Timeless Books.

——1994. Warp and Weft: Garments, Coverings, and Containers. In Diana K. Myers ad Susan S. Bean(eds.)., *From the Land of the Thunder Dragon: Textile Arts of Bhutan.*, pp.91-141. New Delhi: Timeless Books.

Myers, Diana K. & Françoise Pommaret. 1994. Bhutan and Its Neighbors. In Diana K. Myers and Susan S. Bean (eds), *From the Land of the Thunder Dragon: Textile Arts of Bhutan.*, pp.47-69. New Delhi: Timeless Books.

Ngawang. n.d. 1668/1728?. dpal 'brug-par lung-lha'i gdung-brgyud-kyis bstan-pa'i ring-lugs lho-mon kha-bzhi-las nyi-ma shar-phyogs-su byung-zhing rgyas-pa'i lo-rgyus gsal-ba'i me-long (*The mirror illuminating the history and tradition of the arrival of the glorious Drukpa into the southern Mon country of four approaches in the east*). Manuscript in 24 folios of 35x8½ cms.

Nishioka, Keiji & Satoko Nishioka 西岡京治・里子. 1978.『神秘の王国―ブータンに"日本のふるさと"を見た夫と妻11年の記録』(*The Mysterious Kingdom: Life of the Bhutanese from 1964 to 1975.*). 東京：学習研究社 (Tokyo: Gakushu Kenkyusha).

Norbu, Tsewang. 2008. *The Monpas of Tawang: Arunachal Pradesh*. Itanagar: Department of Cultural Affairs, Directorate of Research, Government of Arunachal Pradesh.

Pandey, B. B. 1996. *The Buguns: A Tribe in Transition*. Itanagar, Delhi: Himalayan Publishers.

Phuntsho, Karma. 2013. *The History of Bhutan*. Noida: Random House

Pommaret, Françoise. 1997. Ethnic Mosaic: Peoples of Bhutan. In Christian Schicklgruber & Françoise Pommaret (eds.), *Bhutan: Mountain Fortress of the Gods*, pp. 43-59. New Delhi: Bookwise.

——1999. The Mon-pa revisited: In search of Mon. In Toni Huber (ed.), *Sacred Space and Powerful Places in Tibetan Culture: A Collection of Essays*, pp.52-73. Dharamsala: Library of Tibetan Works and Archives.

——2000. Ancient Trade Partners: Bhutan, Coach Bihar and Assam (17th-19th century). *Journal of Bhutan Studies*, 2(1):30-53. The Centre for Bhutan Studies.

Sarkar, Niranjan. 1993(1974). *Dances of Arunachal Pradesh*. Itanagar: Directorate of Research, Government of Arunachal Pradesh.
Sharma, B. Deben. 2005. *Lhops (Doya) of Bhutan: An Ethnographic Account*. New Delhi: Akansha Publishing House.
Sharma, R. R. P. 1988(1960). *The Sherdukpens*. Itanagar: Directorate of Research, Government of Arunachal Pradesh.
Sinha, Raghuvir. 1988(1962). *The Akas*. Itanagar: Director of Research, Government of Arunachal Pradesh.
Stein, R. A. 1972(1971). *Tibetan Civilization*. (translated from French to English by J. E. Stapleton Driver). Stanford University Press: Stanford. R. A. スタン『チベットの文化』山口瑞鳳・定方晟訳, (*Tibetan Culture*) Translated from French into Japanese by Zuiho Yamaguchi, Akira Sadakata) 東京：岩波書店 (Tokyo: Iwanami Shoten).
Tenpa, Lobsang & Thupten Tempa. 2013. *A Brief History of the Establishment of Buddhism in Monyul: Tawang and West Kameng Districts Arunachal Pradesh, India*. Itanagar: Department of Karmik & Adhyatmik Affairs, Govt. of Arunachal Pradesh.
Tilman, H. W. 2016 (1946). *When Men & Mountains Meet*. London: Lodestar Books.
Thinley, Kunzang. 2008. *Seeds of faith: A Comprehensive Guide to the Sacred Places of Bhutan*, Vol. 1. Thimphu: KMT Publishers.
――2009. Founding of Zhongar (Mongar) Dzong. In Tshering Dorje et al. (eds.), *Fortress of the Dragon: Proceedings of the 4th Colloquium*, pp. 131-159, Paro: The National Museum of Bhutan.
Trier, Jesper. 1972. *Ancient Paper of Nepal*. Jutland Archaeological Society Publications Vol. 10, Copenhagen: Gyldendal.
Trotter, H. 1877. Account of the Pundit's Journey in Great Tibet from Leh in Ladakh to Lhasa, and of his Return to India via Assam. *Journal of the Royal Geographical Society of London*. 47: 86-136.
Wakita, Michiko 脇田道子. 2019.『モンパ―インド・ブータン国境の民』(*The Monpas: People of the Borderland between India and Bhutan*). 京都：法藏館 (Kyoto: Hozokan).
Wangchu, L. 1999. Oral Literature of Monpas of Tawang on Creation of Universe. In Pandey, B. B. (ed.), *Creation of Universe: Oral Literature of Arunachal Pradesh*, pp.131-134. Itanagar: Directorate of Research, Government of Arunachal Pradesh.
Wangchuck, Dorji Wangmo. 2006. *A Portrait of Bhutan: Treasures of the Thunder Dragon*. New Delhi: Viking/Penguin.
Wangmo, Sonam. 1990. The Brokpas: A Semi-nomadic People in Eastern Bhutan. In Nari Rustamji and Charles Ramble (eds.), *Himalayan Environment and Culture*, pp.141-158. Shimla: Indian Institute of Advanced Study.
White, John. Claude. 1971(1909). *Sikhim & Bhutan: Twenty-one Years on the*

North-East Frontier 1887-1908. Delhi: Vivek Publishing House.

Yamamoto, Keiko 山本けいこ. 2001.『ブータン―雲龍王国への扉』(*Bhutan: The Door to the Kingdom of the Thunder Dragon*). 東京：明石書店 (Tokyo: Akashi Shoten).

Yú Nǎi Chāng（于乃昌）(主编) 1995.「冂巴族」『中国民族文化大观』Yu Nai Chang (ed.) (Menba Ethnic Group) Guān Dōng Shēng (ed.) *A Panorama of Chinese Ethnic Culture*) 关东升（主编）、pp. 355-496、北京：中国大百科全书出版社 (Beijing: Encyclopaedia of China Publishing House).

Xīzàng Shèhuì Lìshǐ Diàochá Zīliào Cóngkān Biānjí Zǔbiā （XSLDZCBZ) 西藏社会历史调查资料丛刊编辑组编. 1987.『门巴族社会历史调查』第1卷、第2卷. (*A Sociological and Historical Survey of the Menba People*, Vol. 1 and 2. 拉萨：西藏人民出版社 (Lhasa: Tibet People's Publishing House).

パンフレット（Pamphlet）

Managing Committee of Gontse Gadem Rabgyel-Ling Monastery. 1997. Mystic Land of Monyul. Bomdila: Buddhist Culture Preservation Society.

あとがき Afterword

　本書の刊行を決め、原稿を書き始めたのは、2020年秋であった。ちょうど新型コロナ・ウィルス感染症が流行していた頃だったが、私自身の身体に病巣が見つかり、翌年1月に手術を受けることになった。幸い、手術はうまくいき、数カ月後には執筆を再開した。しかし、2022年春に今度は夫が末期の肺癌と診断され、それからわずか4カ月後に帰らぬ人となった。彼の理解と支えがあったからこそ、私は人生の大半を仕事に打ち込むことができ、退職後も、娘を安心して夫に任せて海外調査ができた。45年間連れ添った伴侶を突然失い、茫然自失の状態だったが、それでも死後の諸手続きをこなさなければならず、しばらくの間、書く気力を失っていた。本書の刊行に4年以上もかかったのは、私の能力不足もあるが、こうした一連の困難を乗り越えるために時間と労力を費やさなければならなかったことが大きな要因だった。

　インド、ブータンの各地で、数えきれないほど多くの方々のご支援とご協力をいただいた。私が最も長く滞在したタワンでは、プルパ・ラムとその家族、友人達に大変お世話になった。インド独立前のタワンに生まれた彼女の両親は、歴史の生き証人のような方々だった。特に父親のトゥタンは、ダライ・ラマ法王14世がチベットからインドに亡命した際に、タワンに滞在していた法王のために毎朝、薪と水を運んだ。トゥタンは、タワンからボムディラまで、法王の母君にも同行した。残念ながら、トゥタンの妻は2016年に、彼自身も2022年に亡くなられた。

　紙漉きの村、モクトウに滞在した際には、ホテルやレストランは一軒もなかった。しかし、毎回ペマ・ドンドゥップ（通称ドン）夫妻の家に泊めていただき、温かいもてなしを受けた。モクトウで紙を漉いていた方々も、高齢者のほとんどは故人となられてしまい、本書を直接お渡しできないのが残念でならない。

　メラやサクテンでも当時のガップ（村長）や村役人、ご僧侶をはじめ、多くの友人、知人たちに支援をいただき、貴重なご教示をいただいた。

　慶應義塾大学の博士課程では、鈴木正崇名誉教授から研究のすべてにわたっ

て指導をいただいたが、遅れていた本書の執筆に関しても、常に励ましをいただいた。ここではお名前をすべて挙げることはできないが、他にも、多くの友人、知人からご指導、ご教示をいただいた。このように多くの方々にお世話になり、ご指導いただいたにもかかわらず、不十分な内容や間違いがあるかもしれない。その点はすべて私に責任がある。

　写真の使用を許可してくださった方々のお名前は、それぞれの写真のキャプションに明記させていただいたが、改めて下に挙げさせていただいた。本書に掲載した地図は、友人の高橋洋さんに作成していただいた。

　終盤になって、出版社を変更しなければならなかったが、快く本書の出版を引き受けてくださった法藏館の戸城三千代編集長には、感謝している。デザイナーの大石一雄さん、前回に続き編集を担当してくださった光成三生さんにも大変お世話になった。これら、すべての皆様に心からお礼を申し上げたい。

2025年3月

脇田道子

写真・イラスト、実物の使用を許可してくださった方々（敬称略）
チャンタソン・インタヴォン、石上陽子（イラスト）、水野一晴、松本榮一、西岡里子（グツム）、山本けいこ、T. A. Bodt、David Sangtam、Ismael Lieberherr、Karma Tshering、The Royal Textile Academy of Bhutan、The British Library、Lama Tashi Wangdi、Neten Dorjee Thongdok、Siok Sian Pek-Dorji、Tshering Phuntsho、Ugyen Pelgen。
※メラに住むSang TshomoとDema Yangzomは、私のためにウールのンゴウシンを再現してくれた。

Afterword

In the autumn of 2020, I decided to publish this book and started writing. This was during the COVID-19 pandemic, and in addition, I was diagnosed with a lesion, for which I underwent surgery in January of the following year. Fortunately, the operation was successful, and I was able to resume writing a few months later. However, in the spring of 2022, my husband was diagnosed with terminal lung cancer, and he passed away just four months later. His understanding and support had enabled me to continue working for most of my life. Even after I retired, I was able to leave our daughter in his trusted care and go overseas for research. Although I was in a daze after the sudden loss of my partner of 45 years, I still had to deal with the various procedures after his death. For quite a while, I lost the energy to write. So, this book took more than four years to publish, partly due to my lack of ability, but mainly because I had to spend time and effort to overcome all these consecutive difficulties.

I received the support and cooperation of countless people in various places in India and Bhutan. In Tawang, where I stayed the longest, I am very much indebted to Mrs. Phurpa Lhamu and her family and friends. Her parents, who were born in Tawang before India gained independence, were like living witnesses to history. In particular, her father Thutan carried firewood and water every morning for the His Holiness Dalai Lama when he was in Tawang on his journey from Tibet to his exile in India. Thutan also accompanied the Dalai Lama's mother on her journey from Tawang to Bomdila. Unfortunately, Thutan's wife passed away in 2016, and he himself passed away in 2022.

When I stayed in the paper-making village of Mukto, there was not a single hotel or restaurant. But I received a warm welcome every time I stayed in the home of Pema Dondup (popularly known as Dhon) and his wife. Most of the elderly people who made handmade paper in Mukto have now passed away, and I regret that I cannot personally hand over this book to them anymore.

In Merak and Sakteng too, I received valuable guidance from the *gup* (village headman) and village officials of the time, as well as from monks and many friends and acquaintances.

I received guidance from Professor Emeritus Masataka Suzuki during my doctoral studies at Keio University. He also encouraged me to complete and publish this book, despite its delay. I also received guidance and instruction from many friends and acquaintances whom I can't all mention individually by name here. Despite the help and guidance I have received from so many people, there may be insufficient content or mistakes. I take full responsibility for these.

Those who permitted me to use their photographs are clearly credited in the captions of the respective photographs, but I have listed them again below. All the maps in this book were produced by my friend Hiroshi Takahashi.

Towards the end of the project, I had to change publishers, but I am grateful to Michiyo Toshiro, editor-in-chief of Hōzōkan, who willingly agreed to take over the publication. I am very grateful to designer Kazuo Oishi and to Mitsuo Mitsunari, who was in charge of editing again this time.

I would like to express my heartfelt thanks to everyone.

March 2025
Michiko Wakita

* People who permitted us to use photographs, illustrations and actual items.
Chanthasone Inthavong, Yoko Ishigami (illustrations), Kazuharu Mizuno, Eiichi Matsumoto, Satoko Nishioka (*gutsum*), Keiko Yamamoto, Timotheus A. Bodt, David Sangtam, Ismael Lieberherr, Karma Tshering, The Royal Textile Academy of Bhutan, The British Library, Lama Tashi Wangdi, Neten Dorjee Thongdok, Siok Sian Pek-Dorji, Tshering Phuntsho, Ugyen Pelgen.
※Sang Tshomo and Dema Yangzom, who live in Merak, reproduced a woollen *ngoushing* for me.

著者略歴 Biography

Michiko Wakita
脇田道子

1951年、東京生まれ。早稲田大学第一文学部日本史専攻を卒業後、旅行会社に28年間勤務した。1976年に初めてインド、ブータンを旅して以来、両国の各地を訪問したが、1995年に初めて訪れたアルナーチャル・プラデーシュ、2006年に初めて訪れた東ブータンのメラ、サクテン地域に特別な学問的関心を持った。退職後、立教大学と慶應義塾大学の大学院で合計10年間学んだ。専攻は、文化人類学で、2014年慶応義塾大学大学院社会学研究科より社会学博士号を取得。2019年に、『モンパ―インド・ブータン国境の民』を法藏館から出版した。メラとサクテンに関しては、2010年「ブータン東部におけるツーリズム導入に関する一考察」(『慶應義塾大学大学院社会学研究科研究紀要』)などの論文がある。しかし、本書以外のほとんどの書籍、論文は日本語で書かれている。現在は、日本ブータン研究所研究員。

Born in Tokyo in 1951, she graduated from the Department of Literature at Waseda University, specialising in Japanese history, and then worked in a travel agency for 28 years. She first travelled to India and Bhutan in 1976 and has since visited many places in both countries. She has a special academic interest in Arunachal Pradesh, which she visited for the first time in 1995, and Merak and Sakteng in eastern Bhutan, which she visited for the first time in 2006. After retirement, she studied for a total of 10 years at the graduate schools of Rikkyo University and Keio University in Tokyo. Her major was cultural anthropology, and in 2014 she completed a PhD in Sociology from the Graduate School of Sociology at Keio University. In 2019, she published The Monpas: People of the Borderland between India and Bhutan with Hozokan Publishers. She has also written articles on Merak and Sakteng, such as 'A Study of the Introduction of Tourism in Eastern Bhutan' (Bulletin of the Graduate School of Sociology, Keio University, 2010). However, apart from the present book, most of her books and papers are written in Japanese. She is currently a researcher at the Japan Institute for Bhutan Studies.

2013年1月、タワン僧院のドンギュル祭にて

At the *Dungyur* Festival at Tawang Monastery, January 2013.

Themotheus Adrianus (Tim) Bodt
ティモテユス・アドゥリヤヌス(ティム)・ボット

1979年、オランダのアーネム生まれ。2017年、スイスのベルン大学で言語学博士号を取得し、ロンドン大学東洋アフリカ学院(SOAS)で、スイス国立科学財団および英国学士院の博士研究員フェローシップを修了。ティムはヒマラヤ地域に生涯にわたる興味を抱いており、チベットとブータンで働き、ネパールとアルナーチャル・プラデーシュ州で調査を行った。2020年に博士論文"Grammar of Duhumbi"を、2018年に"Duhumbi Storybook"を、2020年に"Duhumbi Dictionary"を、2024年には、祖語を再構築した"Proto-Western Kho-Bwa"を出版した。また、同地域の言語および民族言語の歴史に関する多数の学術論文も発表している。ネパールのクスンダ語の記録、記述、復興に携わった後、現在はアイルランドのトリニティ・カレッジ・ダブリンのアジア研究の准教授であり、欧州研究会議のプロジェクトLo-Rigの主任研究員として、ブータンのゴンドゥク語とモンパ語の記述に取り組んでいる。

Born in Arnhem, the Netherlands, in 1979. He holds a PhD in Linguistics from Bern University in Switzerland and completed Swiss National Science Foundation and British Academy postdoctoral fellowships at SOAS University of London. Tim has a lifelong fascination for the Himalayan region, worked in Tibet and Bhutan, and conducted research in Nepal and Arunachal Pradesh. He published his doctoral dissertation *Grammar of Duhumbi* in 2020, the accompanying *Duhumbi Storybook* in 2018 and *Duhumbi Dictionary* in 2020, and the reconstruction of the proto-language *Proto-Western Kho-Bwa* in 2024. He has also published numerous academic works on the languages and ethnolinguistic history of the region. After working on the documentation, description and revitalisation of the Kusunda language of Nepal, he is now Associate Professor in Asian Studies at Trinity College Dublin in Ireland and the Principal Investigator on the European Research Council project Lo-Rig, describing the Gongduk and Mönpa languages of Bhutan.

モンパとブロクパの衣装民族誌
アルナーチャル・プラデーシュ西部、ブータン東部、チベット南部

2025年4月25日 初版第1刷発行

著　者　　脇田道子
寄　稿　　ティモテユス・アドゥリヤヌス・ボット
発行者　　西村明高
発行所　　㈱法藏館

〒600-8153
京都市下京区正面通烏丸東入
電　話　075 (343) 0030 (編集)
　　　　075 (343) 5656 (営業)

装幀者　　大石一雄
印刷・製本　亜細亜印刷株式会社

Ⓒ Michiko Wakita 2025 *Printed in Japan*
ISBN978-4-8318-6294-5 C3039
乱丁・落丁本の場合はお取り替え致します
禁無断複製